# Humane Society

## Stories about tragedy and golf

Enhanced non-fiction by

## Jonathan Shute

Magnas Press • Minneapolis

Magnas Press titles may be purchased for business or promotional use or for special bulk sales. For more information, please write to: Bulk Sales Department, Magnas Press, P.O. Box 19331, Minneapolis, Minnesota 55419.

This is a work of fiction based on actual events in the author's life.

All of these stories first appeared in electronic form as an open source novel project on the World Wide Web. The author wishes to thank the editors and administrators of the Everything Development Company and their parent, Blockstackers Intergalactic for their support in the compilation of this work.

Magnas Press books are available by mail order only, via our web site, www.magnas.com or by direct mail inquiries to: Magnas Press, P.O. Box 19331, Minneapolis, Minnesota 55419. For more information about purchasing this book, send email inquiries to info@magnas.com

ISBN 0-9726345-0-9

Acknowledgements

My sincere thanks to Arlene and Jim Trusten,
Ben Collins, Curt Wig, Ryan Postma,
Nate Oostendorp and, above all,
to Mary Shute.

*For my Mary*

# Contents

Foreword by Ben L Collins Ph.D.
Introduction by Ryan Postma (dem bones)

## Part One

## Part Two

## Part Three

# Foreword

It is commonplace that some of the best fiction that we read is found in autobiographies. That is not so with Jonathan Shute. Allowing for a bit of hyperbole and poetic license, most of what you are about to undergo are the true experiences of a rather brilliant man, who, though relatively young in years exhibits clear and amazing insights into the world in which he lives. He sees through the phoniness and hypocrisy of many of those he encounters yet does not become a cynic. Although he is confronted by many Professor Panglosses, he does not conform, like Candide, but will cultivate his garden only after fertilizing it. Mr. Shute does not find that this is the "best of all possible worlds," but being stuck with it, he and his book might just serve to ameliorate it.

I have known Jon and his family for almost three decades, and watched him and his siblings "grow up." I am delighted in the way they have turned out. Even when he was quite young, I sensed a potential in Jon, but the present work far surpasses my expectations. It represents a rare maturity and talent.

In an effort to maintain continuity and cohesion, some of the more purely philosophical chapters – many of which are my favorites – have been omitted, for they would have served the present edition as mere, though often brilliant, digressions. I have encouraged the author to consider incorporating them into the work as a whole in future editions.

Like many works which depict the growth of a young person as he develops an awareness of the world around him and how he will choose to "combat" its challenges, this book is an excellent example of the *Bildungsroman*, or coming of age novel.

Ben L Collins Ph.D.
Professor of English, Emeritus
University of North Dakota

# Introduction

*"The story of one's life can be made interesting to the world at large, if one tries hard enough."*

-Danny Wildman

What you've got here is a book. They're not around much anymore. This information age we find ourselves in eats paper like popcorn and every morning another watermark goes digital. People scribble furious notes to themselves in electrons instead of ink. Trees are becoming optimists. Nonetheless, you still see books in stores and libraries; you probably remember them from when you went to school. I understand there's a place in the Amazon that's just full of them. They get stacked on shelves too high to reach in third-rate family restaurant franchises. They're often used as paperweights or doorjambs. Ten year old children sit on the larger ones in order to see over their place settings at the dinner table or to drive cars. God wrote one. This here is a book.

Specifically, this book is a series of 61 narratives first published on the web site Everything2.com (E2). As a publisher and editor, I couldn't be more proud to see these stories make their way to the printed page. E2 has been online for just over three years and is the home of many a writer. For the majority of them it's a literary outlet that constitutes a part-time diversion for their amateur interest in communicating and explaining their experiences, and most of the time that perspective takes the form either of factual descriptions of people, places and things or of poetic abstracts. It's harder to capture the middle ground. To find the Truth in a cup of coffee or while standing in line at the bank. It's hard to be literary about experience. It's even harder to make it something that someone else wants to read.

In my role as an editor of thousands, I often have to counsel people *away* from recounting their stories. Most people can't make the mundane interesting. I often have the difficult task of explaining why "My Summer Vacation" doesn't hack it outside the fifth grade classroom. From now on, this book is going to be where I point the would-be autobiographer. They'll receive a copy with a note reading "Please stop - here's why." The nineteen year old kid who is pretty sure last night's acid trip is today's modern novel in the form of a run-on sentence; the forty-five year old man who in all those years had yet to come to terms with his complete lack of inspiration.

Jonathan Shute has done their writing for them. He's finished their stories and is well on the way to writing ours. He lives in Minnesota. He will not stop.

Editing the aforementioned thousands, I spend countless hours reading what is fundamentally the same thing over and over. I type countless sentences, with neither art nor form, explaining the same things to people whom, in my mind, amount to fundamentally the same person. I get a lot of same. I fight its cancer with lollipops and a delete key. I won't stop either. I won't stop because once every few months a writer begins submitting words that go something like this:

> I'm sure that the phenomenon goes by many names but I know it as "The crossword puzzle effect." You hit a wall in solving a crossword puzzle and set it aside. Pick up the puzzle a moment later, the answer appears obvious and you wonder how you could have been stymied in the first place. It must be a cross-cultural phenomenon because I've seen it in the fortune cookie sound bites from Lao Tzu as well. He didn't address crossword puzzles specifically but I'm pretty sure that he was talking about the same thing when he said, "If one ceases to strive for understanding, one can know without understanding."

I always suspected that the first person to come up with a unified field theory or the cure for cancer wouldn't be wearing a lab coat and a pocket protector. I pictured a man or woman sitting on a park bench listening to the birdsong and watching tree branches bend in the breeze. The layman philosopher would appreciate the essence of the forest from his humble perch while the physicists and mathematicians groped the bark and examined pinecones, slaves to the details they sought. Enlightenment would visit the philosopher on the park bench macroscopically, the seamless amalgam of an intricate universe laid bare to the most casual observation, when viewed from a proper distance with an open mind.

Mathematics and the self-defining laws of physics seem a clunky way to address the delicate latticework of small miracles that conspire to create such a mammoth one. A kangaroo could be defined mathematically but it is much easier and more edifying to simply view the kangaroo as a whole. The creature's peculiar magic is lost in quantum analysis and little of value is gained in the effort. The grandest mysteries, like the parameters of gravity and the cure for cancer, seem far too large to approach with a clinically focused mind.

If you catch me lingering on a park bench or gazing out the window for hours on end, apparently detached, I'm working on a unified field theory.

-Excerpt from Why the Willow Weeps,
  Everything2.com


There is a precision of language here, a mathematic of words and letters. An engineering of ideas. The phonetics alone are symphonic - read it without knowing what the words mean. Part of you always will. That's called poetry and there aren't very many people who can write it down. We can all feel it, it ripples through us like a rainstorm, a seizure of soliloquy, but few can make it be felt. Three dimensional. A beautiful idea plotted out in prose with a song just beneath the surface. Ley lines. Architecture:

> *"Enlightenment would visit the philosopher on the park bench macroscopically, the seamless amalgam of an intricate universe laid bare to the most casual observation, when viewed from a proper distance with an open mind."*

When you can look forward to a sentence like that every so often, a pearl in a pigpen, when you can publish that sentence for that author - even if only temporarily, a place-hold for the inevitable book deal - you've got an excellent reason to get up in the morning. That's really about all you could ask for.

In any case, when your ten year old uses this book as an extension of his right leg so he can reach the gas pedal, remember - somebody just might write a story about it. Let's hope it's Jonathan.


Ryan Postma (dem bones)
Editor-in-Chief,
Everything Development Company

# Part One

# Suburban Stigmata

B illy hit his head frequently as a child. He's older than I am so I missed the first few concussions but a couple of the ones that I witnessed would have subdued a lesser soul. Our mother would fret a little but our father had become desensitized to massive cranial trauma by the time I was coming up.

In a typical episode we'd be chasing one another down the hall and Billy would crack his skull open on the corner of the door. His face covered in blood, our father calm, our mother suitably horrified by our father's calm. This type of drama became so common that it no longer merited a trip to the emergency room. My father would bandage Billy's noggin with homemade butterfly stitches and hope for the best. Billy lived harder than the rest of us so we all expected him to die young.

We were an average suburban family at first; mom, dad, five kids, two dogs. We attended church every Sunday but I got the impression early on that we were merely going through the motions. Our father had attended the seminary and decided the ministry wasn't his cup of hotdish but our uncles and grandfathers were Lutheran preachers so there was considerable pressure to toe the line.

As children we were aware of a vague hypocrisy but were given little choice in the matter. We went to church every Sunday and I attended Vacation Bible School, sort of a day care center with a message. We made dioramas of Biblical scenes in shoeboxes and sang about Jesus. "Jesus loves me, yes I know, for the Bible tells me so." I dug it. It was unconditional love every Sunday and every summer.

The message given to the small children in the church was airy and benign. They thumped the grown-ups with the heavy stuff in the big room with the uncomfortable benches. They told us that Jesus loved children most of all, which was a comfort to me at the time. I didn't understand anything about the 'dying for our sins' part or how the Easter Bunny and Santa Clause fit into the big picture but Jesus seemed like a pretty cool guy.

I would have thanked them to leave well enough alone and cease my religious education then and there, leaving out the angry, betrayed Jesus and the wretched death he suffered on the cross. These images were seared into my young mind and gradually replaced those of the gentle man surrounded by happy children. The bloody Jesus reminded me of Billy and my nightmares of his face drenched in blood. Just as it was with Jesus, Billy emerged from his traumas unaffected and I came to connect the two in my mind. This connection was cemented one Easter morning in the driveway of our suburban home.

Billy was ten or eleven and I was his shadow. Little more than half his age, I followed him everywhere he would allow me and hung on his every word. Everybody loved Billy and my parents made no secret of the fact that he was their favorite of five. They may have doted on him because they believed that he wouldn't survive his reckless childhood but there was definitely something special about Billy.

That morning we were all preparing for the Easter service at church, girls in dresses and hats, boys in suits and ties. Billy and I were ready before the rest and had begun some preliminary reconnaissance of the house for Easter eggs, while our sisters fussed over their dresses and hair. Our parents hid the eggs the night before, for the ritual hunt that would follow church.

Our father interrupted the search by sending Billy to fetch something from the car and I followed dutifully. The morning was grand and sunny and though I dreaded the lifetime we were about to spend sitting on those nasty benches at church, I was full of joy over the end of the long winter.

What happened in the driveway that Easter morning is recorded in my mind with a clarity that is stunning and permanent. It is, at once, my most disturbing and most comforting childhood memory. Billy made it to the station wagon ahead of me, opened the car door, climbed onto the back seat and was reaching into the back of the car as I approached the open door.

He emerged from the back seat of the car in a crazy burst and nearly knocked me down as he jumped out onto the driveway. He was waving his hand in front of my face, insisting, "Jonny look, look at my hand!" I can't hear his voice in the movie in my mind but I can see his hand so clearly I could describe the ridges of his fingerprints.

There was a wooden toothpick sticking through the middle of his right palm, equal parts of it protruding from the back of his hand and the front. A small trickle of blood oozed from both sides.

We stood for a long moment, silent, as we scrutinized the gore from all angles. "Does it hurt?" I asked him, both of us still wide-eyed with shock. "It stung a little going in, like a mosquito bite."

We stared at his hand some more. The realization was immediate to me and certain. Billy's hand looked just like what they did to Jesus, on Easter morning no less. Billy's realization was no less immediate and no less certain. Our sisters would have a screaming fit when they saw his wound and he must show them immediately.

They did.

Our mother offered only light resistance to our father's home remedy but our sisters screamed and cried with new vigor as Dad went for the pliers. Billy smiled hard at the anguish he was causing the girls and only grimaced slightly as the toothpick was extracted. I thought for a moment that the tumult he had caused would get us out of church but no dice. Some antiseptic and a Band-Aid for each side of his little hand and he'd be as good as new. The episode was quickly forgotten by everyone but me.

I was a serious little kid and there was little doubt in my mind that I had just witnessed some kind of serious event.

# Y is for Yak

"Mary's teacher seems to believe that Mary has a little bit of a problem with exaggeration, Mrs. Thomas."

The shrill teacher disrupted the principal's mellow tone. "She doesn't have a problem with exaggeration, she lies outright." Mary's mama was flabbergasted. She turned on the teacher and spoke in a calm even voice. "My little girl has never told a lie in her life!"

The teacher was seething, her face and neck burning bright red, veins throbbing near her temple as she spoke. "Your little girl has been telling one whopper after another. I think it may be pathological."

The Principal moved to separate the two women, gesturing for them to sit down and calming them with his oft-practiced fatherly tenor. "Let's not get too excited, we're all adults here. Mrs. Thomas, let me try to explain. The incident occurred while the class was working on the alphabet. Mrs. Wallace was using flash cards depicting an animal to represent each letter and every time she showed a new letter, Mary interrupted."

"She didn't merely interrupt, she claimed to have every animal at home as a pet. 'A' is for 'Armadillo', I've got an armadillo named Sam, 'B' is for 'Bobcat', I've got a bobcat named Trudy. The children thought it was funny but it was disruptive and I can't allow that."

Mama smiled broadly for the first time that morning.

"We do have an armadillo but his name isn't Sam, it's Salmon P. Chase.  Trudy is really her sister's bobcat, she has her own bobcat named Butch but she hasn't spoken to him since he ate Caesar."

The Principal shot a glare at the dumbstruck teacher then returned Mama's warm grin.  "And Caesar was..."

"Caesar was Mary's newt. Her Daddy warned her that he would come to a bad end with a name like that but Mary insisted."

"Wait just one minute!" Mrs. Wallace exploded from her chair. "Are you also going to sit there and tell me that you have a gorilla and a crocodile cohabiting at your house?"

"Oh no, Mrs. Wallace, did Mary tell you that?  The croc lives near the pole barn on the far side of the pond.  He pretty much keeps to himself.  We haven't had a gorilla around since the trouble with Oscar. We didn't know until it was too late that Oscar had a terrible crush on me.  One day he saw my husband kissing me and he went into a murderous rage.  We eventually had to ship him off to the Zoo in Iowa; same with the emu but that was mostly because of the smell."

The Principal was gleefully running through the alphabet in his mind and imagining the menagerie.  When he arrived at the letter 'X' his smile waned.  Mary's defeated teacher guessed at his dilemma and in a resigned monotone muttered, "'X' is for Xylophone, she's got one of those too."

Mama beamed.  "Mary can play all of the songs from that Dr. Doolittle movie.  She always wanted her daddy to get her a Pushme Pullyou like they had in the film.  Remember that? It was a fantasy animal with the head of a llama on each end.  We had the darndest time convincing her that it was a movie trick and there was no such critter in real life.  Her daddy told her that a real yak would be better than a phony two-headed llama so she finally settled for Annabelle."

"Let me guess, Mrs. Thomas, 'Y' is for Yak?"

"Oh she adores that yak.  I think it stinks worse than the emu but Mary doesn't seem to mind."

# The truth book

The Wish Game we played as children always started with such promise. Someone would introduce the simple question and our conversation would drift happily toward the ether. "What would you wish for if you could have only one wish?" Some wise guy would always wish for a million more wishes or unlimited magical powers but such "unrealistic" options were summarily excluded.

The game often degenerated to a chorus of wishes for money. Someone would say a million dollars, the next a billion, then a trillion. When we reached the frontiers of our vocabulary we wished for a "gazillion" or a "bazillion" or simply "infinity dollars." For most of us the grandest wish in the game became our greatest goal in life, sadly, the acquisition of money.

These money wishes left me unsatisfied so I would continue the game on my own, trying to think of the best possible wish. If I couldn't have magical powers or a million more wishes I wanted to have the truth book. The book would have ever-changing pages that would provide an answer to any question I could ask. If a grown-up was bullshitting I'd be the first to know and when someone claimed to speak with the authority of God, they'd get busted quick.

Some wishes do come true because I am communicating to you now using just such a device. A computer connected to the Internet knows everything that is knowable and my laptop computer looks a lot like a book with ever-changing pages. A naysayer would argue that the Internet is bottom heavy with misinformation and detritus. I would counter that even bad data is useful in any quest for the whole truth and those distortions and falsehoods provide the shadows that allow the facts to stand out in the light.

I hope my friends got their gazillions.

# The Bunny Man

The big yellow truck with the nervous little man at the wheel came to the track every Thursday morning. The racetrack did all of its business between Friday and Sunday so the delivery of hot dog buns on Thursday was critical. The race fans were interested in only two things, the probability of witnessing a dreadful automobile crash and getting their hands on one of Don's famous dime dogs.

"The Happy Bunny Bread Company" made deliveries to both residential and commercial clients but the Minnesota Speedway was the anchor of its trade. The track went through more Bunny buns in a single weekend than the rest of the bread company's customers ate in a month. The Thursday morning delivery to the track was vital, so the Happy Bunny people assigned their most reliable driver.

Willy Gibbs was now pushing retirement age and he had been working for the bread company since he was eleven years old. His father actually founded "The Daily Bread Bakery" when Willy was a child but had been forced to sell out to the Happy Bunny people during the darkest days of the depression. His father stayed on after the sale and managed the company until his tragic death in the kneading machine in '38. Little Willy swept floors and cleaned the ovens until he was old enough to drive a delivery truck.

He took pride in his work and developed a genuine affection for almost everybody on his route.  After some fifty years of delivering to the same addresses, Willy felt as if he was a member of many families. He had seen scores of people make the entire circuit from cradle to grave and had a hand in feeding every last one them.  Willy's job was a vital one, in his estimation, and he came to think of himself as an instrument of God.  He provided the daily bread for scores of hungry children.

Each morning, just before climbing into the big yellow truck with the blue bunny on the side, he'd recite the Lord's prayer aloud. Willy would mist up a little bit every time he got to the part about "our daily bread," thinking about his father and the little bakery he began. His father had given his life to answer this humble appeal and there was no doubt in Willy's mind that he was doing the Lord's work.

"Give us this day our daily bread
and forgive us our trespasses,
as we forgive those who trespass
against us..."

Don was a rapscallion, not a scoundrel.  This world was a playground to him and he reveled in poking fun at those who thought it otherwise.  His pranks were rarely mean-spirited but the practical joker walks a fine line between tragedy and comedy and the banana peel isn't so funny if you're the one with a sore ass.

Don opened the first automobile speedway in the state of Minnesota but he had done so reluctantly.  His chosen profession of barnstorming was legislated out of existence by a new bureau of the federal government called the Federal Aviation Administration.  When he received the "cease and desist" warning, on fancy government letterhead, he thought it was some kind of practical joke.  Why on Earth would the government care if he broke his neck in an aeroplane mishap?

The young daredevil continued crashing his old punch board and bailing wire biplane until the day he slammed into the side of a particularly stubborn hay barn.  Don landed in the hospital with a broken collarbone and a roomful of unsmiling federal thugs.  The G-men placed him under arrest for "reckless flight," as he lay in his hospital bed and Don came to the realization that the FAA wasn't joking.

He had a hankering for danger after decades on the edge so he turned to the next best thing.  If he wasn't allowed to crash aeroplanes any longer he would switch to ground based mayhem and "The Minnesota Speedway" was born.

Don soon discovered that the fifty cents a head he was charging for admission barely supported the purses and the fees he paid to keep an ambulance handy.  He became a master showman in the tradition of P.T. Barnum and had no trouble putting butts on benches but he would have to expand his profit potential if the track was to survive.  One day his ten-year-old daughter stumbled on the missing ingredient.  Little Mary complained that she was starving to death in the ticket booth so her mama brought her a plate of hot dogs and home fries.

The race fans were openly envious of her little banquet so Mary munched on the home fries and sold the two hot dogs to the highest bidders.  She got seventy-five cents for one of them and a shiny silver dollar for the other.  To her amazement the bidding war edged the value of the dogs past the price of admission and a companion industry was born.  The little girl was often called on to work the ticket booth so she was accustomed to handling money but these were lean times and she had never even seen a silver dollar before.  Mary couldn't wait to show her father.

Don was quick on the uptake and built the concession stand before the next weekend's races.

---

The delightful little girl who met him every Thursday at racetrack charmed Willy Gibbs but he dreaded the stop nonetheless.  Little Mary was a peach but there was something unsettling about the girl's father. The owner of the Minnesota Speedway was not the kind of man that Willy Gibbs admired but the racetrack consumed Happy Bunny buns by the truckload so his duty was clear.

Mary's father seemed like a huckster to Willy, little better than a con man doing the Devil's work, flaunting his joie de vivre all the while. It was widely known that the speedway appealed to a base interest in potential tragedy and Willy believed that such a thing was indecent. He lived with his widowed mother and took her to church every Sunday, where the preacher would rail against "The Oval Demon" and the sin it engendered. The Reverend sometimes referred to Mary's daddy by name, from the pulpit, as a trafficker in blood lust and beer. How, Willy wondered, could a man like that be blessed with such an angelic little daughter?

"Daddy, Daddy, the Bunny Man's coming!"

Thursday was Don's favorite day. The weekend was a blur of activity with the races and Monday through Wednesday was spent cleaning up the mess. Thursday was his day to admire what he'd built and to rest a bit on his laurels. Thursday also marked the arrival of the bread delivery guy who he lived to torment.

Don decided that if there was a God, that he must have put people like Willy Gibbs on this Earth simply for comic relief. Don couldn't abide people who took themselves too seriously and his mission in life was to see to their deflation. Willy Gibbs reminded him of those humorless bastards at the FAA who had grounded him and poor Willy would have to pay for their transgression.

Mary's daddy began to mimic his daughter and call Willy "The Bunny Man," sometimes to his face and always with a broad smile. The Bunny Man seemed to have no sense of humor whatsoever, which only served to fuel Don's amusement. He would try to outdo himself every week with a new prank hoping to either drive The Bunny Man insane or make him smile; whichever came first.

Willy didn't appreciate Don's sense of humor one little bit but he reigned in his outrage for the good of the Happy Bunny Bakery. The racetrack was paying his salary, after all and he couldn't afford to alienate the owner. When he discovered that he had been made the butt of one of Don's practical jokes, he would simply shake his head and quote scripture.

Don felt that the religious readings he received from the Bunny Man were more than adequate spiritual guidance and he'd boast that it saved him from wasting a perfectly good Sunday in church.

———————

"You know what to do, sweetie, when the Bunny Man goes to the concession stand, you go for his truck."

"Should I take them all, Daddy?"

"No, no, honey, we don't need all of them.  Just grab six or seven, whatever you can carry."

Little Mary called it "The Bunny Man Game" and relished the larcenous bonding with her father.  Her daddy was the smartest man on Earth so she never questioned his motives.  One time he told her to put William, their pet goat, into the back of the Bunny Man's truck and at first she wondered why.  William had a grand old time tearing into the baked goods so Mary figured Daddy was saving money on goat chow.  She didn't have to ask him why he wanted to steal the empty bread racks from the Bunny Man's truck; she knew what they were for.

"Well I sure appreciate you carrying all those hot dog buns to the concession stand for me, Willy.  That damned barnstormer's back kicks in when the barometer dips."

"It's, uh, my pleasure Mr. Thomas.  Where do you want me to stack them?"

The look on Willy's face indicated anything but pleasure as he grunted and groaned under the combined weight of twelve steel racks full of weenie sheaths.  He didn't like to leave his truck unattended for any length of time, ever since that little episode with the billy goat.  The owner of the bakery took the goat losses out of his paycheck that week and threatened to fire him for his carelessness.

"Oh, right over there is fine.  How's your mother, Willy?"

The Bunny Man was exceptionally gullible so he fell for Don's conversational delaying tactic.

"Mother is fine, she gets a little owly when her lumbago acts up but the doctor says..."

A flash of worry crossed his face and ceased the friendly chitchat abruptly.

"I've got to...umm...I'd better be...uh...getting back to the truck." Willy's face betrayed him with a nervous twitch. "Say...uh, you got that goat in a cage now?"

"Yes siree, Willy, I've made cages for the lot of them. C'mon I'll show you."

"I'll...uh...take your word for it. I'd better be getting on to the rest of my route, thanks anyway."

Willy was making a move for the truck when Mary's Daddy grabbed his arm.

"Aw, it'll only take a second. I welded the cages together myself and I'm sorta proud of 'em. C'mon Willy, there's a couple of 'em right over there, behind the house."

———————

The two men walked from the concession stand toward the house, while Don carried on about how much money those pirates wanted for store bought cages and how he'd gotten a great deal on the arc welder. The Bunny Man didn't hear a word of it though, because the Bengal tiger in the cage behind Don's house transfixed him.

Willy had seen one before, in the National Geographic, but the glossy photograph didn't do the feral beast justice.

"Dear Lord! Is that what I think it is?"

"If you're thinkin' she's a big bad Asian kitty cat, you're thinkin' clearly, my friend. The race fans go all gaga over her. I got her on the cheap 'cause she killed a zookeeper in Topeka; tore him to shreds. Quite a mess, I hear."

"Are you sure those cages are secure? You've got children, for Heaven's sake!"

"Sheba could gobble up little Mary without stoppin' to chew, no doubt about it but those cages are tighter'n the preacher's daughter, if you catch my meaning."

The Bunny Man would have been aghast had he heard Don's coarse reference but he was too busy scrutinizing the grated metal squares that comprised the cages. They seemed oddly familiar.

"Where'd you come up with all of the metal grating?"

Mary's Daddy smiled his biggest Thursday smile and told the Bunny Man the whole truth.

"Aw, just some stuff Mary found lying around."

# Defying Gravity

Jimmy Buffett saved my life when I was ten years old.

Worry was my constant companion as a child. I was a serious little kid with the weight of the world on my shoulders and during the worst of it my hair began to fall out. Thinning hair at the age of nine would have been bad enough but to exacerbate my stigma it all fell from the same spot. I had a silver dollar sized bald area on the top of my head that was gradually expanding in a near perfect circle.

The ridicule on the school bus was the worst of it. In class the teacher would intervene if the other children became cruel but on the bus I was on my own. I didn't sleep well so I had dark circles under my puffy eyes and my siblings teased me because my lips were too big for my face. There was no doubt that I was a goofy looking kid and with the bald spot ever expanding I could expect to look even goofier.

I can remember clearly the day that I hit bottom. It was a sub-zero winter morning and instead of enduring the ridicule on the school bus I decided to walk the mile and a half to my elementary school. I hadn't gone a block before I realized I had made a terrible mistake. My feet were frozen solid, my nose hurt from the cold and I still had more than a mile to go.

When I arrived at school the other children pointed at me and laughed out loud until the teacher sent me to the nurse's office. The nurse took one look at me and called my Mother to come and take me home. Cold makes most things contract but for some reason it had the opposite effect on my ears. They swelled to twice their normal size and glowed bright red for days. Between my big lips and my bald spot, my dark eye circles and my massive glowing red ears, I must have been a pathetically comical sight.

There were many nights that my worry wouldn't let me sleep at all. I'd lay awake cataloguing my various anxieties and grow more depressed the following day for my lack of rest. This cycle reached its logical conclusion the day that my ears became swollen and my freakishness could no longer be denied. The prayer I had been taught to say before bed was usually delivered quickly and mechanically, without much thought given to the words.

"Now I lay me down to sleep,
I pray the Lord my soul to keep.
If I should die before I wake,
I pray the Lord my soul to take..."

On that night I delivered the prayer solemnly, word by word, emphasizing the last line and repeating it over and over again.

———————

My parents divorced soon after my swollen ear episode. It was the best thing for all concerned and my fretting actually eased slightly in the absence of domestic conflict. My Mother remarried and I spent the summers with her and my new stepfather aboard a houseboat on the St. Croix River.

It was in that marina where I met a real live pirate who exposed me to a world view that was far superior to my own. He spoke of a great philosopher who believed that this was the best of all possible worlds and that we had all won the cosmic lottery by waking up here.

The pirate explained to me that this sage had been ignored by the mainstream but that all thinking people would ultimately embrace the truth of his message. He was referring, of course, to Jimmy Buffett and his Coral Reefer Band.

I grew to love Jimmy like a father and if I tell you he is my spiritual leader it's only because it's true. He taught me not to take myself or anyone else too seriously and to smile by default. He told me that tragedies very often become comedies and that, "they'd better become comedies fast or else you're in a lot of trouble." Jimmy said there was nothing to worry about and I believed him.

———————

My face eventually grew to match the size of my lips, my ears returned to more normal proportions and my bald spot sprouted an even growth of hair. I still have the dark circles under my eyes but Mary says that with proper lighting and from a certain distance I'm handsome in a way. I smile now, by default.

The anxieties would resurface at Christmastime, when family issues and religious hypocrisy were most conspicuous. That is, until I found out that Brother Jim was born on December 25th.

# Show and Tell

I was in the first grade when I brought the picture to show and tell. It was a photograph of my father and another man standing behind a table with a huge mound of cash. My father was a lobbyist for the state retail federation and the half a million in small bills represented the damage done by shoplifters every day in Minnesota. I didn't understand what a lobbyist was but it was a cool picture and it made my father look awfully important.

He developed a campaign called STEM; Shoplifting Takes Everybody's Money, to call attention to the cost of petty theft to the consumer. It was a high profile endeavor and it resulted in my father being named one of the state's ten outstanding young men that year. It was, by terrible chance, about the same time that I was caught shoplifting.

---

I wasn't a happy little kid. My first sentient moments coincided with the melt down of my parent's marriage so every memory of early childhood has yelling in the background. My siblings and I were shielded from the fray for the most part but the muffled arguments made their way through the walls of my bedroom at night. At the age of six or seven mom and dad were at the center of my little world and the discord between them devastated me. I covered my head with the pillow but the echo of the bitter exchanges persisted.

One night I discovered that I could stop the arguments simply by making the scene. I'd wander into the living room in my pajamas and tell my mom I couldn't sleep and the debate would be quieted. I know now that she was relieved for a break in the battle when she comforted me and asked me if I thought some cocoa would help. As an adult I understand the terrible swirl of emotions in a spousal dispute but as a child I thought that if the bickering stopped everything would be all right.

She'd make me hot chocolate the old fashioned way, with powdered cocoa, sugar and milk. The preparation required standing over the stove and stirring the pot continuously to avoid scalding the milk, so the process happily separated the combatants long enough for tempers to cool. I'd linger over my cocoa as long as I possibly could.

My childish attempt at conflict resolution was inadequate and my parents ultimately found their way to divorce.

———————

I had seven cents exactly in my hand, a nickel and two pennies. The grocery store was about ten blocks from our house and I held the sweaty coins in a death grip the entire way. At the time, a penny would buy more than one piece of candy so great sacrifices were made in accumulating such a sum but I was driven. The packets of Swiss Miss instant cocoa were in aisle four, next to the Ovaltine, and they cost exactly seven cents each.

I cannot convey the hollowness I felt when I reached the instant beverage aisle and found that they had raised the price to eight cents. The commercials for the cocoa haunt a little corner of my mind to this day and remind me of my mother and the comforts she offered. A gentle maiden's voice sings, "Swiss Miss instant cocoa will warm you up inside."

I looked at the nickel and two pennies in my hand and then at the price below the box of cocoa packets a half a dozen times before I finally grabbed one of the packets and stuffed it clumsily into my pocket. As I did so I fumbled the coins in my other hand and they scattered onto the linoleum aisle. I nervously collected them and made a hasty dash for the exit.

The store manager grabbed the back of my collar as I was walking through the second set of doors. He told me that he saw what I had done and that I was in a lot of trouble. How could this be? I looked both ways before I snatched the cocoa and was sure there was nobody in sight. I made a feeble denial and the manager told me that they had me on film. He asked me for my telephone number so he could call my parents to come and get me.

I think about that grocery store manager sometimes, decades later and wonder if he ever fully recovered from my wailing display. All of the sorrow over my mother's absence and the shame of my crime and the angst over the arbitrary price of cocoa fused into a storm of vocal grief. I literally spewed tears and mucus at the thought of my father finding out what I had done. He was, at that very moment, riding the crest of a campaign to curb shoplifting and the embarrassment it would cause would be total.

The good news is that the store manager saw my willingness to pay yesterday's price for the cocoa as a mitigating factor and my pathetic theatrics pushed him over the edge. He let me off the hook with a stern warning and sold me the packet of cocoa for seven cents.

My secret is safe to this day unless my father reads this.

# The worm has turned

"Jump up and down Jonny, now!" His voice was hushed so as not to wake the neighbors but his tone had an emphatic edge. "You've got to jump up and down as hard as you can." He was shouting and whispering at the same time. I was pretty sure he was tugging my chain and that the impact of a 99 pound eleven year old would do little to scare the earthworms to the surface but when Billy said "jump," I jumped.

Billy had been a fisherman, to the exclusion of almost everything else, since he was old enough to bait a hook. His excursions were usually solitary endeavors, like most everything else he did, so on my rare opportunities to join him I did as I was told. He carried a cardboard milk container, opened at the top and half-filled with soil, with a small pen light duct taped to the side. He was just a shadow crouched behind the tiny cone of light across the yard but I could tell he was scoring big. The small pinhole of light was dancing around the yard like a firefly and his whisper was more excited than before, "keep jumping, Jonny, just a few more."

I hopped dutifully until my head started to throb and Billy finally called me off. "The janitor's yard is cherry, man. I got two of 'em as long as my forearm." Our own yard was hard scrabble and gravel but the Elementary School janitor pampered his little patch of God's country. Every spring he spread a layer of natural fertilizer and every day he gave her an even dose of rain. The rap on him was that he hated kids because he had none of his own, just he and his wife and his fertile lawn. Billy knew we were taking a considerable chance harvesting the janitor's yard but the pickings were good so we took the risk. I always harbored a terrible fantasy of getting caught in the act some night and having to suffer the janitor's wrath every day at school.

Billy detached the pen light from the milk carton and was admiring his work as we trotted across the street to our house. I tossed a glance over my shoulder to make sure the coast was clear just in time to catch the curtains on the front window of the janitor's house rustling. "Aw, we're busted Billy, I just saw his curtains move. He saw us, man."

"Nah, he didn't see us, he'd have hollered."

————————

The millpond was on the opposite end of town and it was a hell of a long march on short legs. Before I was ever allowed to tag along I had to promise not to whine and I had to prove that I had enough coinage for my own bottle of Dr. Pepper. There was a little bait store near the fishing hole with one of those Andy Griffith Show bottled pop dispensers out front and after a three mile walk in the summer sun, the fifteen cent bottle of cold soda was the highlight of my day. The truth is I didn't care much for the actual fishing but being allowed to hang with the big kids was priceless. If we had been walking across town to throw rocks in the water I'd have been an eager volunteer.

Billy was always venerable and wise to me so it didn't seem odd in the least that the crusty old guy at the bait shop called the fourteen year old kid "Old Man."

"What do you got for me today, Old Man? You got some creepy crawlies in there I'll bet!"

Billy set the milk carton on the counter without a word and the old guy squinted at the contents, lips moving with his silent accounting. "You're keepin' the biguns I s'pose?"

"Yeah, I'm gonna use the two foot longers on top, the rest are yours."

The old guy furrowed his forehead and cast a banker's glare at my fourteen-year-old brother, "Two dollars, a Dr. Pepper, a stick of beef jerky and a pack of Lucky's. Final offer, Old Man."

"Water-proof matches?"

"Ah, you're a little pirate but these are prize specimens...I'll toss in the wet sticks."

"Deal."

The bait store owner assembled Billy's loot in a paper bag, then plucked a handful of dirt and the two largest earthworms from the milk carton and put them into another. Billy picked up both bags, nodded a silent goodbye, turned and left. The screen door slapped behind him and my brother didn't pause when the proprietor yelled,

"So long Old Man, good luck...to the fish!"

———————

Pulling apart the worm was the worst of it for me. Billy claimed that if you did it right you could separate the worm in sections so both the small section and the rest of the worm would wriggle with life. I don't mean to give you the impression that I was an eleven year old Buddhist or anything. I came up among God fearing omnivorous Lutherans so my views on the sanctity of life were as arbitrary as the next guy's but something about the methodical dissection of the worms really bugged me.

If I dwelled on it for too long I realized that the slow sectional torture of the Earthworm was only prologue to the vivisection of yet a larger critter. Call me a cupcake but I lost my stomach for the whole deal.

"Hey Billy, you ever hear of Aristotle?"

"Yeah, some wise guy from ancient times, why?"

"He said that worms were the Earth's intestines, I looked it up in the Funk & Wagnall's."

"So, what's your point?"

"I just wonder if he's right, ya know, is it cool to be rippin' apart the Earth's intestines, that's all. And you know what else, it would really suck to be the fish."

Even as a teenager Billy was a stoic cat. He wasn't Bwana so much for what he said but what he didn't. He'd fall into these long thoughtful pauses and wouldn't utter a word until he'd something to say. When he did speak it was like those old E.F. Hutton commercials and everyone would crane to hear. I was a little nervous about how he'd respond to my casual indictment of his life's passion but I was his little brother and felt it my duty to mess with him.

"It would suck to be the fish, but Jesus was a fisherman so it can't be evil."

"No way man. My Sunday school teacher, Mrs. Anders, said that he was a carpenter and that the fisherman thing was a metaphor."

"A what?"

"A metaphor. She says it's like you're talkin' about one thing but you mean something else."

"That sounds useful."

"I don't get it either but she said they meant he was a 'fisher of men,' not a fisherman. I think he ate a lot of bread or something."

One of Billy's long pauses ensued that lasted right up until the last worm was used and all but a few of the Lucky's smoked. Billy yanked the stringer full of Striped Bass from the pond and said that we'd better move if we were going to make it home by dark. I was wishing I had never brought up the whole "Earth's intestines" thing and I was afraid that I had really pissed him off this time.

He barely spoke a word in the two hours or so it took for us to get home so I made a last ditch effort at conciliation by offering to help him clean the fish. He knew I hated gutting the fish more than anything else in the world so he gathered I was trying to make amends.

"Sure, there's a mess of 'em and I could use the help."

Billy always burned a cigarette after cleaning fish to get the smell out of his nose and since I helped him with the dirty work, he offered me his second to the last Lucky. This was big, man. He'd never let me smoke around the house where our father might catch me and he'd certainly never empty a pack on me. I was forgiven for busting his chops about critter torture and intimating that his life's obsession might be less than cool.

We sat on the back porch and alternated puffs off the cigarettes with paranoid glances for evidence of our father. Billy fell into his solemn pause for a moment or two, flicked the last of his burning butt onto the driveway with a splash of orange sparks and spoke as he stood.

"Did you know that tennis is free? No shit, you buy a racket and some tennis balls and you can play all day for nuthin', I don't see the percentage in it."

"Tennis is cool. We've got all that stuff in the basement. We ought to go bat it around some time."

"We'd be idiots not to, it don't cost nuthin'."

# Christmas, bloody Christmas

Aristocracy demands a certain amount of inbreeding to insure the perpetuation of wealth. In the old days you had to marry your own cousin to keep hoi polloi away from the keys to the empire. In the modern day there are enough rich people to ensure genetic diversity so, while they still marry among their own kind, there is less risk of mutation and degradation of the species.

In what can only be a nostalgic nod to their blue-blooded ancestors, the wealthy have maintained the tradition of keeping purebred dogs and cats. Geneticists will tell you that such a thing can't go on forever and that the various breeds will end up gasping for life in the shallow gene pool. Susceptibility to disease and congenital infirmity will eventually thin the ranks of all of these breeds to nil.

The casual cruelty of intentionally breeding a critter out of existence sounds bad enough on its face but there is a more insidious evil lurking beneath the surface. Look carefully into the eyes of your rich Aunt Tilly's Pomeranian sometime and you will be greeted with the chilling reality that there is no "there" there. The poor animal is experiencing the final stages of evolution interrupted and if Aunt Tilly's lucky, the result is merely massive retardation. The Pomeranian along with a hundred other breeds has become the animal kingdom equivalent of the hillbilly kid in Deliverance, without the redemptive banjo prowess.

The purebred dog is a perverse anomaly and an affront to the critter's natural inclination to hump anything that moves. Before you plop down money for a store bought dog with a pedigree, understand that potential retardation is the least of your worries. With each successive batch of pureblooded critters, as with the human aristocracy of old, there is an increased likelihood of outright insanity.

———————

It was our first Christmas as rich people so I couldn't wait to get at the booty underneath that tree. The previous year I netted an ugly sweater, a stocking full of fruit and mixed nuts and a book shaped package of ten rolls of lifesavers candy. At the time, the candy seemed a massive extravagance because my parent's humble means usually demanded functional gifting. We'd get socks and underwear on a bad year and perhaps one toy that didn't require batteries on a good one. Our father always told us that if we complained we'd get a stocking full of reindeer turds so we kept our mouths shut and counted our blessings. All of that was in the past. The rich are different all right; for one thing they get a Hell of a lot better Christmas presents.

Our father had just been promoted to President of something or other and after he divorced my mother he hit the lottery in the second wife department. The new step-mother was heiress to a sporting goods empire and in the early 1970's was pulling down an allowance of $50,000 a year for doing little more than redecorating the mansion and watching soap operas. At the time you could buy a brand new car for $3,000, so fifty large was truly large and it was just the tip of the ski slope.

Her father, Grandpa Charley, might just as well have had a license to print money. He reinvented the downhill ski at the exact moment that the nouveau riche adopted the Aspen culture as their milieu and Grandpa Charley cashed in big time. He had an exclusive deal with the Olympic Committee and product placement in James Bond movies so everybody who was anybody demanded his product.  If you ever want to get really, really wealthy, all you need to do is come up with something that rich people absolutely need two of.

We were at our new step-grandfather's house the night before, on Christmas Eve, when we caught our first glimpse of how the other half lived.  Gated communities are relatively common now but at the time it was an exotic concept.  The entire township was fenced in and there were armed guards at every entrance.  Grandpa Charley shared a private lake with a former United States Vice President and his house was a shrine to conspicuous consumption and hedonism.  Charley's pedigreed Lhasa Apso had her own bedroom with a doggy door that led to a little doggy Disney World in the back yard.

In our house we opened presents on Christmas morning but Charley's side wasn't into the delayed gratification thing.  Christmas Eve at Grandpa Charley's was an exercise in wacky excess, ridiculously expensive trinkets parceled out randomly like crumbs thrown to pecking pigeons.  There were nine kids in our hybrid family ranging in age from six to sixteen and Grandpa Charley gave us each an envelope containing $5,000, along with a pile of spendy presents.  The most extravagant gift I had received when my mom and dad were still married was a ten dollar bill, the Christmas before their divorce.  I remember staring at that ten spot for hours, dreaming of what I could buy with it, dizzy over my wealth.

The whole broken home thing might not suck as bad as I feared.

––––––––––

The deal at Grandpa Charley's on Christmas Eve was just the gravy.  The real bonanza would happen on Christmas morning when we'd attack the small mountain of presents at our house.  We were now rich in our own right and with the necessity to fit nine children and two dogs under one roof, our own house was something like a mansion.  When my father bought it I remember him commenting that the wallpaper and carpeting alone cost more than he paid for our former dwelling.  Our stepbrothers and sisters took it all in stride, having grown accustomed to grand surroundings but it was new and exciting to my siblings and me.

Our mother came away from the divorce with little more than a mobile home and a waitressing gig at The International House of Pancakes, so dear old dad must have done something right. We'd get a third Christmas with our mum at the trailer park but we knew that the presents there would degenerate back to socks and underwear. The genuine warmth of the humble little Christmas at mom's mobile home, food with actual love in it and gifts made of cloth, was a more sincere affair by far but I know that it saddened her that she couldn't compete with our father's grand style.

I could hardly sleep the night before our first Christmas in the mansion. I lay awake in my bed that night thinking about the five thousand bucks from Grandpa Charley and how cool it was gonna be to be rich. Our living room had vaulted ceilings that allowed for an enormous Christmas tree and around its base lay an equally enormous complement of gifts. There was a pile of presents some twenty feet in diameter and as tall as a ten year old encircling that decaying pine and I was gonna be the first little monkey down those stairs in the morning if I had to stay up all night to do it.

As it turned out there wasn't much risk of anyone in the house sleeping late on that Christmas morning. The growling and howling and terrible death screams that emanated from our mansion woke up half of the people on our block. The neighbors on either side of us both called the police when they heard my little stepsister screaming. Poor old Alice next door was a busybody and had her nose pressed to the glass in her breezeway, near enough to actually see the blood splattering on the windows of our living room.

————

Our new stepfamily came equipped with a demonic little poodle named Muffin and for our first Christmas in the mansion my dad bought the gargantuan St. Bernard for show. He had big money and a big house so it seemed only fitting to purchase a really big dog. Samantha was a drooling monstrosity that acted nothing like the gentle oafish St. Bernards in the movies. Her growl sent a chill down your spine because you knew that she was big enough to do real damage if she snapped. Years later Stephen King wrote a book called "Cujo" about a killer St. Bernard and readers must have assumed it was a complete flight of fancy. It read like a documentary to me and mine.

I'm a lifelong dog lover but I had no affection for either of those soulless beasts. Muffin, the yippy little poodle from Hell, seemed to have only two brain cells, the one that caused the high pitched yip and the one that compelled her to skittle across the floor on painted toenails to yip at you from another direction. Samantha the St. Bernard was simply insane.

I often wished that the yippy poodle would come to a bad end but I never dreamt it would be such a gory exhibition. When my little stepsister started screaming, the whole family rushed to the living room for the Christmas morning spectacle none of us will ever forget.

The feral St. Bernard had what was left of Muffin clenched in her jaws, shaking the carcass back and forth violently, spraying blood and pieces of expensive poodle all over our Christmas presents and the newly redecorated living room. Little Muffin was surprisingly resilient. What was left of her head was still connected to what was left of her torso and she managed to yip and whine throughout her vivisection. The little poodle had an impressive blood supply, nearly enough to coat every surface in the living room.

By the time we wrested the bloody mop of entrails and rended flesh from the mouth of Cujo it looked as though someone had hurled a poodle grenade into the house.

I wish that I could put a happy spin on the bloody mess but I cannot. When the police showed up they called the animal warden and our St. Bernard was unceremoniously dispatched to dog heaven with a hypodermic. We were shocked speechless when our stepmother ordered the kids to collect the pieces of Muffin for potential reassembly. Her ears, tail and at least two of her legs were entirely detached. What was left of her cranium looked like a lump of raw hamburger with eyeballs and was connected to the torso by a few narrow strands of nerve and sinew.

Our wealth afforded little Muffin elaborate reconstructive surgery and nothing short of a miracle of veterinary medicine. For something like the cost of a new Corvette, the evil little animal was sewn back together and somehow managed a full recovery.

When the stepfamily and the money vanished a few years later I gained a new appreciation for the simpler things in life. The socks and underwear under the little tree at my mother's mobile home had an honest utility and the humble gatherings at Christmastime in the trailer park never degenerated to bloodshed and mayhem.

The soulful mixed breed mutts from the Humane Society were a Godsend.

# If I ever lose my legs

It seems disrespectful to stand atop the grassy Indian mounds to get a better look at the river but most people do it anyway. I admit that I climbed up on one of them once but not without a thoughtful nod to the Ojibwa or Lakota brave whose shoulders I was standing on. The view of the river from the top of that hill is spectacular so anybody buried there would have expected to share the perch with future generations.

The St. Croix River has the distinction of being the only river in the world that is protected against environmental mischief along its entire length. If you squint you can almost see the river the way that the Indians saw it hundreds of years ago, before the advent of the white man and the powerboats.

The Army Corps of Engineers dredge the river on a regular basis to keep the narrow channels clear and the resulting sand from the riverbed is piled up to form sand islands. The St. Croix is less than the artery of commerce it was in fur trading days so the river is now dredged primarily for recreational boat traffic. The islands created as a byproduct provide a place to park the boat and party.

The sand islands were named informally for their location or a defining feature and the names stuck. The most prominent of these is in the middle of the main channel near the town of Hudson, Wisconsin and is known as "Beer Can Island." The island is situated directly across from one of the largest marinas on the river so it is a wildly popular party destination for the weekend warriors. In spite of the river's designation as an environmentally protected sanctuary, the party animals made a permanent mark with their jetsam. No great leap of imagination is necessary to determine why it's called Beer Can Island.

There is a bulge in the river near Beer Can Island known as Lake St. Croix but don't let the name fool you, it ain't a lake. Even at its widest point the river moves along at a pretty good clip and Lake St. Croix in particular has a wicked undertow that kills on a regular basis. Every summer the partiers descend on the pristine river by the hundreds and every summer the Sheriff has to use the dragging hooks to fish out the ones who had too much fun.

Even so, the greatest danger for the drunken boater is not the undertow so much as the other drunken boaters.

---

The best thing about chumming around with Captain Tony was that he had the keys to the only jet boat on the river. The "New Canoe" was a sleek little fiberglass number that could skip across the water as fast as a car could roll on land. The concept of jet boats has been around since Archimedes invented the water screw but they didn't become a functional reality until the mid-1950s. Captain Tony was the first guy on his dock to own one. Jets are common on the river these days and uniformly despised for their noise and velocity. If you've ever been on the tarmac for the lift-off of the Concorde or a Harrier Jump Jet you have some appreciation for the volume involved.

The primary appeal of jet boats for most people is that they go really fast, really quick but that was never my cup of chowder. Every now and then Tony would open her up and the G-force would slap you back in your seat with your cheeks flapping and the blood rushing to the back of your brain like an astronaut in a NASA simulator. You can calmly shave and sip your coffee at seventy miles per hour in an automobile but the same speed on water finds most normal people trying very hard not to wet themselves.

The versatility of jets is a wonder to behold.  They draw less water than a canoe at low speeds and at planing velocity they can skip across the surface with less than an inch of draft.  In the absence of a propeller, they are able to jump over floaters or sandbars without worry and allowed us to visit parts of the river we would otherwise never have seen.

The vessels are like fiberglass projectiles in the wrong hands and most sane people would rather be sailing.  I've heard Captain Tony accused of some scurrilous things but sanity was never one of them.

---

It took three houseboats and twelve grown men to drag Tony's jet boat off of Beer Can Island.  He made a drunken wager that he could drive the boat completely across the island, spitting sand through the impeller and he was only half wrong.  Jet boats operate under the same principle as jet airplanes, sucking in and spitting out water rather than air to create forward momentum.  Tony was correct in assuming that the jet could spit sand as well but he badly miscalculated the effects of heat and friction.  He lost not only the five-dollar bet but the six hundred-dollar jet-drive and the eleven hundred-dollar Oldsmobile engine as well.

Tony didn't believe that a limit existed until he bumped square into it.  We saw him blow five engines in four summers testing the limits of that poor little boat.  He ruined the thing once without ever leaving the slip when he discovered that by aiming the jet drive straight down he could nearly achieve flight.  The water cooled engine got tired of sucking air and expired with an impressive display of smoke and screeching metal before it ever obtained significant altitude.

Tony was an old school biker who had made good with a successful business so he acted with the authority of someone who had righteously conquered both worlds.  The great philosopher Kinky Friedman said that to make it in this life you either need fuck off attitude or fuck off money and God loved Tony so much that he gave him both.

Anyone who knew Captain Tony loved him dearly and everybody else was likely scared to death of him.

He looked something like a cross between Hulk Hogan and medieval depictions of Satan. His face and naked pate always burned bright red with a rugged topography of throbbing veins, accentuated by a ring of stark white hair that surrounded the bald spot on top of his head. The white moustache and goatee added the finishing touches to his diabolical appearance. When his shocks of long white hair were tied into a neat ponytail he simply resembled a badass biker with sunburn but when it was left to blow in the breeze he was the absolute picture of a modern pirate.

Tony lost the use of his left leg to polio and the shriveled limb was kept rigid with a series of braces and a heavily weighted shoe. He walked just like a peg-legged pirate, throwing the dead leg forward with a thump of the heavy shoe and following with the good leg. Decades of using his upper body to drag himself around and to wrench on Harley Davidsons gave him absurdly muscular arms and a barrel chest that contributed to his menacing appearance. If you teased Tony about acting like Long John Silver he'd throw you a smile so warm it could melt a doubloon and answer you in a salty brogue.

"Aye, matey, it's the pirate's life for me."

———————

When the Sheriff's boats roared into the no wake zone of the marina at forty knots, sirens blaring and lights flashing we expected the worst. Their wake caused every boat in the marina to bounce like a bobber and tug violently at the dock lines. The boaters who weren't aroused by the yelping air horns and shrill sirens were called to attention by the contents of cupboards and drawers clattering loose in a dozen bobbing galleys. The Sheriff was usually the enforcer of the no wake area near the marina so the commotion they caused was doubly upsetting.

There were two Sheriff's boats from each side of the river and a Coast Guard runabout led the charge. When they made a beeline for

Captain Tony's slip, the stiffs on the dock must have assumed that his reckless lifestyle had finally ruffled the wrong feathers. Even the people who appreciated Tony's dangerous sense of adventure and pirate-like pillaging of this life expected him to hit the wall eventually. The ones who were frightened of him or antagonized by his unashamed hedonism were eager voyeurs to his presumed comeuppance when the Sheriffs approached his boat.

My buddy Joey and I were loading beer into the ice chest under the back seat of the jet when the commotion started. It was the 4th of July weekend and the river was asshole to elbow with dangerous amateurs so Captain Tony was taking us away from the fray in the jet. We were going to go camping on the string of islands north of the high bridge where the drunken propeller boats couldn't follow. My first thought when I saw the Sheriff was a selfish one. Would Tony let Joey and me take the boat if the cops dragged him off for some act of piracy?

The Sheriff was terse but respectful as his boat slammed into Tony's expensive metal flake paint job.

"We need the jet, Captain and we need to get the beer out of that ice chest now!"

Tony shot a glare at the man for smacking into his pride and joy but was quickly subdued by the Sheriff's explanation.

"A lady got her legs sheared off over by Beer Can Island. We need you to buzz the channel to help us find them. Doc says they'll float for awhile but our propellers will make hash out of 'em."

The woman was lazing on an air mattress near the island when a drunken bon vivant in a twenty-seven foot Chris Craft ran her asunder with his propeller. He must have thought he had hit a floating log because he continued on his dangerous way without hesitation. The boat was five miles downstream when he was finally apprehended and he had his lawyer on the marine telephone before his beer got warm.

There's nothing like a drunken manslaughter rap to suck the fun out of Independence Day so the reckless man must have held out sincere hope for her survival.

———————

If you ever lose a limb and need someone to help you look for it I recommend finding someone who's already lost one of his own, for the sheer enthusiasm he will invest in the effort. When the Sheriff's deputies tried to solicit volunteers to walk the shallows around the island to look for the severed limbs, everybody had someplace else they needed to be in a hurry. In a matter of minutes the island was eerily vacant and the legs were presumably lost to the current. Captain Tony sprang into action as though he was charged with looking for his own lost limb. The Sheriff barely finished gesturing to the location of the incident before the jet roared to life and shot toward the channel.

Joey and I were still tossing cans of beer out of the ice chest when Tony spotted the first leg. Fortunately for me it passed on Joey's side of the boat so I didn't have to fish the thing out of the water. He tossed it in the ice chest and closed the lid quick with his eyes screwed shut but he wound up shuddering with the creepy wilburs for about a month afterward. The second leg was trickier and I don't think anybody but the Captain or maybe Johnny Weismuller could have gotten it back.

Tony was an amazing swimmer for a guy with only one useful leg himself. Joey and I were thirty years his junior with all of our limbs intact and he could swim circles around us, then pull himself onto the transom of the boat with ease.

We were moving slowly upstream in the channel when the Captain saw the second leg floating swiftly with the current in the other direction. He dived from the boat without a word, so my buddy and I didn't know we were pilot-less until we heard the splash. Joey grabbed the wheel and spun her about to chase after Tony who was now moving faster downstream than both the dangerous current and the severed limb. He dived beneath the surface several times before we caught up with him and his final dive lasted so long we feared we had lost him to the undertow. Joey must have driven the boat right over him because he splashed to the surface behind us and scared the Hell out of us both when he tossed the woman's leg onto the aftcover of the jet boat.

Tony wasn't even winded from his superhuman swimming feat when he pulled himself back up onto the boat and took the wheel. Joey and I both fell to the deck with a thump when he throttled toward the Med-Evac helicopter on the pier. He packed the legs in beach towels full of ice and handed them to the paramedics who had waited hopefully for the success of the search. Captain Tony, like most good pirates who lead lives of grand adventure, was a master of understatement.

"You better hurry, boys, she'll be wanting these back."

For all of his selfless effort, Tony was only a partial success that day. One of the legs was badly mangled by the propeller and could not be reattached but the woman can now stand on the other and walk with the aid of a prosthetic limb. Hers was a limited miracle but a miracle nonetheless and she had a notorious rabble-rousing, one-legged pirate to thank for it.

Both the Sheriff's department and the Coast Guard wanted to give Captain Tony a letter of commendation and a plaque but he declined them when he learned that he had left the job half-done.

# Turning the other cheek

Most of the kids in my neighborhood worked at the brickyard at one time or another. The proprietor didn't concern himself with pesky child labor laws so he had an eager work force of street urchins to do his bidding. At twelve and thirteen my buddies and I were too young to get regular jobs so we were glad for the opportunity.

The boss would take the older kids with him on "salvage runs," to collect chunks of wall from recently demolished buildings. He sometimes had permission but most often these missions were done with stealth during the demolition crew's lunch break or over the weekend when the site was abandoned. The younger ones would then chop the concrete and mortar off of the salvaged bricks and stack them neatly on a pallet for resale. He paid us half a penny to clean them and half a penny to palletize them, then sold the bricks back to the builder for thirteen cents apiece.

The work was dangerous and injuries were commonplace. The masonry hammers were ground to a razor's edge so the slightest error could result in a horrific blood letting. A buddy of mine missed the brick on a wild swing of the hammer once and cut a forty stitch gash in his leg. In another moment of carelessness my older brother Billy all but severed his thumb. The salvage runs, however, made the brick cleaning seem like child's play.

They called it "making a run" and meant it literally. The boss would act as lookout leaving his son Kevin to lead the crew. They always returned with tales of brushes with the law or grim reaper that more often than not included some act of profound stupidity on Kevin's part.

He was a big guy and wasn't shy about using an appeal to force if you disagreed with him. He was uniformly ridiculed behind his back but his physical bulk and relationship with the boss prevented any direct criticism. When Kevin wasn't out on a salvage run he was tormenting the little kids in the brickyard. He'd hide behind a wall and pelt us with rocks or steal our cleaned bricks and put them on his own pallet. If we complained to the boss, he told us to quit if we didn't like it.

One day Kevin was screwing around with us as usual, taking our cleaned bricks and hurling them as far across the yard as he could. He didn't notice my brother rounding the corner of the building as he pitched the last brick. A couple of us yelled a tardy warning just as it ended its arc on the top of Billy's head. He crumpled to the ground in a heap and I'm sure that I wasn't the only one who feared the worst.

We hadn't even time to run to his aid before Billy shot to his feet and stood with a disturbing swagger. He looked exactly like a marionette that had been suddenly yanked upright and left to dangle from invisible strings. He wavered on his feet for a long moment, blood streaming over his face and onto his shirt. He tipped his head slowly from side to side and I remember thinking at the time that he was checking for loose screws. As he regained his composure he looked around on the ground near his feet and spotted the brick missile, now broken in two, slightly stained with his blood.

He picked up the two pieces of brick and looked directly across the yard at Kevin. We all stood motionless as he crossed the yard, a half brick in each hand, straight up to the trembling bully. It was apparent from his shifting posture that Kevin was wavering between his fight and flight instincts. I hated that jerk as much as the next guy but I was afraid for him as Billy closed the gap. The brick tore open a flap of scalp from the top of his head down to his ear, which moved in grotesque syncopation as he walked. I could see a terrible clarity in his eyes.

Kevin flinched a little when Billy handed him the pieces of brick. Tiny spittles of blood punctuated every syllable as my brother spoke with unnerving calm.

"It's all fun and games until somebody gets hurt."

———————

I have to admit I felt both relieved and let down. My brother was my hero and I couldn't understand why he'd let Kevin off so easily. He simply drove himself to the hospital where they sewed his head back together and that was the end if it.

Kevin was overly nice to everybody for about a month after that. As the brick throwing incident faded in memory he began to slip back into his menacing ways. He avoided interaction with Billy and he left me alone by association but he began hassling my friends and the other kids as though nothing had happened. The real trouble started when his father bought him the pellet gun.

He convinced his father that bird leavings were lowering the appeal of the patio brick display and that he could solve the problem. Kevin contented himself with the extermination of birds until there were none left to kill. He moved on to mammals and would proudly announce each new species in his carcass collection. I heard him complain to his father that it took so many of the small caliber pellets to bring down a raccoon that it was hardly worth the effort. This guy was a monster and I thought worse of my brother for not beating him to death while he had the righteous legal defense.

Kevin became bored due to the growing scarcity of wildlife and as might have been predicted started shooting at us. He later claimed he was shooting our pop cans and bicycle tires and never meant to hit us at all. The fact was that he had honed his accuracy to the extent that he believed he could take a cigarette out of someone's mouth from across the yard. He was attempting just that when my buddy Mark ruined his fun by moving slightly and catching the .22 pellet with his face. The shot missed his eyeball by centimeters so his vision was spared but it shattered his eye socket and called for an ambulance ride and emergency surgery.

We didn't realize at first what caused Mark's swollen face and shriek of pain, we assumed a chip had flown into his eye. As he was loaded into the ambulance he began screaming "I got shot, I got shot!" That's when one of my friends voiced the obvious question, "Where's Kevin?" He had been conspicuously absent throughout the entire ordeal and the mention of his name triggered something like a Greek chorus of two dozen voices in unison.

"The pellet gun."

The brickyard office building housed a four-story bell tower as its centerpiece. It no longer had a bell but made the perfect sniper's nest for a bored sociopath. Billy knew just where to find the lone gunman. I swelled with pride as my brother sprinted up the stairs for the showdown.

I never asked Billy what happened in the bell tower that day and he never told me. The rest of the kids and I were waiting quietly at the base of the stairs, straining to hear evidence of the ass whupping but we heard nothing. We shrunk a little when Kevin came down first, still carrying the pellet gun and apparently not yet beaten to a pulp. Billy rounded the corner just behind him and told us we were going to have a company meeting outside.

Kevin was still holding the pellet gun when Billy yanked him up onto the flatbed as though he was a bag of dirty clothes. The rest of the kids and I circled the elevated platform as our hero silently menaced an admission of guilt and tearful apology out of the bastard. When Billy told him to "finish the job," Kevin backed away and cowered like a whipped dog. My brother took a single step toward the beaten bully and he leaped from the truck and ran for the office, where he quietly waited for his arrest after calling the police and confessing.

My brother was "Billy the giant slayer" and my stock among the street urchins rose accordingly. Better still he did it with some kind of pacifist, voodoo Gandhi deal that not one of us even pretended to understand. Kevin did a long stretch in the reformatory for shooting Mark in the face and that was the last we ever saw of him. However long he was inside wasn't long enough and I'm afraid it only delayed his evil.

I presume that by now he has graduated to real prisons and proper beatings.

# Fandango

My best friend's brother killed a guy with a beer bottle. It was an accident by most accounts and I think that all he ended up having to pay for it was a short stretch for involuntary manslaughter and a few more years on the probationary leash. It happened at a crowded party in a private residence in front of dozens of witnesses. Somebody said the wrong thing about somebody else's girlfriend or wife; the bottle was hurled and instant karma got them both.

I never got to know my buddy's brother very well. We met only once, as children and I have no recollection of him whatsoever. I'm sure that he is a nice enough person once you get past the fact that he killed a man in anger. My opinion on the issue might change if I was closer to the killer or a friend to the victim but from where I'm sitting, justice was immaculate and swift. The bottle thrower learned that hostility is a beast that is difficult to control once unleashed and the victim learned the hard way to keep his big mouth shut.

About half of the people I run into are angry about something and since all of us are fragile, accidentally killing people must be a fairly common phenomenon. I told the story about the deadly beer bottle to a guy at the bar and he began rifling through the newspaper he had on his lap. In the Metro/State section of that day's paper was a story with a similar ending. Two men had been evicted from a nearby bar for hell raising and they resumed their fight on the sidewalk in front of the tavern with deadly results.

To say that fistfights in real life aren't anything like in the movies is a gargantuan understatement. The next time you are enraged enough to throw a fist you should pretend that you are holding a gun because hostility has a way of getting out of hand. According to the newspaper account of that particular fracas there was only one punch thrown. The victim fell to the sidewalk, hit his head against the curb and that was all she wrote.

The perpetrator in that case wasn't as lucky as the beer bottle guy because he wound up with 7 to 10 for the manslaughter rap. That's a long time to sit and dwell on one careless word or one spilt drink.

————————

When the film "Billy Jack" came out the resemblance of the title character to my brother Billy was startling. It wasn't so much that Billy looked like Tom Laughlin, though they did share some remarkable physical similarities but it seemed that they had modeled the character of Billy Jack after my brother's peculiar worldview. The details were obviously different but the aggressive pacifism of the stoic Billy Jack seemed eerily similar to Billy's own.

If you haven't seen the film, you should, but not for its cinematic brilliance because it hasn't any. The hero, Billy Jack, champions the cause of an open school populated by peace loving hippies who become so irksome in their mellow communal utopia that the modern viewer will likely root for their demise.

The message of the film, if there is any coherent message at all, is confusing and contradictory. Non-violence is portrayed as the ultimate good but it would seem the only way to accomplish it is with frequent ass kicking by the martial artist and former Green Beret, Billy Jack. The hero is what they used to call a half-breed, equal parts noble Native American and Anglo-Saxon white devil and he returns from the white man's war in Vietnam to wage reluctant battle against racist rednecks in America.

———————

Billy began his training in the martial arts to learn to defend himself against tough guys but the discipline eventually seeped into every area of his life. If you have ever known a seriously devout martial artist you've seen the paradoxical serenity that such well-focused violence can engender. I suppose it must be calming, in a way, to know that you can beat the living crap out of any idiot you encounter. He studied Shodokan, Japanese style karate, under a world renowned master but ultimately developed and practiced his own training regimen that would have made his sensei blush with pride.

Name a warrior skill and Billy had been to the end of it and back again. Throwing stars and fighting staffs were mastered mostly for fun but the long sparring sticks looked a lot like pool cues and held the promise of some real world application. He would tell you that the knife throwing was merely to hone his hand eye coordination but the outline of a humanoid on the old door he threw them at betrayed a darker potential. Eventually he could turn and throw from fifty feet in a mostly darkened room and hit a piece of electrical tape the size of a dime.

In addition to the normal rigors of the dojo, his workout regimen included several hours each day of ritual self-flagellation to thicken his skin against assault. Many of the exercises he performed were shocking and difficult to witness. It took him awhile to convince his girlfriend to punch him in the face as hard as she could but I think that she actually grew to enjoy the sessions.

The depth of his commitment to toughening and pain tolerance are best illustrated by an exercise that he performed first thing every morning when he got out of bed. Billy lived in a crummy little efficiency apartment at the time, with an uncarpeted concrete floor that doubled as a sparring partner. When he awoke he would kneel on the edge of the bed with his hands clasped behind his back and fall chest first onto the unforgiving cement. He considered his exercise a failure if he let out a whimper or lost his wind and repeated the punishment until he got it right.

I questioned his sanity at the time but came to understand why it was more important for Billy to be able to absorb a blow, rather than deliver one.

———————

We both ran with gangs in those days but me and my punk friends were more like the little rascals in the "Our Gang" films than the Crips or the Bloods. Billy's buddies were the genuine articles, dealing quantities and stealing wheels, kicking ass and breaking hearts. His best friend from the bad old days is still inside for beating up a couple of cops who mistook him for a cupcake.

I wanted to be just like Billy when I grew up so I bugged him to spar with me and teach me to be a karate man. He was kind of a little guy but his mastery of the science of fighting drew hushed respect in every room that he entered. I watched him back down guys twice his size with little more than a heavy look and oh, how the Sheilas swooned for a genuine badass.

By the time Billy was qualified to teach the martial arts he wanted nothing to do with hand to hand combat. He told me that I shouldn't enter into a fistfight unless I was prepared to kill a man and if that was the case, I should buy a gun instead. All of his training could be distilled to the effectiveness of knowing a couple of dozen ways to take the life of a human being with one strike.

"It ain't like in the movies, Jonny, a real fight lasts a couple of seconds, tops. Why the Hell would you trade punches with an idiot when you can crush his larynx or jam his nose up into his brain and kill him dead?"

"I just want to learn to defend myself if things get ugly."

"The best defense when things get ugly is to run away, little man."

———

I liked fishing well enough; I just hated catching fish. I used to put my line in the water with a sinker and no hook to keep up appearances and spare the prey but Billy got wise eventually. When he tied a hook onto the end of my line I only pretended to bait it but to my dismay the shiny hook alone snared the occasional sunfish or striped bass.

I started giving Billy grief about the casual cruelty of his hobby and he hated me for it. He had a single-minded enthusiasm for fishing since he was old enough to walk and showed little interest in anything else. I was no longer welcome on most of his fishing excursions.

There is a quiet violence in fishing for sport that Billy had always been able to minimize through respect for his prey. He never took more from the pond than he could clean and eat that day and his opponent was regarded with reverent dignity right up until the filet knife ended its existence. It was obviously a bloody endeavor but Billy treated it with far greater solemnity than the beer-bellied yokels did on the Saturday morning fishing shows.

He behaved more in the Native American tradition, living synergistically with nature, quietly grateful for its gifts. There was nothing intentionally cruel in the way Billy treated the fish or the live bait and I felt terrible for tweaking his conscience on the matter.

Our father traveled frequently on business so the older kids were charged with looking after the younguns and Billy was forced to pal around with me whether he wanted to or not. He'd rather swallow a hook himself than take his whiny little brother fishing anymore, so alternate pastimes were explored and tennis emerged as our primary activity. Our old man was a tennis buff so there was a pile of equipment in the basement and since court time was free at the elementary school on the hill, it fit perfectly within our budget.

We were as unlikely a pair of tennis players as you will ever see. The country club set would have winced at my cut off blue jeans and Led Zeppelin T-shirt but Billy's wardrobe would have sent them fleeing the court in hysterics. He had taken to wearing a pseudo-Native

American fringed leather jacket everywhere he went, summer and winter, with matching flat-brimmed heavy leather hat. How I'd love to have a photograph of him standing there, all bad-assed Billy Jack in leather with his pale, bony chicken legs sticking out of borrowed white tennis shorts.

Everything goes better with beer and tunes so Billy would pull his Charger right up next to the tennis courts and put the speakers on the roof; trunk open for accentuated bass thrust and easy access to the cooler. He had a cassette deck in the car that could play both sides of a tape in a continuous loop so ZZ Top Fandango blared across the tennis courts, over and over again.

The quality of ZZ Top's music increases in direct proportion to the amount of beer consumed so by the time the beer chest was empty we'd have Fandango cranked up to eleven.

---

The beer cooler was half-empty and ZZ Top's Fandango had made three or four complete loops around the tape deck by the time we were joined by tennis players on the other court. They were giving us dirty looks and I remember thinking that it might be a good time to change the tape or perhaps turn the volume down a little until they became acclimated.

"Hey, Wilbur, you think we should kill the tunes?"

"Kill the tunes? It's the best little ol' band from Texas for chrissake. Screw 'em if they don't like ZZ Top. We were here first."

ZZ Top is sort of the tequila of rock and roll music. You don't sip tequila you slam it.

"Hell, I'd turn it up louder but the speakers keep vibrating off the roof of the car."

There were three of them playing on the neighboring court, two big clunky guys going doubles against a wiry little athletic looking dude on the other side. The single guy was obviously a serious tennis player or at least he considered himself as such because he was attempting high velocity overhand serves that would have been worthy of Pete Sampras if they didn't keep slamming into the net for repeated losses against less skilled opponents. Every time he missed a serve or double faulted he'd swear loudly or smack his expensive racket against the fence or the hard clay court.

The angry guy's theatrics became increasingly vocal, curses that would make a dock worker blush, almost drowning out ZZ Top's kick-ass live version of Jailhouse Rock. When he finally blew his top, I suspect that the real culprit was his false sense of grandeur with a tennis racket and that his high opinion of his own skill doomed him to failure. He blamed the tunes.

"Turn that fucking noise off NOW!"

He directed his edict at Billy but I immediately moved to turn down the music. My brother shot me a stern look, waved me off and took matters into his own hands.

"That's no way to ask for something, buddy. How'd you ever get so old without learning please and thank you?"

The guy lost it. His spendy composite racket shattered when he slammed it to the ground and ran toward my brother with murder in his eyes. As I moved toward Billy's side of the net, both of the angry guy's companions moved to stall my progress and hold me in place, one on each arm.

Billy shed the tasseled jacket to play tennis but he kept his trademark leather hat on as always. He did everything but shower wearing that hat; the two of them were inseparable. When the angry guy knocked it off of his head and challenged Billy to fight, I got a chill down my spine.

––––––––––

It's funny that at the time the worst thing I could imagine is that Billy would kill the guy and have to go to prison over something stupid. It never even occurred to me that he might be in physical danger himself. When the angry guy cold cocked him in the jaw and Billy did nothing to stall the fist, I didn't know who to be afraid for.

"C'mon you punk. You're gonna just stand there while I kick your ass?"

Billy worked his jaw a little and checked for loose teeth with his tongue as he spoke.

"That all depends. Are you going to kick my ass because you don't like ZZ Top and have terrible manners or because you're a crappy tennis player?"

Boom. The left hook caught the other side of Billy's jaw hard enough to loosen his children's teeth. When the angry guy dropped back into a karate stance and started cocking his leg for a kick I tried to wrestle free from the grip of his companions to no avail. I would have been all for calling it a day and running away but that didn't seem to be an option so I tried to goad Billy into offensive action.

"Get 'im, Billy, before he cracks open your coconut!"

Boom. Such a sloppily executed roundhouse kick wouldn't have been much of a threat if the target wasn't just standing there with his hands by his side. In bare feet the sissy kick would have just glanced off of Billy's forehead but the rubber soled tennis shoe cut a gash that followed the line of his eyebrow and began the first in a long series of flowing wounds.

"I'm a brown belt from Chicago and you're gonna wish you'd never run into me."

Billy spat blood with every word as he responded to the angry guy with unreasonable calm.

"They must have a different kind of martial arts in Chicago because the first thing sensei taught us was respect."

The hothead resumed his assault, punching Billy over and over again, squarely in the face until blood was flowing from both nostrils and cuts in both of his lips. The gash above his eye became a chasm, torn wider with every smack, splattering droplets of blood around a wide circle on the clay court. Billy stood entirely still, feet planted in the exact position they were in before the madness commenced, like a statue anchored to a pedestal.

Just when I thought the angry guy had come to his senses and stopped the terrible beating he caught his breath and unloaded the big guns. It appeared to be pissing him off that he couldn't knock Billy down so he kept kicking him harder and harder, first his chest, then his abdomen, then his kidneys.

Billy just stood there bleeding.

I can now summon as tough an exterior as the next guy but I was only thirteen years old at the time. I gave up yelling for Billy to fight back and began to cry, certain I was going to watch my brother die that day.

—————

The angry guy's companions seemed to sense that they were on the brink of an accessory to manslaughter rap because they eventually became emphatic in their own appeal to stop the spectacle. By that time the perpetrator was bent over in exhaustion, incapable of delivering much of a wallop, huffing his wind as though he had just finished a marathon.

They collected their tennis equipment and their volatile little friend and drove off into the sunset. Billy was standing in the exact same spot he had been in when the beating began, bleeding from a dozen wounds, Fandango still blaring from the car stereo.

I got to drive the Charger for the first time ever that day because both of Billy's eyes were swollen shut. You should have heard the girl at the Kentucky Fried Chicken restaurant shriek when we walked in the door and asked if we could use their restroom to get him cleaned up. His face looked like ground round and his entire torso was a mass of bloody shoe prints and wildly colored bruises. He was absolutely painted in his own blood from head to foot and that poor girl must have assumed he had fallen out of an airplane.

Billy spat one of his front teeth into the sink and as I unrolled toilet paper for temporary bandages he lisped,

"Tennith ith kinda rough, maybe we oughtta try golf."

# One man's trash

If it was up to the harbormaster, D dock would have been untethered and left to drift downstream long ago. Class distinctions were firmly delineated in the marina, as in the larger world, and the denizens of D dock were the unwashed masses that the privileged set took up power yachting to avoid. The marina manager had more in common with the working stiffs than the blue blazers but his loyalties followed his ambition.

The layout of the marina had been determined decades before by a committee of dedicated snobs who had gone so far as to compartmentalize the slips according to wealth. The decision was made to assign letter grades to the five main docks, A, B, C, D, and S. The silly rich committee members would be on A dock, of course, upwardly mobile weekend warriors on B. C dock was for poseurs and wannabe's and D was left to the wretched refuse.

S dock was for sailboats exclusively but in the regal opinion of the yacht club, S stood for satisfactory because they paid their bills on time. The fat cats in command were power boaters and the only thing they held in lower esteem than poverty was a wind driven vessel. Sailboats were a nuisance, like a log drifting in the channel, zigzagging back and forth across their righteous petroleum driven path, barely in control of their own progress.

They'd have called it F dock were it not for the fact that one of the snobs owned a sailboat for show.

---

S dock looked brand new because the sailors hardly ever showed up. On the rare occasion they visited the marina they didn't dwell around the slip as the power boaters did so there was little in the way of wear and tear on the dock. Most of the sailboats were merely status symbols, objects 'd art, and their skippers barely qualified to captain a dinghy. It seemed a shameful waste that those gorgeous vessels should lay idle for months at a time but the owners could afford other diversions as well.

A walk down D dock was a treacherous affair because the money allotted for marina maintenance dwindled as it passed through the letter grades. A dock was sturdy and kept in meticulous repair, as was B dock with its covered slips and hand railings. Things started to slide a little by the time they got around to C dock, some of the light fixtures were perpetually broken and the painted slip numbers were left faded and peeling. The money always ran out by the time they got to D dock and it was left in abject squalor, the Cabrini Green of the boat basin.

The docks were supported by empty fifty-gallon oil drums, welded shut to insure their buoyancy. When a weld on one of the barrels yielded to corrosion it sank to the bottom, or was sucked down river with the current. The lost barrel would leave a soft spot on the dock that gave way to the pedestrian's weight, something like traversing a floating trampoline. If a barrel went missing on one of the wealthier piers it was replaced within the hour, but the humble D dock was left to nature's inevitable decay. Perhaps one in three of the original floatation barrels remained and half of those were taking on water.

In addition to keeping the dock afloat, the proper allotment of empty drums enforced the linear nature of the pier. In their absence, D dock took on a serpentine quality which, in conjunction with the soft spots, created a bobbing weaving path that would make a circus acrobat edgy. Some poor soul fell in the drink nearly every day off of D dock but the frequent appeals to the marina for maintenance were greeted with crocodile tears and the profitable sale of floating key chains.

I'm slow to criticize the rich folk for allowing the deterioration of our dock because it only brought us closer together. The rest of the marina was inhabited by isolationist pufferfish who rarely commingled and for whom boating was little more than another means to flaunt their wealth. The residents of D dock had to rely on one another for their very survival. We'd fish our unfortunate neighbor out of the river when the sloshing pier gave way, or rush out in a heavy storm to help guide our fellow into a dangerously shifting slip. We became a family, bound by arduous necessity and our genuine respect for the river and each other.

It should come as no surprise that D dock was the soul of the scene. Real people inhabited that pier, with dogs and children and towels drying on a clothesline strung across the poop deck. They drank and partied together with a familial ease that the upper crust found unseemly and distasteful. The rabble seemed to have a genuine affection for one another that the islands of aristocracy over on A dock could never comprehend.

It seemed to us that the fat cats with a more solid footing were missing the boat.

———————

I actually owe a debt of gratitude to the slumlords who let D dock slip into decay because I parlayed the hardship into a lucrative summer job. Every time somebody took an unintentional plunge off of the wobbly dock, I was paid a couple of bucks to dive in and retrieve whatever they'd been carrying. My services were in constant demand to fetch Weber grill components or car keys or jugs of wine from the riverbed. My greatest success was the challenging recovery of a hapless boater's errant toupee. The tiny globule of fake hair drifted with the current before coming to rest on the bottom and it took me dozens of groping excursions into the murky depths to earn my two-dollar commission.

I was visited with inspiration the day that a woman fell into the drink and was separated from her charm bracelet. It wasn't an expensive bauble but it carried a trinket from each of her children and grandchildren and was, in her estimation, invaluable. Heavy shiny things were child's play next to a drifting hairpiece so her cherished heirloom was recovered in a single dive. She was so delighted when I returned it to her that she forgot to pay me and I was so humbled by the joy she displayed that I never thought to ask.

Diving for jewelry, albeit costume jewelry, put me in the mind of sunken treasure and it occurred to me that the rich people over on A dock must fall in the river from time to time as well. Their docks were sturdier but they were tottering old bluebloods for the most part, entirely capable of falling in the water unaided. It seemed unlikely to me that they'd adorn themselves with ornaments that merely possessed sentimental value. When they took the plunge they'd be giving up high-class booty, pearl earrings, diamond broaches or the keys to the Lotus. They would never think of hiring a river rat to do some scavenging, they'd simply ring up the insurance company or the locksmith.

I bought a diving mask and waterproof flashlight the very next day.

———————

The guy at the liquor store gave me twenty bucks apiece for the two crated magnums of French champagne. The sterling silver flatware in the rotted walnut case yielded only forty dollars for scrap because some of the spoons went missing. The jewelry angle was a big disappointment, one necklace, one empty money clip and the braided gold band of a ruined wristwatch.

My failed quest for sunken treasure gave way to the accumulation of fascinating archeological data about how the other half lives. What I saw was the waterlogged evidence of a slash and burn boating class that didn't believe in making the long walk to the dumpster. Beneath the boats on humble D dock I found little more than sand and sunken barrels. The riverbed below the million dollar vessels on A dock was blanketed with trash from stem to stern.

Beneath the top layer of jetsam lay an older stratum and beneath that one another more ancient. Before I reached pure sand I found tin cans, actually made out of tin, that dated from around the turn of the century. Not only were these people filthy pigs, they seemed to have been descended from a long line of other filthy pigs.

As luck would have it, their trashy lifestyle was the source of my greatest windfall as a scavenger. The current breed of floating slobs was of little use to me but their great-grandparent's refuse carried substantial antique value. They were fond of Coca-Cola, it seems and the frivolous abandon that accompanied their wealth compelled them to toss the empties over the side. I even found a few bottles that had never been opened and still contained the original contents.

You'd be amazed what some cats will pay for a couple of cases of empty Coke bottles that predate World War I. If I told you what they gave me for the full ones you'd go out tomorrow and buy a diving mask.

# On conspicuous consumption

**D**ue to a terrible mix-up at Powerball Headquarters, all but one of my little numbered Ping-Pong balls remained in the hopper for Saturday's drawing. This is a disturbing turn of events and will, no doubt, have a detrimental effect on the Consumer Spending Index. Ripples will be felt in the area of charitable giving as well because I had planned to only piss away half of the money on myself. The rest of my windfall was to be dedicated to a philanthropic entity, operated from the deck of my yacht, that would provide cell phones and Sport Utility Vehicles to the less fortunate.

Such a blow would have devastated a lesser man but I was able to summon the inner strength to go on, to fight the good fight. I arrived early enough this morning to snatch the vitriolic letter of resignation from my manager's inter-office mail box and have resumed my humble role with the unwashed masses.

————

It's been said that a boat is a hole in the water, surrounded by wood, into which one pours money. Any boater could tell you that this is a laughable understatement and inaccurate to the extent that the hole is usually surrounded by fiberglass.

If you want peace and quiet, visit any marina on a weekday. The poor shmuck who owns that gorgeous boat won't turn up until about noon on Saturday because he's working overtime to impress you. It might surprise you to learn that working stiffs, not unlike yourself, own some of the biggest and showiest vessels in the harbor. Weekend warriors.

I pretty much had the marina to myself Monday through Friday. There was the English professor down the dock but he kept to himself for the most part. You'd hear the rat-a-tat-tat of his Underwood as he hammered out his novel, punctuated by the occasional splash, as he'd cannonball into the river to refresh. The semantics professor was only half-kidding when he threatened to take a place in the city on the weekends for some peace and quiet.

There was only one other boater on the dock who hung around with us during the week and that dude had it snapped. Sammy had more money than God and he wasn't shy about showing it off. His boat would have inspired envy in even the most ascetic soul. "The Lucky Ducky" was a seventy-two foot Hatteras that he "stole from a dizzy widow" for $750,000. Sammy made sure that everyone in the marina knew that the yacht was worth three times what he'd paid for her and that he owned her outright. His cancelled personal check for the full amount was framed and hanging in the wheelhouse.

Sammy had the biggest, baddest bobber in the whole damned marina and you could detect it in his walk.

---

I did odd jobs around the marina, as a kid and I couldn't wait to get on board that beautiful Hatteras. She had teak trim and decking, a high maintenance material that requires frequent applications of oil and sealer to protect it from the elements. I made the mistake of telling the fat cat owner that I was so eager to get my hands on his boat that I'd have done the teak gratis. He took this as my initial negotiating position and wound up paying me something like two dollars an hour; for nearly a hundred hours of grueling labor.

Nobody in the marina really knew what Sammy did for a living, beyond the vague speculation that he was involved in some manner of fund raising. "Hey, aren't we all? Old Sammy's just better at it." The nice people on D dock didn't hate him for his good fortune but they were happy for him in the same manner that the fourth runner up is happy for Miss America. The summer I toiled for slave wages on the decks of "The Lucky Ducky," I was given a first hand glimpse into the mechanics of his wealth.

Sammy wasn't just your ordinary run of the mill fundraiser, he was *the* fundraiser for a high profile malady. He told me that he generally made four phone calls per day, just after lunch time, to corporate CEO's and wealthy individuals. He only dealt with transactions in the six or seven digit range and his commission was five percent of the gross. On a typical donation of five million dollars, Sammy would bag $250,000 for his efforts. Good gig if you can get it.

I noticed him doing the happy dance one day on the poop deck of "The Lucky Ducky," as I oiled the teak railings of the flying bridge above. I called him "Captain Sam," as would any good sycophant and hollered down to find out what he was celebrating. "Hey, hey, Captain Sam, don't tell me you won the lottery again?" Sammy smiled hard and explained that he had just closed the books on a five-year commitment from a major industrial firm for four million dollars per year.

I did the ciphering in my head and hollered back, "Woo Hoo! That's a cool million for the boat fund, Captain, not a bad day's work!"

His demeanor darkened in an instant and he scowled at me from the poop deck like Captain Bligh, "It's not about my commission, young man. I'm in the business of curing disease and saving lives, nothing more. I'd do it for free."

———————

We should all be thankful, I suppose, for Sammy's efforts on behalf of crippled children.  Technically speaking, his fund raising prowess is focused on finding a cure for the disease so he isn't really acting on behalf of the currently afflicted.  We have to hope that quality of life issues, like wheelchairs and leg braces, are being attended to from someone else's yacht.

The five million or so that he subtracts annually from the cause is merely fair compensation for his good works.  Sammy doesn't see himself as a fat cat with a bitchin' boat, he is Mother Theresa with a cell phone.

If you are engaged in fund raising yourself, you might want to take Sammy's name out of your Rolodex.

He gave at the office.

# Hello in there

It was a long walk to the nursing home. The place was never our initial destination but we seemed to end up there two or three times a week near the end. The Ebenezer Extended Care Facility was on the far side of town, miles from home and marked the frontiers of our pedestrian hooliganism. On the days we walked to the nursing home we had to call for a ride home or blow off our curfew.

My buddies and I called ourselves "The Men of the Oasis." Our name derived from the fact that Minnesota winters are a harsh challenge to street urchins so a part of every day was spent searching for warm places to congregate and smoke cigarettes. We would gain access to an empty warehouse or office building and declare the space our conquered oasis from the cold. Compared to what gangs are like today we might as well have been wearing Boy Scout uniforms but in our minds we were a force to be reckoned with.

The nursing home was always open and always warm so it became one of our favorite hangouts. They offered free hot chocolate and donuts for visitors so the place was truly an oasis. Many of the seniors were decrepit and unresponsive but a handful of live ones made up for the rest. One of the old guys, Oscar, spent the whole day on a bench near the front door and harangued everyone who passed by. He'd yell, "Who the hell are you and what the hell are you doing here?" to every visitor. It was particularly funny when it was a clergyman or a doctor he was yelling at. Oscar would say something like, "Hubert H. Humphrey didn't know his ass from apple butter," and we'd absolutely bust a gut.

When the staff realized that we were juvenile delinquents and not actual old people visitors they asked us to leave. Oscar rose to our defense and told the head nurse that we were his grandchildren and that we had more right to be there than she did. He stood unsteadily and shook his finger at the fifty-something nurse and said, "Remember which side your bread is buttered on, girlie!"

We were never hassled again.

––––––––––

Jane was a hottie, no doubt about it. The sepia toned photograph on her dresser was from her wedding in 1899 and she was breathtakingly beautiful. She buried her husband thirty years ago and had been waiting patiently to join him ever since. Jane had haunting, infinite gray eyes and she was no less lovely at ninety-two, than at sixteen.

Her husband Charlie was among the last casualties of World War II and was actually killed after the final cease-fire. Word of the Japanese surrender hadn't reached the jungle airstrip that was his charge and an uninformed sniper ended his life a full week after the end of the war. Charlie was a month away from retirement and a full Colonel's pension as a veteran of both World Wars. He was twelve hours away from his reunion with Jane in Hawaii when the curtain was drawn.

Jane was sixty-two when she lost Charlie and though she bemoaned the sacrifice of their retirement together she presumed they'd be reunited soon enough. When she was born the average life expectancy was something like fifty-five so she could not have anticipated the decades of terrible solitude. The nurse told us that Jane hadn't spoken to a soul since her arrival at the home ten years before.

The daughter who wanted to be rid of her died years ago and she had no other living relatives.

The Chaplain who delivered the news of Charlie's death had given her a Bible that day and she read it from cover to cover in one sitting. She spent every day of the thirty years since, waiting to die, with her brain in a book. When she finished reading the last paperback in the nursing home's meager library, she quietly devoted the remainder of her estate to its expansion. When I met Jane the library contained more than ten thousand volumes and she had read every word of every last one of them.

———————

She told me that I had Charlie in my eyes and I was her favorite. I'd get lost in a conversation with her and my buddies would get bored and split. Jane had an amazing memory and could relay the exact phrasing of a minor work she had read twenty years before. Pick a subject and Jane had studied it to completion, though she had no formal education beyond the eighth grade. I was thirteen years old and I fell in love with Jane and her infinite gray eyes.

I was with her when she died and it occurred to me what a terrible loss the world suffered with her absence. The wealth of knowledge and the dots connected behind those eyes went unrecognized and would pass unmourned. I looked around the cafeteria as the paramedics took her away and noticed the other ancient faces for the first time. I saw the same deep pools behind every sad expression and realized that the rest of the old geezers had been all but invisible to me until that moment.

We seem to equate old with useless and I'm afraid we do so at our peril. We herd up the wisest among us and put them out of sight and out of mind. Most will take their secrets to the grave.

Reading a great old book is not done as a service to the book but to the reader.

It is ultimately selfish.

# The Lord's Barn

The cost of war is usually measured in body bags or amputated limbs. The more subtle expense of shattered minds and shortened life spans are less direct and more easily overlooked. Many thousands of Vietnam veterans will expire within the next ten years or so, twenty years before they're due, as a result of the hidden price of that war. If you know a veteran of the conflict in Southeast Asia who has reached the age of fifty-six, shake his hand. He has defied the odds and the actuarial tables.

Of the dozen or so Vietnam vets I have known, about half were what my friend Mark refers to as "Rear Echelon Mother Fuckers," while the remainder were engaged in daily bullet avoidance. The Veteran's Administration makes no distinction between the REMFs and the boys on the front lines when they peg the average life expectancy of a Vietnam veteran at fifty-five. The horror of war is visual as well as visceral so I suppose that anyone "in country" is picking up part of the tab for the life-shortening stress festival. Go ahead and buy Mark a thank you beer before his fifty-fifth birthday, just to be on the safe side.

Without the accounting of the REMFs we would know little or nothing about the scene because most of the combat veterans who lived to tell about it don't want to. Chances are they are still trying to make sense of it themselves or more likely, trying in vain to forget that it ever happened.

It's just as well that they don't hit us with all of the gory details. We don't really want to know.

————————

Jim still slept with one eye open and a .32 Berretta under his pillow at night, five years after the last NVA regular or Vietcong guerilla took a shot at him. A clinical term like "post-traumatic stress" is a horribly misleading euphemism for the weight that he carried. You will not likely hear a combat veteran describe his lingering menace in such antiseptic terms. You probably won't hear him describe it at all.

Many nights he'd awake screaming a tardy warning to a long dead brother in arms, gushing jungle sweat in the cool bedroom of his Minnesota home. On more than one occasion his wife found herself staring down the barrel of that semi-automatic pistol when she startled him from a rare deep sleep. She learned not to make any sudden movements if he leveled the Berretta and unlatched the safety. You can add the worst kind of insomnia to the hidden cost of war. That poor man didn't get more than a few hours of decent shuteye per night, since the summer of '67.

Jim wasn't drafted, he enlisted in the Marine Corps and was shipped off to Asia before any widespread protest of the war began. By the time he found out he was engaged in an unpopular fight, he had already served two tours in the jungle and caught enough lead to kill more than one man. The most prominent of his scars were both caused by the same bullet, the entrance wound in the geographic center of his chest and the exit wound in about the same place on his upper back. A large caliber bullet tore right through the middle of his body and he miraculously survived but golf ball sized lumps of scarred flesh made him relive it every time he took off his shirt. How disorienting it must have been to return home and find the people he was fighting for more eager to shame than honor him.

He didn't know anything at all about hippies or yippies or "Hey, hey LBJ, how many kids did you kill today?" He was too damned busy, up to his neck in the blood of a Marine platoon with only a handful of survivors and none of them completely intact. Jim knew all about Audie Murphy and John Wayne and The Green Berets; about honor and country and the fight for democratic principals. His government asked for volunteers to fight the good fight and by God he stepped forward. I can only hope that he turned a deaf ear to the "baby killer" nonsense from the people on whose behalf he thought he was bleeding.

We all have epochal periods in our lives, those character defining stretches that may have been stark at the time but with age become romanticized in the retelling. We should all be so lucky to bounce a grandchild on our knee in our 80s and recount the life changing experiences that made us who we are. Jim lived long enough to meet his grandchildren but didn't have much that he wanted to share with them about his pivotal period.

I knew Jim for thirty years and never once heard him utter the word Vietnam.

---

As if the terror of the jungle and the lack of ticker tape weren't enough, shortly after his return to the States he began courting a woman with five children. She was recently divorced with little monsters ranging in age from nine to seventeen and he was barely twenty-five himself when they were wed. I was the youngest of the five, as undisciplined as he was gung ho, incapable of letting the sun go down without doing something obnoxious, illegal or downright evil. I think I caused that poor dude more consternation than the Vietcong and I'm afraid I acted in league with them to shorten his life through stress.

The very first night I came to live with them, my bags weren't even unpacked yet and Jim had to field a phone call from the police in the town where I used to live. They needed to ask him some questions about his juvenile delinquent step-son and they needed him to pay fourteen dollars in damages or he could be arrested himself. The incredulous expression on his face was priceless as the cop explained to him that I had stolen the fire extinguishers out of a place called "The Lord's Barn." Jim was raised a strict Catholic and the question was etched in his face.

What kind of unholy bad seed would take the fire suppression equipment from The Lord's Barn?

It was all a big misunderstanding, man. The Lord's Barn was a hangout for hoodlums, operated in a rehabilitated barn, adjacent to a church parking lot. It was run by a couple of volunteers with money from the church collection plate. The administrators were a lady cop and the wife of a Federal Marshal and they sought to give street urchins a safe home away from home. The place had pool tables, foosball tables and vending machines and nary a whiff of religious guidance. The respectable name and the soft hearts who ran the joint made it the perfect cover for all of our delinquent enterprises so we made the Lord's Barn our base of operations.

The barn was decrepit, with loose clapboard panels everywhere so we had access to the premises at all hours. After they fixed the gaping holes we were still able to get inside by scaling the silo and shimmying through the feed tunnel like farm rats. It was our scene so we never messed with it or stole anything, ever. It would have been child's play to empty the vending machines and game tables but it was never even discussed. We were hooligans and ne'er-do-wells but even we wouldn't rip off The Lord's Barn. The place was held in such reverence that when Mark started shooting us with the fire extinguisher, I didn't just grab one and shoot back. I said that we should take it outside.

There were four of us that night, with both Marks and Terrible Ted and we each grabbed a fire extinguisher for full-scale war in the open air. The jets of high-pressure fine white powder were far more impressive under the spotlights of the church parking lot so we waged our battle there, without giving a thought to our visibility or the consequences. Those things have incredible thrust and when they're not aimed directly at your buddy's head they can achieve amazing range. Under spotlights on a windless, pitch-black night the effect of the billowing clouds of fire retardant was spectacular.

…Until the cops arrived.

They showed us a great deal of mercy since we could have been nailed with a breaking and entering rap and a variety of goofier offenses. Rain would soon wash the parking lot clean and there was no real damage done so they promised to let us off the hook if we paid to recharge the fire extinguishers.

I was just getting ready to go live with my mother in an entirely different city and I doubted these local yokels would go through the trouble of tracking me down for such a minor sum as fourteen dollars. I actually had the dough but that was my gambling money.

———————

With that phone call from the police on the night that he first welcomed me into his home, Jim became one of my fathers. I had a perfectly good father already but I've never seen the rule that you're only allowed to have one. Jim isn't my step-anything. To his credit he resisted the natural urge to kick my skinny little ass right then and there and although he never quite managed to make a Marine out of me, it wasn't through negligence on his part.

When I so much as voiced disagreement with my mom's choice of television channels, he'd throw me one of those death looks that only combat vets possess and hiss, "Don't get lippy with your mother." Thanks to Jim, such a thing never occurred to me. He was an adoring husband to my mum and a great father to me and fifty-five is too damned young for such a decent man to die.

I didn't cry much for Jim right away because I was more than a little relieved for him. He suffered numerous ill effects throughout his life from the wounds he sustained in the war and at least I know that he's getting some well-deserved rest. The water works didn't really start to flow until I faced my prematurely widowed mother.

He received a twenty-one gun salute from a grateful nation at Fort Snelling National Cemetery in St. Paul. Jim was born on Pearl Harbor Day so it is poetically fitting and to me heartrending that he died on Memorial Day. I used to tease him about his birthday being so easy to remember because it was "A date which will live in infamy." I can almost hear his posthumous retort.

"Just *try* and forget Memorial Day, pal."

# Dangerous Ideas

I'm a firm believer in the concept of creative visualization. The idea is beautifully described in the Richard Bach book, "Illusions, The Adventures of a Reluctant Messiah." In the book, Mr. Bach puts forth a proposition that echoes the sentiments of every romantic philosopher who has ever taken breath: This is the best of all possible worlds and we have some say over our own reality.

If you are willing to suspend disbelief for the few hours it takes to absorb the charming allegory, you might just be swayed.

The story was published in the post hippie 70's, as America struggled with its ideological hangover. The summer of love was gone forever and cultural apocalypse seemed imminent. Everybody was Kung Fu fighting instead of Imagining and Woodstock became Kent State in the time it takes to grow a decent patch of marijuana.

During the darkest days of disco Mr. Bach revived a few million latent idealists with his optimistic little book.

---

My older brother picked up "Illusions" at a bookstore downtown, to pass the time while he waited for his bus. The story was so compelling that he missed three buses in a row as he stood reading in the aisle of the bookstore. He missed the fourth and final bus standing in line to pay for the book he had already read.

The basic premise of the tale is the same as Plato's "Allegory of the Cave," that the world of ideas is the real deal and that everything else is little more than a shadow on the wall. The book is interspersed with snippets from the messiah's handbook but it might just as well be Socrates speaking.

*"Imagine the universe beautiful and just*
*and perfect.*

*Then be sure of one thing:*

*The Is has imagined it quite a bit better*
*than you have."*

Or conversely,

*"Argue for your limitations and*
*sure enough they're yours."*

I was about thirteen years old when I read the book and I couldn't wait to tell my English teacher about it. He encouraged the class to read more fiction and this was a tantalizing fiction indeed; that every man might be his own messiah. I thought he'd appreciate the story's Platonic pedigree, if nothing else.

Not only was the teacher unimpressed with my choice of fiction, he held me up to ridicule in front of the entire class.

"If young Mr. Shute wants to waste his time and energy on Pop Philosophy that's his prerogative but I expect better of the rest of you."

I was dumbstruck. How could that sweet little book inspire such venom, in a teacher of all people? His derision was so intense I feared it would climax in a book burning. At first I wondered if he had even read the thing but his tirade continued and removed any doubt.

"That's secular humanism young man and it might just as well have been written in the Devil's own hand."

He was spindling the paperback book and pacing back and forth, red faced, inappropriately hostile.

"Moby Dick" is literature; your little fantasy book is trash, nothing more. It was composed by an imbecile for the amusement of other imbeciles."

I was not well read in the seventh grade so I had to take the man at his word about Moby Dick. I wouldn't find out until years later that Herman Melville was a tedious blowhard and that Moby Dick was his tour de force. Taste, in a matter as arbitrary as fiction, is bound to be subjective. In my humble opinion, if you can wrassle your way through Moby Dick in less than a week, without losing the will to live, I don't want you at my cocktail parties.

Mr. Turner's fanatic spectacle mellowed to a patronizing taunt.

"Perhaps our young philosopher is similarly edified by the comic strips in the Sunday newspaper."

The class tittered and for a moment I felt very small. I remembered a passage in "Illusions" that was devilishly appropriate to his belittling remark so I stood from my desk and paraphrased Mr. Bach as he had paraphrased Plato.

"I'll take the truth wherever I can get it, thank you!"

His condescension may have earned a wave of giggles but mine got a round of applause and a ticket out of his class for the rest of the period.

# Big Larry and the G-men

I felt a dreadful foreboding when the secretary told me to go to the conference room instead of the Principal's Office. We rated the seriousness of a confrontation by the number of grown-ups it took to do the confronting and if they needed a conference room I was in deep.

Principal Larry, his own bad self, was at the inquisition as were both of his Assistants. Matters of discipline were normally handled exclusively by the sadistic minions, to shield Larry from actual contact with the students whom he feared and despised. If they had to drag Big Larry into this I had gone too far.

I counted the stern faces twice to make sure I had an accurate tally, sixteen all told and at least three were armed. It was an intimidating assortment of parents, teachers, counselors and cops but most distressing was the two menacing suits in the dark corner whom I could not identify. They looked like Hollywood G-men and my little voice was screaming, "Run away, run away!"

I hadn't any idea what I had done to merit this grand theater of angry adults until I noticed the ream of computer paper on the middle of the conference table. I realized at that instant that the two guys in the shadow weren't from Central Casting.

I'd be the first to admit that I had discipline issues in high school.  My willingness to engage teachers in argument and my anarchistic nature clashed with their conventional world-view.  I had been permanently barred from all of my classes, except of course "Discussion and Debate," and spent my days between the library and a computer terminal in the counselor's office.

They invented a job for me in the counselor's office running a computer program to help other students with career counseling.  The personal computer had not yet been invented and the dumb terminal connected by modem to a mainframe was a complete mystery to the office staff.  They knew it involved something called the ARPANET and that it magically connected them to Universities across the country but none had learned to operate the strange device.  Due to my house arrest in the counselor's office I had plenty of time on my hands.

The plan seemed obvious to me and beautiful in its symmetry.  I would connect through the mainframe to the computer at U.S.C. as I always had, only instead of going to the directory that contained the career counseling program I would breach the University's rudimentary defenses and find the Central Scrutinizer. Once inside I planned to give myself a positive balance at the Bursar's office and perhaps a Masters Degree in computer science.

The password to edit student records required nine characters so I guessed that it was looking for a Social Security number.  I wrote a basic program that would call the California computer, insert a random nine-digit number and redial in the event of failure.  The program would make the first call at 8:00 p.m. on Friday when the office was empty and continue over the weekend until it completed a connection.

I made one small mistake in forgetting to turn off the printer.

The noisy Teletype chugged on all weekend and created a four hundred and fifty-page account of my every transgression.  When the Head Counselor found the evidence on Monday morning he didn't know what I was doing but he knew that it wasn't kosher. He alerted just about everybody who had a telephone.

———————

There wasn't any such thing as computer crime so the collected authorities were unsure how to proceed. When a Canadian kid hacked into Citibank a couple of years later they wrote laws-a-plenty but it seemed that I was happily ahead of the criminal curve.

As the roomful angrily debated my fate my father stood from his chair, shook his head in derision and said, "He's just a kid," and walked out. The inquisition disintegrated under the truth of his statement. When I told the Head Counselor I was quitting school he warned me against it and said that I should come back for my senior year and "blow the top off the place."

I presume he meant academically.

# The melancholy monkey

There is an episode of The Twilight Zone called "People are alike all over," in which two Earth astronauts crash land on Mars. One of the astronauts has unguarded optimism about the Martian civilization they will encounter and the other is cynical, expecting to find nothing new under the sun. The hopeful astronaut dies in the crash and the pessimistic one is left to cope with the Martians.

The inhabitants of Mars earn the skeptical astronaut's trust by presenting him with living arrangements that would be familiar to him. He is given an Earth house with all of the amenities of a typical suburban dwelling and told that he can live out his days in peace.

The house turns out to be a cage in a Martian zoo.

———

The zoo seemed like a perfect place to take a girl on a date. It is wholesome and benign, alive with happy children and the wonders of the animal kingdom. There is, however, a subliminal metaphor of animal urges and unashamed nudity, which can only propel a date in the right direction. It doesn't seem to make sense but the best way to get down and dirty with a nice girl is to start with something wholesome and benign.

I met her in line at a convenience store and she was a knockout. She was way out of my league but I thought I'd give it a stab. "Would you like to go to the zoo with me?" The zoo thing kills 'em; they collapse like a house of cards.

"Sure, I haven't been to the zoo since I was little. I'm Cindy, what's your name?"

Cindy seemed too good to be true. She was movie star beautiful and picked me up from my bus boy job in a brand new candy apple red Corvette. I thought I was dreaming when she asked me if I wanted to drive. I looked around the parking lot twice to make sure I wasn't on Candid Camera before climbing in the driver's seat of her car.

By the time we got to the zoo it was clear that Cindy had issues. Big as a house, crazy as a loon issues. Over the course of the twelve-minute trip to the Como Park Zoo she mentioned suicide more than a dozen times and murder twice. I found little comfort in the fact that she seemed six times more likely to take her own life as somebody else's.

When we got to the zoo she bounded out of the car with the enthusiasm of a child and actually skipped toward the monkey house. What is charming in a six-year old schoolgirl is scarier than hell in a twenty-three year old crazy chick and the nervous man in the ticket window had to presume she was out on a weekend pass and I was her guardian.

She rambled incessantly, to the curious stares of little old people and children on field trips, of how she felt as if she lived in a zoo.

"It is so hard to be beautiful, everybody staring at you all the time, everybody wants something from you. Sometimes when they're looking at me that way I just want slash my wrists and spray blood all over the ogling bastards!"

Nervous teachers and school children moved away from us in waves, "Come along children, time to go to the rare bird exhibit."

We eventually had the monkey house to ourselves and her ranting was moving me to believe that, in her case, suicide was probably a viable and fortuitous solution. I leaned against the glass of the chimpanzee exhibit, resigned to her bizarre chatter, and tried to focus instead on the playful chimps.

One of the captive apes caught my eye and held my gaze. He climbed the tree branches that had been erected as his jungle gym. As he reached the top branch of the simulated tree, he grabbed one of the ropes that hung from the ceiling as simulated vines. The little guy never broke eye contact with me as he looped the rope around his neck over and over again. He was looking directly in my eyes when he fell from the branch with the rope coiled around his neck.

I saw his fall in the slow motion that accompanies shocking events and began to yelp a warning to the custodian at the far end of the exhibit when I realized that the chimpanzee was only kidding. He had surreptitiously held on to the last coil, so that instead of snapping his neck, he swung playfully with his one handed grip on the rope. He repeated his macabre theatrical play over and over again, staring at me the entire time.

I don't go to the zoo anymore.

# On casual cruelty

The awkward silence ensued when I said that changing lanes without signaling is worse than the massacre at Columbine High School. The proposition was disturbing to the roomful of relatives at Christmastime but it was, nonetheless, both figuratively and literally true.

With all of the wailing and gnashing of teeth over spree shootings and random violence it seems that nobody really wants to address the core issue of casual cruelty. Well-focused rage will always grab the headlines and distract the masses but the root cause of such displays is never far beneath the surface. The young murderers in Colorado were driven, by their own admission, by little more than the taunting of their classmates and the culture that encouraged it.

If there is anyone left in America who doesn't understand the motivation behind these horrible dramas it is for lack of honest effort. The small stones of cruelty you cast today cause unfathomable ripples and result, with increasing frequency, in the pockets of local horror you see on CNN. If you cut someone off in traffic today or if you were rude to a telemarketer on the phone, you are responsible for the killings at Columbine.

———

I invented road rage. I'm not proud of this fact but the sincerity of my essay depends on the confession.

I was sixteen and my driver's license was three days old. The complexities of operating an automobile held my full attention, from the ten o'clock two o'clock grip on the wheel right up to the faithful use of the turn signal. I scrupulously kept a full car-length distance for every ten miles an hour of speed and made a full, three-second pause at every stop sign. They showed us a Disney film in driver's education class called "Courtesy is Contagious" and I adopted the movie title as my driving mantra.

I was rolling down a hill at twenty-eight miles per hour, riding the brakes slightly to stay within the posted limit of thirty. The fact that my foot was on the break pedal was the only thing that prevented a terrible collision. The other car was waiting to exit the driveway of the Apostolic Bible Institute at the bottom of the hill. The driver saw me approaching and was clearly debating whether or not to cut in front of me or wait for my car to pass the driveway entrance.

The car inched closer to the street, braking, creeping forward then repeating the process. I passed the point where I could safely slow to accommodate the other car and at that moment the driver succumbed to the darker angels of his or her nature and hit the accelerator. To save a few milliseconds of driving time, or perhaps to gain pole position at the next stoplight, this ignoramus had risked both of our lives.

I stomped the brake pedal to the floor with both feet and with tires squealing, avoided impact with the other car by inches. Courtesy may be contagious but so is idiocy. When my heart returned from my stomach and I regained control of my vehicle I was seeing red. I noticed stickers all over the back of the offending vehicle indicating a vicarious relationship with various police agencies, which only served to fuel my anger.

I decided to follow the car until it stopped and confront the reckless driver face to face. If it was a man I was prepared to punish his impertinence with fisticuffs, if a woman, with a stern lecture. Road rage is too polite a term for my vexation. I followed the car for miles before I realized that the driver recognized my intentions and chose to keep moving to prevent the confrontation. My temper cooled after following the car for twenty minutes or so and the better angels of my nature intervened and halted the chase.

When I returned home from school a few days later my mother handed me a calling card from the local chief of police. She said that they had been to the house earlier that day and that they needed to interview me about my participation in a stalking incident.

With high drama the Chief of Police pulled out his wallet and showed me a photograph of his daughter and asked me if I recognized her. I told him honestly that I did not. He told me I had been stalking her and that I may not have committed any crime yet but he would put me on their list of suspects to be dragged in for questioning in every case of sexual impropriety.

I wish now that I had the courage to stand up to The Man and explain why I had followed his daughter's car that night but I did not. I was intimidated by the roomful of badges and guns and the building full of cages. I was sixteen years old and they were telling me that I would be marked for life as a sex pervert because the dangerous driver happened to be female. In previous dealings with the police during my hoodlum youth I had internalized the first rule of the path of least resistance; deny everything. I instinctively disavowed any memory of following her intentionally and intimated that his daughter may simply be a little bit paranoid.

I curse myself to this day for not summoning the courage to stand up for myself and tell him that his daughter was the rogue who deserved punishment. I will never know whether or not she eventually caused the death of an innocent for my inaction.

———————

"The Golden Rule" smacks of a false idol crafted in precious metal. Do unto others as they would do unto you is too easily interpreted as do unto others before they do unto you. The eastern concept of karma provides a more constructive framework for correct behavior and cultural serenity.  If we knew that our smallest transgressions were to be written in ink on our own ledger, to be paid for in full at a future date, our attention to a clean slate would be total. Western culture perpetuates the nonsensical and insidious belief that the balancing of the books occurs after our death and that we alone are affected by our actions.

"We," in the largest sense, are one organism. *We* determine our fate and that of our fellows and hold sole ownership of every last ripple in this pond.

Every now and then casual cruelty kills overtly and we all agree to ignore the truth and call it a car accident or a suicide.  For every spurned lover or disgruntled employee there is a spurner and a disgruntler.  For every sad, defeated child there is a grinning bully.  For most traffic fatalities there is a selfish bastard who has, in some small way, denied the humanity of his fellow motorist.  We can't imagine why we live in a world where murderous violence is the order of the day, yet most of us need only look in the mirror to find the problem and the solution.

Try thinking about karma the next time you drive your car and for Heaven's sake use your turn signal.

# Part Two

# The latter part of a yellow

Nearly all teenagers reject the wisdom of their parents at one point or another so the most scrupulous care and feeding can still result in the creation of an abrasive little puke. Prisons and cemeteries are full of angsty teenagers who lacked a strong adult role model at the point that they started ignoring advice from mom and dad. Every young person will cling to someone during this period, be it a conscientious teacher or the hopelessly delinquent kid down the street.

A parent's warnings become as predictable as the changing colors of a semaphore and anything fun or interesting seems to get the automatic red light. Puberty made many of us want to gun the engine at the first sight of that yellow caution rather than waiting out a long red and it's a miracle that more of us weren't broadsided in the process.

The young killers at Columbine clung to hateful notions or to nothing at all as they passed through the pivotal vacuum of adolescence. It was so easy for the press to wag a finger at the luckless parents and almost impossible for them to muster a defense. How could their parents not have known that they were stockpiling explosives? Surely if they had taken a more active role in rifling through their children's belongings the weapons cache would have been uncovered and the tragedy averted. The reality was that the parents were among the hardest hit victims and society at large was the co-conspirator. We engaged in mass denial as a community when we pointed the spotlight of blame on bad parenting.

Call me a wacky idealist but I believe that a single caring adult outside of the family could have altered their path. One grown-up who wasn't too busy making money to spend time with them could have swayed one of the boys and he could have swayed the other. A compassionate mentor with no parental axe to grind might have shown them a palatable lifestyle and stopped the bleeding.

It's a near certainty that every parent will be shrugged off at some point and a tragic reality that very few grown-ups are willing to jump in and guide a child who is not their own flesh and blood. As long as our child has the best school clothes and a healthy breakfast, what do we care about the kid who sits next to him on the school bus? Well, we care about that other kid because he will likely be Junior's greatest influence during the most dangerous epoch of his life. Even people without children should care about that other kid because if you don't, he might eventually do you damage.

I'm surprised that more young people aren't dangerously adrift.

————————

The professor at the end of the dock kept pretty much to himself at first. He spent the summers on a tiny houseboat called the "JJ," tapping out his novel one letter at a time. You could hear him halfway down the dock, hunting and pecking on the clunky old Underwood, occasionally cannonballing into the river to invigorate his muse.

Ben was a man of some girth and the tiny houseboat moved as he did. When he stood on the edge of the poop deck to jump in the water, the little JJ listed precariously under his weight. After the sound of a splash the boat bounced around like a bobber in a heavy chop and you could hear dishes and silverware and sometimes the typewriter itself flying about in the cabin. He'd struggle back onto the bobbing little vessel and the "rat-a-tat-tat" continued until sunset.

We first met Ben on one of the days that his typewriter crashed to the deck and required repair. He came over to our boat to borrow tools to fix the typewriter and introduced himself to my mother who was hanging laundry on the front deck.

"Hello, I live over there on the JJ and I wondered if you could loan me a wrench."

"Wrench? Oh, of course we have wrenches, at first I thought you said 'wench' and I was startled."

"Well, I suppose I'll take whatever you can spare."

My mother blushed with embarrassment and I think Ben was smitten. He singled her out as a favorite that day and began to favor me by association.

Ben wasn't anything like the other grown-ups that I knew; for one thing he was much smarter. He was an English professor with a fistful of advanced degrees but beyond that he was streetwise, having come up the hard way in depression era Hoboken. My delinquent tendencies weren't shocking to him most likely because they reminded him of his own misspent youth. I was a little cigarette chomping wise guy but Ben never busted my chops about it or tried to mold my behavior.

It was grand to watch the interaction of the English professor with the regular stiffs on the dock because they were never really sure when he was making fun of them. Ben wasn't mean spirited but he could always be counted on to deflate a pufferfish who had it coming. His wit could slice an idiot into croutons before the victim even detected the sting of his blade, then his charm and humor would bandage the wounds as though nothing had ever happened.

The main thing that separated the professor from the rest of the grown-ups was that he never talked down to me.

———————

If you ever want to get a rise out of the adults in your life, tell them that you plan to quit high school and become a professional gambler. My secret ambition was to be a hobo and ride the rails but I thought that professional gambler sounded jazzier and more ambitious. The fact was that I didn't much care what I had to do for bread, I just wanted out of that creepy high school.

I was three weeks into the eleventh grade and was banned from all but two of my classes for insubordination or being argumentative. All I had left on my schedule was a math class that I was failing badly and a speech class called "Discussion and Debate," in which I excelled. The remainder of my day was spent under house arrest in the counselor's office.

Things were beginning to get out of hand in my math class and I had to face the reality that I wasn't long for that world. The teacher's name was Al Fink, which by itself would have been enough ammunition for most subversive smart-asses. He was the only teacher who encouraged students to call him by his first name and he must have thought that we thought it was because he was cool. Guess again Mr. Fink.

I found out that Al was short for Aloicious and discovered that he liked that even less.

"Listen, Aloicious, if the set of numbers between 2 and 3 are finite, go ahead and write me a list."

"Go to the principal's office NOW, Mr. Shute!"

This cat was obviously clinging to Ptolemy and couldn't grasp curved space. Fink told the principal that I was no longer welcome in his class or anywhere in the mathematics wing for that matter. It wasn't even October of my Junior year and I was persona non grata in more than ninety percent of the building.

I decided to do everybody a favor and quit. Counselors and parents did their thing and told me what an idiot I was and pretty much every grown-up in my life wrote me off as a lost cause.

All except for one.

———————

My life would be very different if Ben had not intervened. I remember my hoodlum buddies and wonder how things might have changed for them with a Ben of their own. He wasn't related to me in any way and had no obligation to see to my well being, yet he was willing to spend thousands of hours on my behalf.

Ben was the only grown-up who didn't tell me that I was an imbecile for wanting to quit high school and actually intimated the opposite may be the case. He said that he had heard of students being admitted to his University before they graduated high school and convinced me to give college a try.

Two months into my second semester of college, the University discovered that I was admitted in error, with a horrific high school transcript and no diploma or GED. I showed Ben the letter of eviction from the dormitory and he drove more than three hundred miles to my high school that very day. He pounded his fist on the principal's desk and said that he wasn't leaving until somebody wrote me a completely fictitious, glowing letter of recommendation.

Even with perfectly good parents and all of the comforts of middle-class suburbia, I would have been in deep tapioca without the kindness of a stranger. When I look around today I see parents zealously protecting their children from outside influence and it saddens me. Not only do mother and father not know best, there's a pretty good chance that they're entirely clueless. When my parents spoke it sounded just like the muffled gibberish of the adults in the Charlie Brown cartoons. Parents are the last people on Earth that a troubled teenager will trust so I'm sure that many go completely untethered.

Without Ben's example, my distaste for the human condition would have been total and I would likely have come to a bad end.

———

The day that the police pulled us over I knew that I wanted to be just like Ben when I grew up and that I had found my mentor.

My old man knew me too well to let me practice driving with his brand new Monte Carlo but Ben feared less for the rusty little Pinto. He bragged that the car could do a two-minute mile on a proper downgrade but comforted my parents with the assurance that it topped out at around forty.

"Do you know why I stopped you?"

"No I don't, officer … sir."

Every hooligan knows that you don't get lippy with the cops no matter what. It's "yes sir" and "no sir" and "thank you sir, may I have another." I was driving on a learner's permit and justifiably terrified of cops so my heart fell to my stomach when Ben tossed in his two cents from the passenger seat.

"Tell him that the Pinto runs on a rubber band and isn't capable of surpassing the speed limit. He needs new batteries for his radar gun."

The policeman heard Ben's wisecrack and his expression turned stony and mean. My insurance rates were already going to be obscene with the built in surcharge for being a teenager. The last thing I needed was a moving violation and for the first time in my life I was wishing that Ben would just shut the Hell up.

"I stopped you because you blew through the latter part of a yellow light at the intersection back there."

The smart-ass English professor chortled loud enough for the cop to hear and in that moment proved to me that it was possible to be grown-up and cool at the same time.

"The latter part of a yellow?  What color is that?"

# Pennies from Heaven

Mark Twain wrote a piece of literary criticism in which he warned that the writer should use the correct word, not its second cousin. A lazy author will exhume a seventy-five cent word from the thesaurus only to abandon the one-cent version that better tells the story. The results of thesaurus abuse can be comical as in the case of George W. Bush's first college essay. His mother gifted him with an extra large Roget's and admonished him not to repeat the same word twice. He sought a synonym for the "tear" on his cheek and the big book told him to use "lacerate" so he did. The rest is history.

My concern is for the more subtle abuses that only gently deceive the reader but cloud the message of the essay. If the writer is unaware of the meaning of the word "rapscallion" he may incorrectly and slanderously describe someone as a "scoundrel." These two terms were particular favorites of Mark Twain and he would spin in his grave at their juxtaposition. In honor of the great man I will attempt to illustrate, by example, the distinction between the two.

———————

My buddies and I were perpetually broke in college. There was money for beer of course and my Dad sent me twenty bucks a week for cigarettes and sunflower seeds but there was never a surplus. I lived in a dormitory with a room and board contract so I knew that I wouldn't starve to death but the empty pockets were a constant frustration. What my friends and I lacked in resources we had to make up for in resourcefulness.

We were up late one night in the dormitory lounge watching the wedding of Prince Charles and Dianna on CNN. The pomp and circumstance of the royal wedding led our discussion to our own mean financial straits and we agonized over the wasteful display. "You could buy a hundred thousand cases of beer with that one tiara." We passed the bottle of Yukon Jack, hurling drunken sarcasm at the happy couple and a grand time was had by all.

Someone suggested that we pool our resources and buy some canned pop to mix with the Whiskey. When the five of us emptied our pockets there wasn't even enough change for a single can of soda. At that very moment the CNN reporter mentioned that the estimated cost of the wedding was in the millions.

I was arranging our pathetic pile of pennies and dimes on the table and bemoaning our poverty when I was struck by a Heavenly inspiration. If you set a dime on top of a penny you'll notice that the dime sits perfectly within the ridge along the edge of the penny. It occurred to me that if you removed the ridge from the penny you'd end up with a copper colored dime. The importance of this discovery may be lost on the comfortable reader but in our desperate condition it was nothing short of alchemy.

We dispatched one group to scour the floors around the vending machines and under the couch cushions for stray pennies and another to search for a metal file. If I told you that it worked I would be confessing to a federal crime and that would be silly. Suffice it to say that we toasted the Royal pair with properly mixed beverages before a sumptuous buffet of Doritos, Snicker bars and ice cream sandwiches.

———————

It is shocking to me that some people throw pennies on the ground. When I was a little boy my mother told me that they fell from Heaven and I believed her. To prove her theory she showed me that each was inscribed with the phrase "IN GOD WE TRUST" in capital letters. When I found out that people were discarding them as useless I was horrified.

I grew to love and respect the man whose image is pressed onto the face of each coin. "The Great Emancipator" silently comforts the poor and gives hope to the oppressed to this day. Abraham Lincoln, in his humility, directed that if they must use his image for currency that they choose the lowest possible denomination. He reminded me of Father Abraham in the Bible and taught me that you didn't have to reach back thousands of years to find an example of human virtue.

A scoundrel is a person who would discard a penny as worthless scrap. A rapscallion will bend some rules to prove the scoundrel wrong.

# The little green guy

Luigi would stand next to your desk and wait for you to use the wrong verb tense in a piece of Latin oratory. He'd actually vibrate with rage when you hesitated and if you spoke in the present when the text demanded pluperfect, he'd hit you hard with the back of his hand. Corporal punishment is banned in most public schools but modern sensitivies had not yet reached our prairie University. Luigi was generally a kind soul but an ignorance of proper verb conjugation really seemed to piss him off.

We called him "The little green guy" behind his back because he stood about five feet tall and his skin was green. I don't mean to say that he had an olive complexion or a swarthy Mediterranean patina, the man was as green as the Grinch who stole Christmas. He was afflicted with a terrible case of the gout, which caused him to walk in an awkward waddle, teetering on painfully bowed legs and tortured feet. His expression was a perpetual aching grimace and his students struggled mightily to make him smile. Only first semester students called him Dr. Giardello, to us he was Louie, the little green guy and he was beloved.

He spent his summers in Italy and each September a new batch of freshmen struggled to sift through his Italianized English just to begin the labyrinth of Latin. Louie welcomed each new crop of Latin students by telling them that they had enrolled in the study of a dead language and they were wasting their time. He announced on the first day of every semester that anyone who had registered for his class merely for the language credit could leave and never return and they would be given a grade of C. Invariably six or seven people would sign the log on his desk and never return.

His family barely escaped Mussolini's Italy and he lusted for the freedom from tyranny in America. What he found was a disturbing cultural vacuum, the senseless adoption of novel and futuristic at the expense of tried and true. He became a classics professor because he believed in his heart that the toddling America would not survive her ignorance of history. He saw the dwindling interest in teaching and learning the humanities and feared it would become a footnote in the post-mortem summary of the American experiment.

———————

America is the brilliant student with the sadly unrealized potential. Our philosophical pedigree and our command of the science of warfare give us preeminence in every arena we enter, yet our progress is stymied at every turn. The students in Tiananmen Square chanted the name of Thomas Jefferson and carried a likeness of the Statue of Liberty but our Coca-Cola culture was not what they sought.

When we lecture the Chinese government for their cruelty in squashing the protest, the finger we wag is bloody with our own brutal past. When we criticize their human rights record we do so as the country with the largest percentage of its citizens in prison. Our ruthless conquest of the Native American population and our barbaric treatment of the African slave and his descendants are not lost on our global neighbors. These events seem like ancient history to the youthful America but they are among the most recent in a long line of historical human atrocities.

There is little doubt that humankind is evolving as a race and there is less doubt that we've stumbled onto the secret of harmony in human affairs. The American system of Jeffersonian Democracy will likely be the model for the peaceful organization of the first world government but it will be in spite of American actions, not because of them. Our system of government was the product of romantic philosophers and their love of ancient truisms. With inspired eloquence the American architects erected a framework for human affairs which would rest on the shoulders of reason and the lessons of history. It is ironic that the culture shock of true democracy will probably hit America the hardest.

———————

One of the students brought in a package of Pall Mall cigarettes that day because it held a Latin inscription. The phrase "per aspera ad astra," or "to the stars through adversity" happened to be the little green guy's life motto and it set him off on an hour-long rant. He told us that the real meaning of the phrase was that humankind, in its ability to reason and remember, had unlimited potential. He said that the aphorism implied that with the lack of sincere effort we were earthbound and doomed. He told us that we were lucky beyond words to have been born in America's bosom and we had an intrinsic obligation to work harder for the Heavens. He said that our common listlessness and ignorance were greater crimes against humanity than the scourge of Hitler and Mussolini combined.

Louie quivered with sequestered fury as he detailed his harsh passage from the ugly war in Europe to the institutional apathy of the Midwestern American campus. His eyes welled with tears and his entire body trembled as he pounded his chest and admonished the shaken sophomores to "LIVE LIKE A LION, not like a little lamb." By the end of the class there wasn't a dry eye or insouciant soul in the room.

The little green guy wasn't slapping us for using the wrong verb tense. He slapped us because he was afraid we weren't going to make it to the stars.

# Special kids

I have always harbored a secret envy for simple people. Facile intelligence comes in handy when you're watching Jeopardy or bluffing your way through essay tests but beyond that it's an enormous pain in the ass. A staunch intellect invariably leads one to self-examination, which can only result in self-loathing or self-love and neither one of those does anybody any good.

The town I grew up in was home to the state school for the mentally handicapped so every fifth person you met on the street had his own peculiar take on reality. An effort was made to merge some of the mildly retarded children into the mainstream so my elementary school had the same ratio as the general population of the town.

In those days they called it "mongolism," a generic catchall term for Down's Syndrome and any related malady. The "special kids" commuted from the state school on the short bus and were allowed to participate in regular class work with the rest of the children. We made friends with them but it was never quite the same as with our regular buddies because the special kids had to go home to the institution after school.

My own early childhood was a hellish melange of wicked stepmothers and bad scenes so I came to covet their simple serenity and the predictable structure of their home at the state school. They always appeared so happy and content, two qualities that seemed to consistently elude me and mine.

The special kids had something going for them beyond their general good spirit in that they were apparently born without the capacity for meanness. Because they lacked guile they simply didn't expect to find it in others. If you played a joke on one of them or made fun of them for something it was like it just didn't compute. I had a dozen friends who were "special" and I never saw one of them exhibit anything resembling the cruelty of a "normal" child.

What really made me jealous was that they didn't seem to worry as much as I did. They were more engrossed by the matter at hand, less distracted by introspection and far more easily amused. Along with the rest of the "normal" kids, I wasted about half of my life concerned with what others were thinking about me. The fact was that most of the people I worried about were dwelling on themselves as well, so they weren't really paying attention to me at all.

I got ripped off when I was born normal.

———————

Aaron was six feet, seven inches tall when he slouched. He was a crooked man, bone thin, all sharp angles and terrible posture. His head tilted and bobbed lazily forward from his shoulders and gave the impression that it might roll off at any moment. His hair was an unkempt thatch of greasy knotted curls that could never have accommodated a comb. The clothes were Salvation Army rejects, high-water pants and paisley shirts with big collars that weren't stylish when they were brand new.

Aaron usually smelled bad, very bad. His stipend from the county was eighty dollars per week, just enough for a bus pass and bologna sandwiches, with precious little left over for personal hygiene. To the best of my knowledge his clothes were never laundered.

His parents sold their farm in Bismarck and retired to Florida, leaving Aaron to his own devices in Grand Forks. They had very little contact with him when they lived in the state and after their retirement he was entirely forsaken. His mental disability classified him as marginally functional, which meant that he was allowed to live on his own in a subsidized apartment but that there had been some debate about having him institutionalized.

Grand Forks is a University town and the well-coifed, snappily attired collegians had a field day with poor Aaron. He liked to hang around campus to play pool and Ping-Pong in the dormitories and the undergraduates liked having him around as a target of ridicule. Aaron's awkward manner and ungainly appearance made them appear smart and elegant by contrast, so he was encouraged to move freely in their world. He was naive, oblivious to their derision and considered them all his friends.

Aaron was exceedingly quiet and painfully shy, his every syllable was uttered with a little wince of apology for having ever been so bold as to speak at all. When he did talk there was little evidence of retardation, just a slight speech impediment that forced him to focus on the careful formation of each word.

He was an innocent child trapped in a big old goofy body, forced to make his way alone in a cruel and confusing scene.

———

I started hosting the eight ball tournaments in the dormitory game room to make extra money between financial aid disbursements. I went door to door signing people up for the matches, collecting five dollars from each, confident that the tournament itself was just a formality. I was sharking grown-ups in pool halls while these rubes were slopping pigs or driving a combine on the farm. They didn't stand a chance.

I pretty much had my run of the place until Aaron started showing up for the Friday night eight ball tourney. He didn't live in the dormitory and wasn't even a student at the University but the man had a nose for money games. Although he didn't seem exactly right in the head he could shoot a mean game of pool and more importantly possessed the requisite five dollars.

Aaron was obviously touched with some manner of mental infirmity. Sometimes his eyes would get "stuck" on a person or an object and for a minute or five his body would become paralyzed in whatever position it was in at that moment. He'd stand still as a statue no matter what you said or did to distract him and his gaze remained locked on the same spot long after the item of interest moved along.

We had to be patient with Aaron when we let him play in the pool tournament because he'd occasionally freeze up in the middle of a shot and you would just have to wait it out. There didn't seem to be any rhyme or reason to the objects of his fascination, sometimes it was a pretty girl and sometimes just a discarded cigarette butt.

"Aaron, I saw her too, she was gorgeous but she's not there anymore. Go ahead and take your shot. ... Aaron? ... Can you hear me?"

"Yes, yes."

"She was a pretty girl, Aaron but she's gone now."

"Yes."

He might be in the middle of the pool stroke and his focus wouldn't waver from the last spot where the girl had been standing. Aaron wasn't in a trance because you could talk to him about it while it was happening.

"Aaron, are you ok?"

"I'm fine. The doctor says I have a condition."

"What kind of condition, Aaron?"

"He says I get stuck sometimes."

---

When somebody has a hot run on the pool table we say that he's "unconscious" and Aaron was all of that. The few times that he did miss a shot it was the result of getting stuck for too long and testing the patience of his opponent. A sore loser would sometimes become frustrated with the interruption in play and harangue him for his disability, which made Aaron nervous and slightly unsteady. Poor sportsmanship rarely detracted from his overall performance though and I didn't see him lose more than a couple of dozen games in over a thousand starts.

I only lost one or two of the Friday night tournaments before I decided to go with the flow and change the game to partners. Aaron and I didn't lose once as a team.

"How long is he gonna stand there that way? C'mon ya retard, hit the ball!"

"Hey man, lighten up, he's got a condition."

Aaron had a condition all right; a condition that allowed him to concentrate way better than the rest of us and to peel the financial aid money off of every hayseed that passed through the game room at Walsh Hall.

"Can't you do something to snap him out of it?"

"Sorry, man, you can't rush genius. Do you think they hollered at Michelangelo that way? 'Hurry up Mike, the Pope wants the chapel by Thursday!' I think not."

"He smells really bad too, worse than my roommate, it's hard to focus on the game."

"That's my partner, baby!"

————————

After our third or fourth victory as a team I began to wonder what the rest of Aaron's life was like. We were dividing our winnings from the tournament one Friday night and it occurred to me that if I had his amazing talent for pool I would be a very wealthy man. I walked him home and discovered that he lived in abject poverty, among the saddest circumstances I've ever encountered.

His refrigerator contained a loaf of bread and a package of bologna; that's it. There wasn't any mustard and there wasn't any milk. The boarding room had only one electrical outlet besides the 110 volt for the ancient refrigerator and that powered a table lamp and a crappy old radio. There were no other light fixtures or appliances of any sort and no bathroom.

"Where do you go to the bathroom, Aaron?"

"They let me use the one down the hall during the daytime."

"What if you have to go at night?"

"Sometimes they let me use the one at the gas station but not always."

"But where do you bathe?"

"Bathe? ... Oh, they let me use the shower at the Field House sometimes but not always."

"Jeez, Aaron, the way you shoot pool I thought I'd find you living in a mansion. What do you do with all of your money?"

"I get eighty dollars from the government every week but fifty goes to Mrs. Cavenaugh for letting me live here."

"You should be rolling in dough with the talent you have. You could be winning tournaments every single night."

"Oh, maybe some day. I was just learning how to play when I met you. I'm really good at Ping-Pong but the guys at the Field House don't play for money."

"You're telling me that you never played pool before I met you? That's just not possible, you never miss a shot."

"That game is easy because the ball sits still. Ping-Pong is much harder."

———

The "guys" who Aaron played Ping-Pong with at the Field House were the Varsity Table Tennis Team and they had been using him as a practice dummy for years. He bobbled a pool shot or two in his time but he almost never missed a return on the Ping-Pong table.

Aaron may have lacked a traditional style and a strong serve but he wore down every single opponent with sheer resilience. The Varsity team played an aggressive game in the Asian fashion, several feet from the end of the table, smashing overhands with the velocity of a Pete

Sampras Ace. Aaron held up the paddle in front of his chest and simply moved it slowly from left to right to block the ball.

The athletes who were playing on a scholarship told me that he rarely gave up a point and that he had never lost a game. They called him "The Retardomatic Ball Return" just barely out of earshot and occasionally something worse to his face after a difficult loss.

"Aaron that's amazing! Those guys go to college for free because they're good at Ping-Pong and they can't beat you on their best day."

"They say that I play funny and wouldn't be allowed into the tournaments."

"Aw, they're full of it, Aaron. They just don't want to admit that you're better than they are. I'm gonna take you on tour and make us both millionaires. I think that this is the beginning of a beautiful friendship, Aaron."

"I've got lots of friends *now*."

# Humane society

It's sad that the state of American society has descended to a level where no prudent person would consider either hitchhiking or picking up someone who is. The simple human kindness of transporting a stranded soul may be lost forever to the ravages of our mutual fear and mistrust. If my sister told me that she was planning to hitchhike cross-country I would consider her suicidal or worse.

In a simpler time it was a common means of transportation and one would think nothing of crisscrossing the whole of the country with nothing but a thumb. The sleepy truck driver who needed a conversation to stay awake was the most reliable ride but any car with an open seat or pickup truck with an empty bed was fair game.

I'm not old enough to tell you about a time when it was an entirely safe and sane means of locomotion. I routinely thumbed the three hundred miles between college and my hometown more than two decades ago but even then it was getting a little dicey. An ample supply of degenerate weirdness has changed the landscape considerably in twenty years. I wouldn't pick up a hitchhiker now on a dare and I wouldn't hitchhike myself unless my life depended on it.

Most of my trips were between Minneapolis and Grand Forks, North Dakota where the weather is often unkind and the pity ride was my stock in trade. Minnesota Nice is merely a survival technique developed by the natives to cope with the harsh climate. It could be you stuck on the highway the next time so you think twice before leaving someone else stranded. I'd curse the cars that drove by without stopping, "How could those heartless bastards leave me out here to freeze? They've got room for three more people in there."

As often as not I'd make the trip with a buddy and it was much tougher for two to catch a ride than one. What we gained in companionship and security we'd pay for with more time on the pavement and more cautious cars whizzing by. On several occasions we gave up completely for the lack of traffic and spent the night in a culvert or under an overpass.

————————

Dave and I were heading home for the long Thanksgiving weekend and our last ride dropped us off at the Fergus Falls exit, just about the halfway point to Minneapolis. We wasted a couple of hours in Fargo detouring on foot around a massive construction zone and by the time we made Fergus it was getting cold and dark. The traffic was dwindling to nil and we had to face the reality that we would probably be spending the night outdoors.

Late November is a bad time to sleep in a ditch in Minnesota so we decided to trek into town and try to find a place to crash. We didn't have a dollar between us but my buddy Dave told me that he heard that in small towns the police would let you sleep in a cell before they'd allow you to freeze to death. We waved down the first cop we saw and he made it clear that what we were describing to him sounded a lot like vagrancy and that he could arrange for us to spend the entire holiday weekend in a cell. We thanked him but declined his generous offer of incarceration in the Fergus Falls lockup.

We were able to pass a couple of hours in the lobby of a Motel Six by convincing the desk clerk we were waiting for friends to arrive. At about midnight he noticed we were both fast asleep on the chairs in the lobby and he gave us the bum's rush. We slouched, tired and cold, through the November sleet back to the limited shelter of the highway overpass. The wet sleet dampened any hope of finding dry wood for a fire so we burned my Psych 101 notes in an empty coffee can we found in the ditch.

Our original plan had us arriving home in time for dinner so we hadn't thought it necessary to bring money for food. The hunger pangs were fast becoming a more pressing issue than the fight to stay warm. We were haunted by the glow of the massive Perkins Restaurant sign next to the freeway and the horn of plenty it symbolized. Perkins was open twenty-four hours a day and it taunted us that night with its warm booths and bottomless cups of coffee. Our cold concrete and steel crevice was close enough that we could see the happy late night diners and the perky waitresses and actually smell the Granny's Country Omelets in the steam that wafted from the building.

The Perkins restaurant chain has an established custom of flying a massive floodlit American flag over each restaurant. As we shivered over our little coffee can fire with the huge American banner flapping in the background, our patriotic fervor for life in the land of plenty was wafer thin. I noticed that it was after midnight and technically Thanksgiving Day so I pulled the scarf away from my mouth and wished Dave an ironic, inappropriately cheerful "Happy Thanksgiving!"

"Yeah, Happy Fuckin' Thanksgiving to you too!"

———————

Dave had taken on a distressing thousand yard stare, eyes glazed, in the direction of that huge American flag. By the glow of our pathetic little fire, barely shielded from the cutting sleet, I watched his facial expression change from depressed endurance to righteous indignation. He smothered the coffee can fire with the back of his Elements of Physics textbook and stood hunched under the bridge.

"This is America, dammit, let's go get breakfast!"

We walked back across the bridge and headed into town, me following about five paces behind Dave's inspired gait. He led us straight back toward the Motel Six from which we had been evicted so I questioned him.

"Nah, we're not going back to the motel, that desk clerk was wound pretty tight."

There was a small Greyhound Bus terminal next door to the Motel Six and Dave made a beeline for the ticket counter. The nice lady in the cashier's window was startled by the sudden appearance of two desperate strangers at one in the morning. She tore her crossword puzzle where the pencil point had been, then fumbled the pencil itself until it fell to the floor.

"Cccan I...hhelp you?"

Dave sounded more like an eager salesman than a scoundrel who meant her harm, so she gradually relaxed her guard.

"Hi there, we're college students hitchhiking home to The Cities for Thanksgiving break and our last ride dropped us at the Fergus Falls exit. We haven't eaten since noon and didn't bring money for food. If you loan us twenty dollars we'll mail it back to you tomorrow when we get home."

The nice lady reached for her purse without hesitation, extracted a twenty-dollar bill and handed it to Dave. She tore the bottom off of a bus schedule and wrote "attn: Betty" above the address printed on the bottom of the brochure.

"If you send it to that address I'll get it. There's only the three of us who work here and I'm the only Betty."

We thanked her thoroughly, a little surprised at the success of Dave's simple ploy and she minimized the gesture.

"When you two came up to the window I was sure you were here to rob me. I'll ask God to forgive me for being quick to judgement and buy you breakfast in the meantime. You boys have a nice Thanksgiving."

Dave and I were both a little misty over the kindness of a stranger as we exited the Greyhound terminal but we were laughing our asses off in a celebratory gallop by the time we made Perkins.

————

We could see our spot under the overpass from the warm booth at Perkins and life was good. Twenty bucks covered two Granny's Country Omelets, two bottomless cups of coffee and a five-dollar tip for a hottie named Kim. We had enough change left over to buy a copy of the local newspaper and enough time on our hands to scour it from cover to cover.

The Fergus Falls paper had a story on the front page about an animal shelter run by a local resident. When the cages at the Humane Society were full, the recently widowed woman devoted her husband's humble estate to an overflow facility to forestall euthanasia. The heartwarming article compared her to Mother Theresa and intimated that she was not a wealthy person and that she might be missing meals herself to feed the strays.

The woman was, after all, still working the graveyard shift at the Greyhound depot.

# Which way are you headed?

Anything you can do to ease the discomfort of a homeless person is effort well spent. It's easy enough to dismiss them as lazy or foolish and walk away but not without hardening yourself a little in the process. Some of the people on the street may have chosen to live as they do but it's far more likely that they were thrust there by circumstance and lack the optimism to rebuild. The world must have seemed a cruel place for them to subtract themselves so completely but we can prove them wrong. The couple of bucks that you toss to the destitute man on the street can have a dramatic impact on his quality of life and it isn't so much for what he can buy with the money.

For the hour or two that he's allowed to linger at McDonald's over the hot apple pie and small cup of coffee, he can see a scene that isn't wholly mean and selfish. Your gesture didn't just put warm food into one man's stomach; it changed the entire world for the better in his eyes. Most of the street people I've run into are there because they lacked the killer instinct necessary to survive in a dog eat dog world. Once proud men surrendered to a pushy mob and their reward for not shoving back was exile. They rejected the idea of competing with you for a promotion or kissing an idiot's ass and were summarily expelled from the game.

Many people are hostile toward the urban outdoorsman, they yell, "Get a job" or worse and to him their angst is telling. They resent his ability to live his life without the competitive undercurrent that mars their own humanity. The hobo thinks of the people who must be stepped on to get that swell job and the theatrics that must be performed to keep it and simply begs off. He tried it for awhile, living a lie to inspire envy in his neighbors, who were themselves living a bigger lie to keep up appearances. It just wasn't his cup of stew.

Who among us hasn't neared the end of their rope at work or at home and felt like chucking it all? If I had a nickel for every time I bit my tongue to keep from telling the whole truth to an ignorant boss or impertinent spouse, I could afford to give two bucks to every human I encounter for the rest of my natural life. Living on the street is punishment enough, so the hobo doesn't need to be scolded by society for not playing by the rules. He realizes that a job would change his life, he's just not convinced that it would change it for the better. The street person doesn't need our pity either and likely doesn't deserve it; chances are that he pities us.

We should probably just pay the two bucks.

———

It was the night before Thanksgiving and my friend and I were hitchhiking home from school in North Dakota. The traffic on the freeway dried up as the holiday neared and we were stranded overnight in Fergus Falls. We didn't expect the layover and hadn't brought along any money but the kindness of a stranger saved us from a cold, hungry night under the freeway overpass. A nice lady at the Greyhound depot took pity on a couple of impoverished college students and loaned us twenty dollars for breakfast.

We spent most of the night in the booth at Perkins, testing the limits of their "bottomless" cup of coffee and waiting for the traffic to pick up on the highway. The restaurant had undergone a shift change and our new waitress wasn't showing us any love at all. After awhile she quit refilling the coffee pot altogether and seemed to have the support of management, a nervous little dude with a polyester tie who had been giving us the hairy eyeball since we arrived. Our original waitress, Kim, was a sweetheart and even flirted with us a little when Dave gave her the five-dollar tip. The surly crone who replaced her kept hitting Dave's foot with the vacuum cleaner and making it abundantly clear that we had worn out our welcome.

When our first waitress told us she was punching out, we paid the tab and gave her the tip but lingered over the table so long that it felt funny stiffing the new person. We didn't have much money left but collected our remaining coins and left them on the table as a gesture of good faith. Seventy-eight cents all together, three quarters and three pennies, not much but it was all that we had.

As we headed toward the exit, the waitress moved at once to clear our table and startled everyone in the joint with the commotion she caused. She tossed our cups and saucers into the bus tub with such force that we heard the ceramic shatter from across the restaurant. Dave flashed me a worried glance and we both paused to look over our shoulders at the scene she was making. The waitress scooped the coins from the table and ran across the room to catch up to us as we neared the door.

"This is what I get for working on Thanksgiving and putting up with you god-damned bums for two hours? Seventy-eight cents? You just keep your fucking seventy-eight cents, assholes!"

I was halfway out the door when she threw the coinage but Dave caught the full brunt of her fury. One of the quarters made an impressive welt on his forehead and a penny caught him right smack in the eyeball.

"I'm blind! I'm blind! That crazy bitch blinded me on Thanksgiving!"

We instinctively dropped to the deck to avoid the next volley and scrambled to collect the coins scattered around the restaurant entrance. The meek little manager was doing his best to restrain the woman and apologize to us at the same time. It seemed she might wriggle free at any moment and do us some real damage so a hasty retreat to the freeway seemed in order. We didn't even look back to acknowledge the geeky restaurant manager's feeble attempt at lawsuit avoidance.

"Sorry for the trouble, guys. Have a nice day!"

---

We ran to the freeway overpass and huddled in the cement and steel cavity beneath the bridge to get out of the cutting wind. It would be an hour until dawn and another hour after that before the Interstate rumbled to life with Thanksgiving travelers. We knew that between the holiday spirit and Minnesota Nice that catching a lift to Minneapolis would be a cinch but for the time being there was no traffic at all.

"Wow, your eye looks terrible, Dave. It's all puffy and the white part of your eyeball is covered in blood."

"Man, it feels like the penny's still in there. It hurts like Hell!"

"Maybe we should go back and look for a doctor in town. Might be slim pickings though, on Thanksgiving Day."

"You're kidding right? I'm never going back to that town again. We'll catch a ride to Minneapolis when the traffic picks up; we're only a couple of hours away. Damn it hurts! My mom will take me to the Emergency Room when I get home if it still looks bad."

"It's getting worse, bro, your whole eye is puffing up like a bullfrog. It's sort of merging with the welt on your forehead. You look just like Rocky...you know...at the end of the movie."

"She's got a Hell of an arm. I got beaned with a fastball in Little League once and it didn't hurt anything like this.

The full belly from Perkins and the two hour wait for traffic made me want to take a nap in the worst way and that's exactly what I did. Some Interstate Highway bridges make better squats than others do and I'm here to tell you that the one on I-94 in Fergus Falls, Minnesota is almost uninhabitable. It's as if they purposely designed the thing with no horizontal surfaces to sleep on. If you doze off you must remain perfectly perpendicular to the road or you will roll down the forty-five degree incline and onto the freeway.

Dave said he was going to try and ignore the stabbing pain in his eye and get some sleep as well. I cleverly positioned my self a little bit further up the incline, assuming that Dave would act as a speed bump and keep me from rolling all the way down the hill to my death.

"Hey Dave, if you roll down onto the freeway and get run over by a semi can I have your stereo?"

"You're always looking for an angle, aren't ya? I'll bet you stuffed yourself into that crevice just so you'd hit me if you rolled down the hill. Selfish bastard."

"How could you think such a thing? Man, that stings."

"Just giving you shit, Jonny. Happy Thanksgiving."

"Happy Thanksgiving, Dave."

———————

The kid was thumbing his way to Seattle on the opposite side of the freeway when he noticed the two bodies stretched out on the angled concrete bridge abutment. He claimed that he was throwing rocks at the guardrail to see if we were dead or asleep but his aim was terrible and the first rock he threw hit Dave hard on the leg. He woke with a start and rolled all the way down the hill to the shoulder of the freeway, just in time to catch the slushy spray from a passing truck. I woke up when I heard him yelling across the freeway like a madman.

"What the Hell is that all about? You just threw a rock at me, didn't you?"

"I thought you might be dead."

The kid was a little younger than we were, quite a bit smaller than Dave and visibly nervous over having thrown the offending rock. Dave was covered in slush from head to toe, shivering on the shoulder of the road. His swollen eye looked worse than before his nap and he was exhibiting a new limp, rubbing the spot where the rock had hit him.

"So you go around throwing rocks at dead people? What kind of monster are you?"

The kid looked like he was about to cry, pacing back and forth with his head down saying "I'm sorry" over and over again. Dave gestured for me to climb down so we could go over and talk to him. The kid must have thought we were coming over to kick his ass because he shouted a nervous, goofy attempt at conversation.

"Which way are you headed?"

I could tell that Dave's temper had cooled but he couldn't resist a snippy answer to a stupid question.

"Which way do you think we're headed, Einstein? The freeway only goes in two directions, this-a-way and that-a-way. We're going the opposite direction as you."

We crossed the freeway and the poor kid was crying all right, bawling like a baby. He couldn't have been sixteen years old and he told us that he'd been living outdoors for more than a year. He was carrying an open cardboard box that was nearly as big as he was and its only contents were a piece of silky fabric about one foot square and a page torn from a pornographic magazine. Dave calmed the kid and distracted him from his weeping by asking why he was carrying a mostly empty box.

"Oh, it's just some stuff I keep. I'm going to make a shirt out of that fabric when I get to Seattle."

Dave and I exchanged a furtive "this person is clearly insane" look and silently agreed not to delve further into how he planned to make a shirt out of one square foot of cloth. Dave moved on to the next obvious question instead.

"But why such a big box?"

The kid explained that he carried the big box so that people would presume he was a person of substance and be more eager to give him a lift. That made a certain amount of sense to us so we forgave his patchy insanity and became fast friends. He told us that there were potatoes in the Dumpster behind Perkins and we said that we had eaten but thanked him just the same. Dave got the idea at the exact same time as I did and we both started riffling through our pockets for the coins.

I only came up with two of the quarters and a penny but Dave had the rest of it. Even in our rush to escape the restaurant we had somehow managed to salvage all seventy-eight cents and we eagerly handed it to the kid.

"That's really nice of you guys. I've sure got something to be thankful for today."

"It's nothing, kid, you ought to go up to that Perkins and sit inside to warm up for awhile. They've got a bottomless cup of coffee for seventy-five cents. Three cents tax and you've got her licked exactly."

"Bottomless?"

# Introduction to logic

**P**aul knew precisely how many footsteps it took to walk between every building on campus. You could say something like "Administration Building to Jasper Hall?" and he'd answer "1,512," or "Library to the Field House?" and Paul would say "Which doors?" He was almost totally blind so most people assumed that he counted the steps to aid in his navigation around campus. The fact of the matter was that he was exercising his mind as well as his legs.

The miracle of the human brain was the subject of continuous study and experimentation for Paul because he lacked the distraction of visual stimuli. The counting ritual began as a method to determine his precise location but he eventually discovered that he could keep count without paying complete attention. The concept of the divided mind fascinated him and he'd challenge himself by attempting to recite poetry or sing a song without losing his count.

When he lost his place in the poem or the numbered footsteps he'd stop dead in his tracks. You'd sometimes see him standing as still as a statue for minutes at a time, lips moving silently, fingers tapping out an indecipherable code on his trouser leg. Freshmen thought he was just another nutty old Prof but upperclassmen knew better. He might be motionless but his mind was moving at a ferocious clip.

If you were walking across the quad and saw him frozen in place it was best not to interrupt him.

————

Paul was stricken with a degenerative eye disease in his late teens and by the time he went off to college at Johns Hopkins he had lost ninety percent of his vision. A tutor was hired to read his college textbooks aloud when a Braille version wasn't available and he somehow managed to finish his undergraduate program with honors. Paul was admitted to the graduate school in the study of philosophy and so took the radical cost saving measure of marrying his tutor. He received his hard won Ph.D., also with honors, in little more than the standard length of time.

Anyone who has ever been handed a syllabus can appreciate what an impressive feat Paul accomplished. The inability to read would have washed most people out in the second semester, not to mention the additional difficulties he endured with everything from doing laundry to locomotion around the campus. I had perfectly functioning eyeballs and still had trouble making it to class, much less summoning the will to read half of the crap they required of me.

Paul was hired as a philosophy professor at the prairie University and had been elevated to Chairman of the Philosophy Department by the time I made the scene. The freshman classes that he taught were always full because it was widely known that he gave open book tests and quizzes. The presumption was that since he couldn't see his hand in front of his face he was ill equipped to scan the room for cheaters with crib notes.

My first class with him was the Introduction to Logic and Scientific Method and he forever laid waste to the theory that open book tests are easy.

————

Paul was a creature of habit so pranksters had a field day with his vulnerability. Each day he'd walk into class and follow an identical routine, seventeen steps to the coat rack in the corner, hang up the coat. Turn ninety degrees to the left and take fifteen steps back to the table at the front of the room and set down his class materials. As often as not some scalawag would rearrange the furniture slightly and the slapstick comedy would ensue.

The philosophy professor took the monkey business in stride and never once fell to anger or frustration. He'd hang his corduroy jacket on the hook that wasn't there and it would fall in a heap. He'd turn ninety degrees to the left and walk fifteen steps to the table that was now sixteen steps away, drop his books and papers in a messy pile on the floor and begin his lecture as though nothing had happened. The scamps eventually abandoned the mischief when it failed to get any sort of rise out of him.

I knew Paul better than most of the other students because we had a mutual friend on the faculty and sometimes saw each other socially. I had been to his house for dinner a number of times and gained better insight into his complex nature through my acquaintance with his wife. She explained to me that Paul was never really where he appeared to be, that he dwelt entirely within the world of ideas. With the loss of his sight he constructed an elaborate landscape in his mind, a sort of three-dimensional topography of knowledge gained and concepts explored. As the world within him grew more detailed and intricate, his memories of what the other world looked like faded.

The counting of steps and the rote memorization of an entire semester's syllabus were merely devices he used to subtract himself from the situation so he could dwell on deeper matters.

---

The world of people and things was not only subordinate to the world of ideas, it was in his estimation inconsequential. Paul thumped us with the formal fallacies of logic and the subtle power of the syllogism as though they were the most important things in this life. His fondness for the scientific method and deductive reasoning was evangelical and his fervor for the subject matter was contagious to all but the most stubborn dullards. He said that meticulous attention to pure logic was the foundation of philosophy but that we are diverted by the crude lies that parade past our senses.

Every now and then you run into someone who is doing exactly what they were put on this Earth to do and for a minute or an hour the universe makes perfect sense. A Van Morrison or a Vincent Van Gogh will give you the tingling reassurance that most of our potential lay dormant, yet to be discovered much less utilized. For that moment or hour, the weight of the world falls away.

The final exam in Paul's class was a challenge, to say the least. If a professor ever stands before one of your classes and announces that all of the tests will be open book, you can assume they will be the most grueling that you'll ever endure. My advice is to scoff at the ignoramus who tells you that it will be a joyride to an easy grade and to redouble your efforts to pay attention in class.

The Blue Books for the final were a blank slate, save the challenging problem written in his own crooked, labored penmanship on the opening page.

*"Visual input is both a vehicle for and an obstacle to sound thinking. Prove, through deductive and inductive reasoning, that it is better to be blind than sighted."*

# Can you spare some change?

Sometimes the most obvious things elude me and then, when I least expect it, they hit me like a fist in the face. As children we were told that humans live to be seventy-five or so and most of us took the arithmetic for granted. I completed eighteen revolutions around the sun before I realized that the seventy-five year thing was an optimistic generality, a statistical ideal. When the Queen Mum expired at a hundred and one she cleared the way, mathematically, for a forty-nine year old to blow a gasket on the golf course.

Another thing I mistakenly took for granted, as a child, was that hospitals were places where people went to get better. The fact is that most people don't go to the hospital unless they are bumping up against the abyss so it stands to reason that many will fall. A significant percentage of the people reading this essay will go to the hospital to die.

Each of our individual realities will defy statistical analysis and I suppose that's half of the fun. If you can imagine such a thing as an unlimited life span, unfettered by chance or disease, you can picture abject boredom.

In such a world the suicide rate would be one hundred percent.

Every Friday was "Buck Pitcher Night" at The Spud. From four-thirty in the afternoon until closing time, one dollar would pay for six beers and a fiver would knock you on your ass. Upperclassmen usually went on Thursday nights for "Thirty-five Centers," when each cocktail was just a quarter and a dime but they could afford to blow off class on Friday morning. Friday night was amateur night and the tightest budget could buy a buzz at Buck Pitchers.

It was the Friday before Spring Break and most of us were eager to bug out of town for a couple of weeks but The Spud was packed. A dollar pitcher of beer is a siren song to the impoverished student so Daytona Beach would just have to wait. I pissed away almost ten dollars that night and missed my ride home to Minneapolis altogether.

Walsh Hall was the largest dormitory on campus, housing more than three hundred students, but when I got back from The Spud that night it was eerily vacant. I was shit-faced, bouncing off the walls on the way to my room to pass out, when I ran into the only other soul in the building.

Scotty was the Resident Assistant on our floor and Scotty was a humorless fuck. Each wing of the building had an "R.A." to make sure we didn't have too much fun in college and our boy worked overtime. The annoying little twit wasn't even going home for Spring Break. It was no accident that Scotty Timmons was transferred to the party floor and he relished his situation as the new sheriff in town.

My suite mates and I were liberal arts majors with an emphasis on bong technology and beverage consumption, so Scotty focused his redemptive efforts on us. He'd write us up every time he'd catch a whiff of burning rope and he actually called the cops once when we were testing the limits of my roommate's new stereo. How were we to know that Bose 601's could achieve enough bass thrust to dislodge ceiling tiles?

It's humanity's saving grace that all of our wishes aren't granted because we are prone to wish for stupid things. Scotty Timmons was a thorn in my side for more than two years and I often wished the nosy little weasel would come to a bad end.

There is no doubt that Scotty saved my life that night so I'm necessarily ashamed to have ever wished him away.

————————

The R.A. was cracking a book in the study carrel on our wing as I wobbled serpentine toward my room. What a weenie, I thought to myself. What kind of freak of nature would be studying on the Friday before Spring Break?

"Hey Scotty...hic...rock and roll, baby...hic."

The sober resident assistant didn't bother looking up from his Trig textbook. "Another late night at the library, Mr. Shute?"

"Nah Scotty...hic...just a little extra-cur...hic...ular at The Spud."

"Your parents must be proud."

"Aww fuck you Scotty...hic...your parents must be looking into retro...hic...active abortion."

Then it hit me, like a baseball bat to the stomach. Wham! Scotty weighed all of a hundred and fifty pounds with his pockets full but he somehow gathered the strength to carry me to his car and drive me to the Emergency Room.

I was unconscious and the ER physician feared the worst. He sent Scotty back to the dorm to gather my personal information so that my parents could be notified. Scotty returned in twenty minutes with my file and spent the entire night at the hospital awaiting news of my fate. He decided that he would be the one to make the difficult phone call to my parents if things should take a bad turn.

Scotty felt it was wrong that I should die hundreds of miles from anyone who gave a shit about me so he stayed by my side and gave a shit. When I woke up two days later he was asleep in the chair next to my hospital bed.

The prairie emergency team felt they were out of their depth and so packed me off to spend Spring Break in a Minneapolis hospital.

———

I was born with a structural flaw that guaranteed the eventual explosion of one of my internal organs, Buck Pitchers just speeded things up a little bit. The tiny hose that was meant to vacate one of my kidneys was too narrow and the suds from The Spud popped the organ like a water balloon.

I was eighteen years old but for some reason they put me in the pediatric intensive care unit. The cartoon characters on the wallpaper and the big blue bunny on my door conspired with the massive doses of Demerol to make me believe I had fallen down the rabbit hole. After about a month of various surgical procedures and pharmaceutical smack I didn't know my own name.

When I came to my senses I felt nothing but self-pity, "I'm a kid, for chrissake, why me?" When the specialist showed me his plan for the final surgery, with a Flair pen on a paper towel, I knew that the curtain was coming down.

My roommate in the hospital was a couple of years older than me and considerably more mobile. Bobby'd pace around the room, bitching about being put in the pediatric ward and bitching about the food and bitching about the nurses, whom he referred to as simply "Those bitches."

He seemed pretty damned healthy to me and I wondered why he was in the Intensive Care Unit to begin with. He told me that he had Hepatitis C and that it was as serious as a heart attack. Bobby was drinking at Moby Dick's, the notorious watering hole on Hennepin Avenue in Minneapolis, when a stranger accosted him.

A panhandler grabbed his shoulder as he exited the bar and demanded twenty-five cents. My ICU roomie resisted and told the bum to "Get a fuckin' job." The moocher spun Bobby around and punched him square in the teeth, cutting his fist in the process, and bleeding into Bobby's mouth. A tiny blood born pathogen hopped from host to host and the next thing Bobby knew he lived in the kiddie wing at North Memorial Hospital.

————

I had a fourteen inch, half-sutured, gash in my abdomen, with what looked like garden hoses tethering me to a wall of hissing machinery. I thought that Bobby had a lot of damned nerve to whine about his little punch in the teeth. He once told me that I had it made because I was allowed to self-administer my own morphine and he had to beg "those bitches" to get a Tylenol with codeine.

Almost every night we'd see the blue lights flashing in the corridor of the Intensive Care Unit and a crash cart would be summoned to attempt a miracle. Bobby had a dark sense of humor and he used to start singing "Another one bites the dust" every time the Code Blue Team ran past our room.

"...And another one gone and another one gone, another one bites the dust"

We were the only residents of the pediatric ward with pubic hair so Bobby was whistling past some pretty young graves. In the fog of my pain medication I came to believe that he was the Devil incarnate. I wished Bobby would get dead himself.

This life is funny and I don't mean "funny ha-ha." Bobby would sing his song to dying babies and I'd fall deeper into doubt about our existence and its value. Toward the end I concluded that our lot as human beings was entirely arbitrary and without any definite meaning or worth. Bobby proved me wrong when the crash cart came for him.

His life was worth exactly twenty-five cents.

# Mama Passion

You've been cramming and struggling for eight semesters, sometimes getting out of bed before noon, in pursuit of your bachelor's degree in the liberal arts. The intoxicating glow of recognition by your academic peers will seem reward enough at graduation but now is not the time to rest on your laurels. It is never too soon to start planning your career and I'd like to take this opportunity to share a piece of wisdom that I acquired the hard way.

You will be swept up in a heady swirl as you collect your BA in Interpretive Dance and that Ceramics minor can only serve to broaden your commercial appeal. You must, however, keep your feet firmly planted on the ground after graduation and not let your expectations as a man or woman of letters get the best of you.

I'm not bragging but I eventually parlayed my own Political Science degree into a swell bartending job and you could do the same. I know what you're thinking, "Yeah but you prolly had connections and stuff," but this is not the case. I am a self-made man and had to claw my way up from the bottom just like everyone else.

There was, at the time of my graduation, an apparent glut in the supply of political scientists so I had to make my way in an unrelated field. There is no shame in temporary compromise toward a greater goal so I held my head high as I signed on for my first professional situation.

When the potato processing facility needed a security guard, I seized the opportunity.

———————

I overheard the drivers talking about Mama Passion as they dumped their potatoes into the flumes in the floor of the loading dock. I heard one of them say that they had first seen her around the Tater Tot laboratory so I presumed they were talking about the woman who worked in the lab.

Each end product produced by the factory had its own laboratory staff for quality control and the technician who tested Tater Tots was a large woman, whose girth seemed to expand hourly. Her primary duty was to make sure that exactly 70% of the Tater Tots could stand on end but it was clear she was involved in voluntary taste testing as well.

I wanted to join in the conversation with the truck drivers so I chimed in, "She's a big one alright."

They fell silent at once and each of the four men stared at me as I turned the key in my security clock. The driver who had been telling the story about Mama Passion spoke in a strangely hushed reverence; "You've seen her? You've seen Mama Passion?"

"I see her nearly every day, she's over near the Tater Tot line right now gobbling up the profits."

All four drivers stared at me, slack jawed, inexplicably awed by my utterance. The senior driver spoke again in a quiet conspiratorial tone.

"The last poor bastard that ran into her is a raving lunatic to this day, he lives with his mama in Williston. They say he ran screaming out of the factory, into a taxicab and took the cab clear across the state. Nobody's seen or heard from him since but the taxi driver still loses sleep over that $900.00 fare."

The other drivers were inching their way toward their respective trucks, slowly, inconspicuously as the senior driver spoke. "The cab driver says that the guy trembled the whole way to Williston and mumbled the same thing over and over again for seven and a half hours – 'Mama Passion, Mama Passion, Mama Passion...'"

"Aww, you've gotta be exaggerating, she's not that scary, I've seen women twice her size."

"Women? Listen college boy, I ain't talkin' about no woman, I'm talking about a spud gobbling rodent. I'm talking about a rat as big as a Labrador with teeth like a wolverine. I'm talkin' about Mama Passion!"

———

Hardly anybody called it a potato processing facility, it was "the potato factory" and it employed half of the town. The other half of the town were bettering themselves with a college education, which, as often as not, also led to a situation at the potato factory.

The local vernacular included many references to the burg's primary industry and the busiest bar was called "The Spud." If someone wanted to express total joy they would say they were "as happy as a rat at the potato factory."

By all accounts, Mama Passion was a happy rat indeed. A mammal specialist from the University was contracted to investigate and had taken plaster casts of her footprints and samples of her stool. He estimated that she weighed between thirty-five and forty pounds and was at least two and a half feet long without her tail. A plaster cast of the tail itself hung in the biology department and the diameter at its base was almost four inches.

The life expectancy of a typical brown rat in the wild is 2.5 to 3.5 years but the consensus at the biology department was that Mama Passion had been feasting on tubers for a decade or more.

Rat infestation was a constant concern at the potato factory so the facility maintained a full time exterminator on the premises. Jack Trader was a sadistic sort and generally well suited to his detail but he was no match for Mama Passion. He always managed to feign effectiveness with a high body count but everyone knew that he was terrified of confronting the big girl herself.

Jack employed the typical arsenal of traps and poisons with the atypical addition of a twenty-two-caliber side arm. He claimed he wore the hip boots because the flumes were damp but we all knew it was an extra layer of protection against the teeth of the legendary rodent.

———

I finished my last circuit of the factory for the night and returned to the security office to clean out the coffeepot for the next poor chump when the telephone rang. Five-dollar an hour security guards are rarely the last buffer between life and death so I was tempted to ignore a call so near the end of my shift. I now wish to God that I had.

The property was massive and with my luck I would be summoned to unlock a door on the other side of the factory and I'd miss last call at The Spud. The guy who relieved me for the graveyard shift was a meticulous little puke named Willis but everybody called him Barney Fife. Barney was as punctual as the guards at Buckingham Palace and he'd arrive in ten minutes exactly, at the stroke of midnight, as he had done five nights a week for the past ten years.

Barney took his degree in Criminal Justice at the University and was thrilled to be gainfully employed in his area of expertise. He seemed oblivious to the taunts of the factory workers and after a decade he still believed the job to be a valuable "resume builder" in his chosen career of law enforcement. The factory struggled with an epidemic of employee theft so some genius upstairs decided to arm the security guards. Barney had been appealing to management for a firearm permit since the week he was hired and the day we got the memo he drove straight to Kmart and bought a gun.

He was a passive aggressive cat and was the last guy on Earth you wanted to see with a loaded weapon. He quietly chafed under the derision of the factory workers and his face burned red with latent rage when they called him Barney Fife to his face. One of the guys on the

French fry line called him "Deputy Dawg" once and it so angered him that he kept the guy under surveillance for weeks until he caught him doing something wrong. Ol' Barney Fife wrote him up and got him suspended for a month.

Barney had been only a minor hindrance to the black market French fry trade in the past but his authority could no longer be questioned. Nobody doubted that the wiry little Criminal Justice major would wind up shooting somebody, it was just a question of when.

———

I recognized instantly that I wasn't being summoned to unlock a door when I heard the man screaming on the other end of the telephone. The wailing on the phone reminded me of a call I had taken a month before when a couple of rats had gone through the potato-peeling machine. It's not a pretty sight and the poor girl who witnessed the spectacle had only worked at the factory for two weeks. She took a medical leave and never came back.

This call was different though, as it wasn't a teenaged girl doing the screaming but a grown man with a side arm and hip boots. Jack Trader, the company exterminator, dialed the security office from the phone on the loading dock. He had seen a shadowy figure moving behind him in the maintenance tunnel and was calling me for backup when he came face to face with the gargantuan rodent.

He dropped the telephone receiver and it dangled from its cord while he scurried up the nearest pile of potatoes. Jack was screaming his appeal from atop the potato pile to the dangling telephone handset across the loading dock but he was making himself abundantly clear.

"Jesus, Jonny, get down to dock A quick...Aw, Christ Almighty she's coming up after me!"

I could tell Jack wasn't talking directly into the receiver by his distant shout but it didn't occur to me that he wouldn't hear my voice.

"What the hell is it Jack? Is this some kind of goof?"

"OH, SWEET MOTHER OF GOD, CALL THE NATIONAL GUARD!"

———————

I still suspected that Jack was playing a joke on me until I heard the squelch on my two-way radio. Barney Fife was driving past the loading dock on his way to the front gate and heard the shouting.

"Troubadour to Eagle's Nest, Troubadour to Eagle's Nest, do you read me Eagle's Nest?"

"Oh for Heaven's sake Barney, enough with The Guns of Navarone crap, you're a rent-a-cop in a potato factory."

"My name's not Barney, it's Willis and you're supposed to call me Sergeant Peters. I can have you written up you know!"

"Ok, Sergeant Peters, get your skinny ass to the loading dock and find out what all the shouting's about."

"I'm in front of the loading dock now and your insubordination has been noted..." Barney paused and I could hear a squelch on the two-way radio and then the distinct crack of a pistol shot. "Troubadour to Eagle's nest, Troubadour to Eagle's Nest, I'm taking fire from inside the loading dock. I'm going to return fire, call for backup."

"Oh, jeez Barney, don't shoot. Jack Trader's in there shooting at Mama Passion. Repeat, don't return fire!"

My warning fell on deaf ears as Barney had already tossed the walkie-talkie onto the passenger seat of his Chevette and retrieved his Kmart pistol from beneath the driver's seat. I still had the telephone receiver held to my ear when the firefight ensued.

Jack took the worst of it with a slug in the shoulder and another in the kneecap. He had a nasty set of teeth marks in his waders and twelve puncture wounds on the foot beneath them. He'd tell you that the worst part of his recovery was the rabies regimen he had to endure and that the gunshot wounds were secondary. They put him on sixty-percent disability and gave him a big settlement check to prevent a lawsuit.

When Barney started firing blindly into the dark loading dock, Jack ignored the attacking rodent long enough to squeeze off a shot at the over zealous security guard. You'd think Barney was a combat veteran to hear him tell it but the shot barely grazed the top of his head. It followed the geeky center part in his hair almost perfectly and left a comical bald scar where the part had been. He was back to work the next day. Both men lost their permit to possess firearms.

Jack Trader swore up and down that the rat was the size of a Saint Bernard and that he was lucky to escape with his life. Barney Fife's incident report describes a "shadowy figure approximately waist high."

Mama Passion was never found.

# In a building made of bones

I'm a skeptic when it comes to ghost stories so I am reluctant to relay my own. I have, however, seen things that I cannot explain and for which no rational explanation has been offered. The most dramatic episodes of supernatural activity that I've witnessed have gone unreported, more from selfishness than a fear of sounding loony. When the episodes are reduced to words they are lessened.

Most of my experience with ghosts happened in the same building over a two and a half-year period in the mid-1980s. The specific events numbered in the hundreds and became so commonplace that they often passed without remark.

I began to pay close attention to the odd occurrences and immediately found patterns of apparently supernatural activity that were predictable and routine. The skeptic in me quietly investigated each instance, in the hopes of finding a prankster at the other end of the phenomena but none was ever discovered.

Nicollet Island is a 48-acre strip of land in the Mississippi River just above St. Anthony Falls, in downtown Minneapolis. Only two structures exist from the original building boom in the 1890's and one of these was the Island Sash and Door Company. The building was constructed in 1893 of massive blocks of rough-hewn, Minnesota Blue Limestone, quarried from that very site. That same year a disastrous Minneapolis fire made quick work of most of the rest of the buildings on the island but left the stone edifice intact.

In 1913 the building was purchased by the Salvation Army and converted into a homeless shelter for men, which operated for nearly 60 years. By the early 1970's the neglected Nicollet Island had earned a reputation as a haven for transients, hippies and winos. It was, by all accounts, a roguish scene and rumor had it that the police only visited for the occasional corpse removal and never did so after dark. The island was a magnet for the city's wretched refuse and the crumbling shell of the old limestone building had become a squatter's nest.

Limestone is little more than compressed calcium carbonate, the remains of ancient sea creatures, so the building itself was actually made of old bones. Those walls contained the last breath of scores of desperate men and it is little wonder that a restless soul might linger.

As part of the city's gentrification of its riverfront in the mid-1970's, the building was sold to a developer for one dollar. The property was to be refurbished as an upscale hotel and restaurant. Millions of dollars were devoted to the hotel project and millions more on the island as a whole and the results were stunning. The derelict building where winos had gone to die was transformed into an elegant neo-Victorian inn.

I began work as the hotel desk clerk and barman in the pub a year or two after their grand opening.

---

The spirits moved daily through the hotel and their machinations were obvious to anyone who paid attention. Any single incident would be summarily dismissed as a freak occurrence by the casual observer but the activity I chronicled over the course of two years made a believer out of me.

The hotel had twenty-four guestrooms and every room was decorated differently, each with a separate personality and feel. The ghost showed a definite preference for rooms 216 and 316, as these rooms were the focal point of most of his activity. In a typical episode a guest would return to the front desk after check-in and report that their room seemed to be locked from the inside.

Each room had a deadbolt lock operated by a lever on the inside of the room. There was no key for the deadbolt and so there was no keyhole on the outside of the door. The bolt could only be thrown from inside of the room. The first time it happened to room 216 and we considered calling the police for fear someone had thrown the deadbolt and died in bed. The host went outside and scaled the limestone wall in his evening clothes, jiggled open the window and gained entrance. The room was immaculate and empty and locked from the inside.

The next time it happened, the host scaled the building more adeptly for having practiced but when he made it to the window he found it locked as well. He broke through the flimsy window lock and climbed in the window to unlock the door. There were no adjoining rooms or secret trap doors and the walls were three feet of solid limestone. Whoever or whatever locked both the door and the window from the inside exited through non-conventional means.

The locks were changed on every room on the second floor so that the deadbolt could be thrown with a master key from outside the room. Shortly after solving our mysterious problem a guest returned to the front desk complaining that room 316 seemed to be locked from the inside. I looked at the host and he looked right back at me.

"If you think I'm climbing the outside of this building to the third floor you're nuts...this is a brand new suit pal, call a flippin' locksmith."

The guest was getting snippy by the time the locksmith arrived two hours later so we comped her room and changed all of the locks on the third floor as well.

Rooms 216 and 316 continued to be locked from the inside intermittently but since we now had the key it became only a minor nuisance.  Both rooms were still the source of dozens of complaints about everything from extreme spontaneous temperature swings to the guest in 316 who reported that she awoke to find both previously locked windows wide open.

Otherwise rational hotel guests began to request rooms on the opposite end of the building.

---

Perhaps the most haunting manifestation of the ghost, or ghosts happened in the Pub, in the basement of the building.  The memory visits me to this day and I am still left to wonder if the spirits weren't struggling to communicate with me.  On the days I tended bar I noticed an odd arrangement of pens and small scraps of paper lying around when I arrived.  Each day I'd collect the pens and put them back in the cup next to the cash register and throw the scraps of paper in the trash.

I didn't think anything of it until the first time I closed and opened the bar on successive days.  I had been the one who cleaned the bar the previous night and I padlocked the doors when I left.  Ten hours later when I returned to open the bar, the padlocks were in place but the strange configuration of writing implements and scraps of paper were arranged along the entire length of the bar and the back bar.  I examined the pieces of paper closely for the first time and each had only a small squiggle or an odd pencil mark with no discernable writing.

The pens, perhaps a dozen of them, were almost evenly spaced, some perpendicular and some running parallel to the line of the bar.  One of the small scraps of paper lay between each pair of writing tools.

I asked the only other people with keys to the Pub and they hadn't a clue who might have been there in my absence.  That night when I closed the bar I placed small pieces of scotch tape along the seam of each door.  I switched the padlock on the back door with the one from my locker just to be sure.  When I returned ten hours later my padlock was locked, my scotch tape was intact and the pens and paper were arranged almost exactly as they had been the day before.

In that moment my worldview shifted forever and I questioned my skepticism of everything from alien abductions to Santa Clause.

––––––––––

I was working at the front desk of the hotel the night the ghost showed its surlier side. It was about 9 o'clock on a Saturday night and the restaurant was packed. A buddy and I were leaning against the desk, watching the parade of thousand dollar suits and designer gowns go by when he nudged my arm and said, "What's the story with her?" He was pointing at the hotel guest who was descending the stairs into the middle of the crowded lobby, barefooted, wearing only her bathrobe. Her hair was a ragged mess and her face was frightfully pale.

She walked directly up to me and spoke with an eerie calm. "I was stepping into the bath when it happened, it wasn't supposed to kill me."

"Umm, what wasn't supposed to kill you, ma'am?"

She was impassive, oblivious to the murmuring crowd and apparently unaware that she was grotesquely underdressed. The woman was a calm, ghostly zombie speaking in a creepy monotone.

"The ceiling wasn't going to kill me at all. I barely had a toe in the tub when it fell. It didn't even graze me."

"Ma'am, the ceiling fell in your room?"

"Yes, it did...just the part above the tub though."

"Thank God you weren't injured ma'am, I'll move you to another room immediately."

"That won't be necessary. I'm checking out in the morning and I can get by without the tub. I just thought I should let you know before someone else books the room that It's going to need quite a lot of work. And I wanted to give you this."

She handed me a three by five-inch card with the name and description of one of the guestrooms. Each of the rooms was named for a famous Minnesota settler and the cards had been placed in the rooms when the hotel first opened. Over the course of time it became a nuisance to make sure that the correct cards were in the corresponding room so the practice was abandoned years before.

"Oh, that's nothing ma'am, just a little biographical description of the famous settler your room is named for."

"But it's not the right card for my room, I'm in 316 and the card is supposed to be in room 216."

I didn't let on that both rooms were the font of great weirdness in the past and when I noticed that my buddy was about to I gave him an elbow to the ribcage.

"Just a little housekeeping oversight, ma'am, happens all the time. You're sure that there's nothing I can do for you?"

She spoke as though she was under hypnosis, "No, I'll be fine, goodnight."

My buddy grabbed the card from my hand as the woman turned and crossed the lobby toward the staircase. "Those are the hinky rooms, man, your ghost was trying to smush that nice lady." Now it was my friend who was oblivious to the curious stares of the restaurant goers. "There's somethin' about this card, man, did you see her? She looked like a Stepford Wife. She didn't have nuthin' on under that robe either."

I snatched the card back from him and scrutinized it for significant clues but found none. The name held no special meaning to me and the short biographical description of an early milling baron was unremarkable. The date of the man's death caught my eye because it was one of history's infamous milestones. "Hey look, the guy died on the same day as Julius Caesar, March fifteenth."

"Beware the Ides of March, dude."

It was the third week of February when the ghost sent us the sign and my friend and I agreed that I should be extra vigilant when the designated day rolled around. I remember taping the card next to the calendar in my apartment and putting a big red X on the fifteenth of March so I wouldn't miss it.

I'd like to fill you in on what went on in the hotel that day but I can't. The business fell into bankruptcy on the fourteenth and the sheriff padlocked the doors the next morning.

# On situational ethics

"**D**on't keep the money from bottled beer or liquor, it's too easy to count; take the money from soda pop, they can't keep track of that."

The girl who was training me in for my first bartending job was talking so fast I was barely able to follow along.

"If you end up with an absolute stiff, raise the drink price to cover your tip and ring it under open liquor."

I didn't want to appear ignorant so I nodded and smiled a half a smile. I didn't have any idea what she was talking about but I needed the gig. I fibbed a little when I told them that I was an experienced bartender.

After I worked a shift or two on my own I understood exactly what she meant. A certain percentage of the customers would leave no gratuity for services rendered and the bartender could make up for shortfalls with freelance sales and creative arithmetic. Situational ethics.

My father was a bartender and I couldn't, in my wildest dreams, imagine him pilfering money from his employer. He taught us as children that we must never speak ill of our employer, much less steal from him. I have had dozens of bosses since then and among these a fair number of flawed ones. I considered my father's admonition absurd in the face of an obviously malevolent or ignorant restaurant manager but I would not stray from his command. If the boss is bad enough to complain about you should find another job.

Like Ann Landers says, "Nobody can take advantage of you without your permission."

The first time I stuffed the $1.25 from the sale of Coca-Cola into my tip jar instead of the cash register was my last. I wasn't so much haunted by my father's admonition about loyalty to the people who feed you, as by my growing awareness of the vicissitudes of karma. The millionaire hotel proprietor would not suffer financial collapse for my small indiscretion but my little voice made it clear that I would.

I've kept a large photograph of my father next to the cash register of every bar I've tended since that day.

---

The hotel had only twenty-four rooms but it was a fancy joint. The original limestone structure was purchased from the city of Minneapolis for one dollar as part of its riverfront redevelopment project and millions were spent on remodeling. Each of the guestrooms was decorated differently, with actual Victorian antiques and reproductions and no expense was spared in attending to the tiniest details.

The back bar in the Pub was hand carved mahogany and its commission cost more than I would make in five years behind the bar. Ridiculous sums were spent on every fixture so we surmised that it was the pet project of somebody with more dollars than sense. They managed to forestall bankruptcy for about three years.

Harbingers of doom were everywhere during the last weeks and months before the place finally closed. The angry end of the accounts payable list was growing more aggressive by the day and judgements against the owners piled up much faster than reservations for the quaint little rooms. When our paychecks began to bounce the proprietors called an emergency employee meeting.

They adopted a familial tone with us and thanked us for helping them weather the difficult seas. The owners explained that they were having a hard time meeting payroll and that they would thank us to work without one for awhile. We felt like a family, in a way, and the owner's cynical appeal for free labor was satisfied. We took a vote and agreed to continue regular operation of the hotel without pay for a month. In a month's time we would be reimbursed for our accrued hours and the standard payroll would resume.

When the month passed and the supplemental payroll checks bounced we sensed that the end was near. Those of us who worked for tips weren't profoundly affected but plenty of housekeepers, dishwashers and cooks were out on the street. They made the promise to their landlords as the promise had been made to them. When the promise was broken their leases were too. They acted like a family and now they would have to live like one; dwindling resources were pooled for the rent on collective dwellings. In the final weeks of the hotel's operation all of the cooks shared one house, the housekeepers another and the dishwashers a third.

The bankruptcy court finally decided that the owner's alimony arrears would be the primary claim so none of us ever saw a penny. None except Kathy the waitress, whose husband Guido (no kidding) confronted the owner as he climbed into his Saab one night. Guido said he wasn't leaving until Kathy was paid every cent she was due and the nervous little man pulled a wad of money from his pocket on the spot and counted out fourteen hundred-dollar bills.

––––––––

We were allowed access to the padlocked premises to retrieve our personal possessions so I collected all of the board games and record albums I had brought to the bar. I made a pass through the kitchen to say goodbye to the last of the staff but found the owner, alone, struggling to disconnect coolers and other kitchen fixtures. In my naivete I thought he was turning off the gas or something but he was, more likely, pirating the appliances for use in his next restaurant venture.

I came to despise the owner but when I asked myself what my father would do, I could almost hear his voice out loud. I approached the scoundrel and offered my hand to thank him for hiring and employing me. He stood from his crouched position behind one of the coolers and sheepishly reached over to shake my hand when he noticed his own was covered with black grease and slime. He turned his palms upward and both arms were caked with grime to the elbow so we mutually shrugged off the handshake.

I said "Good luck" and left him to his burden.

# Heads or tails?

Jaime's old man was a gynecologist and his mother a psychologist so I'd razz him that they must have flipped a coin. It's little wonder that Jaime turned out to be a smooth talking ladies man.

He grew up on the right side of the tracks in an affluent suburb of Cleveland but he spent the bulk of his childhood and adolescence looking for escape. Jaime didn't so much have a problem with drugs and alcohol, he had a problem with a world full of straights and a life that constantly interfered with his buzz.

He was a star athlete in more than one sport but the culture that he inhabited was not one of sober athleticism. Jim Carroll's Basketball Diaries might well have been written about Jaime and his teammates, whose efforts to score off the field were of primary importance. While lightweights in the stands might be jazzed on a little schnapps they'd lifted from their parent's liquor cabinet, Jaime and the rest of the offensive line chased acid with Jack Daniel's at the pre-game party.

Jaime never met a drug he didn't like and he never found a dosage that could satisfy him. Still in his teens, he'd been to the end and back again with junkie pride, any quantity, any orifice, any time. His parents pulled his ass out of the stew a dozen times before turning to professional help in the happy heartland. Cleveland may rock, but Minneapolis rehabilitates.

I met him at the haunted hotel on Nicollet Island almost twenty years ago, soon after he had begun his treatment at St. Mary's Hospital on the banks of the upper Mississippi. "The land of ten thousand lakes" has many claims to fame, from the invention of Scotch tape to the Governor formerly known as Jesse the Body, but Jaime emigrated for a different reason entirely. Minnesota holds quiet preeminence in the science of detoxification.

Very few people move here on purpose, due to our legendary winters, but fewer still decamp in disgust. Minnesota grows on you. I've always thought it a blessing to be born here and have kept mostly silent about it for fear that the Shangri-La would be discovered and overrun. When a business traveler at the bar would whine about being transferred to the tundra against his will, I'd whisper encouraging words, "Don't moan about the weather, brother, you've landed in God's Country. Winter keeps out the riff raff."

Jaime, like many outlanders, didn't choose Minnesota; it was thrust upon him.

---

Drug and alcohol abuse is a symptom, not a disease. I'm not a physician or a specialist in obsessive behavior but my job involves ministering to the afflicted. I claim my expertise as a professional drug dealer, the legally sanctioned kind, with a shot glass and a tip jar. In my humble opinion, every alcoholic is a potential jogging fanatic and every neat freak is a heroin hound waiting to happen.

There is only one sure cure for obsessive behavior of any kind and that is to replace it with an alternate obsession.

In examining the spectrum of people who exhibit these behaviors you'll find a startling commonality: Elevated intelligence. The best and the brightest are invariably touched by manic obsession of one kind or another and the busiest brains often seek quietude in chemicals. Don't be surprised if you wake up the junkie in the gutter and find a former College Bowl contestant or if the barfly puking in the alley turns out to be Charles Bukowski.

————————

Jaime took the cure at St. Mary's but never counted himself among the hardcore disease victims. Alcoholics Anonymous indoctrinated him at first but he wound up tripping over a couple of the twelve steps. When they told him that he couldn't pal around with anyone who was "using" it pretty much ruled out everyone he was fond of, so he gave AA the slip. He was the living exemplar of the guy who would have been an alcoholic if he'd only had time for the meetings.

When Jaime was released from rehab he took a job in the banquet department at the hotel on the island and changed his obsession like flipping a switch. Waitresses. He was a charming little cat to begin with and the introspective therapy he endured at St. Mary's rendered him more sensitive than Oprah. Girls fell at his feet because he did what other guys only pretended to, he listened to them. Clever bastard.

Skirt chasing is benign in and of itself but it often leads to matrimony and worse, as it did for Jaime. When he slipped on that wedding band, fidelity demanded that he start all over again with a new obsession.

By the time I made his acquaintance he was up to over a hundred rounds a year and he kept his clubs in the trunk throughout the winter. Summertime in Minnesota is fleeting at best, so it's no mean feat to squeeze that many holes into one season; you have to be driven. He golfed at least four times a week, rain or shine, to the joy of his bride who preferred it to backsliding into substance abuse.

Jaime's smart and hilarious and still sober by his own devices. It goes without saying that he's become a wicked good golfer and you should demand at least a stroke a hole if you meet him on a tee box.

He once confessed to me that he missed getting high but that he knew he could never do it half way. He'd either be a dead junkie or a scratch golfer.

Sort of a coin toss.

# Like church only bigger

If Jaime can't make you laugh, you're probably already dead. A good deal of his repertoire is pirated from professional comedians he sees on television but he has a way of surpassing their delivery and making it his own. Many of his pop culture references go right over my head because I work at night and don't see much prime time television but I make a great audience for Jaime because he won't get busted for stealing material.

I didn't get to watch much "Seinfeld" so I had no way of knowing that he was imitating Kramer when we stood at the counter to pay our greens fees.

"You get this, babe, all I've got are hundreds and I don't have them with me."

Or a pretty girl with a predominant chest would walk by and he'd fall back against the wall with slapstick exaggeration.

"Boutros Boutros, Golly!"

He has an odd, nasal cartoon character timbre over smoker's gravel and he talks so fast that you're still laughing over the last thing he said while he's pitching the next one. His dialect can be described as modified gangster-speak, a cross between Daffy Duck and James Cagney. The fast talking gangster thing is just a ruse because Jaime's definitely a lover, not a fighter. An angry man tried to pick a fight with him on the golf course once and he struck the guy dumb by beating himself up.

"Listen, sister, I won't give you the satisfaction. I'm gonna kick my own ass."

Jaime grabbed the collar of his own shirt and threw himself to the ground with inordinate violence, pretending to punch himself in the face and kick his own shins. He continued the self-flagellation long after the situation was diffused and the angry guy wound up laughing hysterically and buying Jaime's beer.

---

Billy isn't as funny as Jaime but he's close and it's an entirely different kind of humor. Dark and thoughtful, he's George Burns to Jaime's Gracie Allen. When they golf together they create a perfect dialectic and become greater than the sum of their parts. You would swear that their performance is rehearsed because they finish each other's sentences like old married people. They have openly debated abandoning their heterosexuality and joining in gay marriage so that they'd be eligible for a family pass at the golf course.

"You know, Jaime, there are tax benefits too?"

"Don't toy with me, babe!"

There is no problem too big or too serious for Billy to wrap his worldview around and he has a firm opinion on absolutely everything. His specialty is curmudgeon satire but the deadpan delivery is so effective that you can never be sure if he's kidding. He had never even heard of Jonathan Swift when he told me that he came up with a solution for over-population, unemployment and hunger.

"Eat the people who are unemployed...duh."

I brought a copy of "A Modest Proposal" to the golf course the next day and accused him of stealing the idea from Swift. Billy read the whole thing while we waited on the tee box, then tossed the book back to me and oozed derision.

"What an idiot. I said the same thing in one sentence."

––––––––––

The banter on the course rarely has anything to do with golf per se, more a four-hour jaunt around the world of ideas with the golf gods sitting in judgement.  Your demons are right there on every shot and every putt, standing on your shoulder, whispering or screaming into your ear.  As you address the ball and make your final practice swing everyone falls to silence except the little voices in your head.

Some people go to church to crank up the volume on their conscience and ask the big questions but not these cats.  They wouldn't last five minutes in church, playing with the little pencils on the back of the pew and ridiculing dogma.  When I told Billy that the golf course reminded me of church because of those little pencils he said that it was exactly like church only bigger and more expensive.

"People in prison should have to golf every day.  Golf builds character, rubs off the rough edges."

"Right babe, it made a character out of you."

Jaime can't pass up a straight line and I can't leave well enough alone.

"But if you sent people to prison and let them play golf for free, everybody would want to go to prison.  Toss in the government health care and three square meals every day and jobless duffers would be scaling the razor wire to get in."

"What's your point?  You think that gathering up all of the people who are too lazy to work and too nervous to steal is a bad thing?"

"Well no, it just sounds expensive, that's all."

"Not more expensive than having your sister raped or your neighbor murdered.  Prisons are bad guy factories plain and simple, you might just as well cut to the chase and kill 'em all as leave 'em cooped up with their own kind.  The only thing they learn in that cage is hate and the longer you leave 'em there, the better they get at it.  After ten or twenty years they let 'em out, lovely.  Lock me in a cage like that and you'd better never take your eyes off of me."

If the conversation gets too heavy Jaime brings it down a notch and reminds us that the golf gods are watching.

"I can barely take my eyes off of you now, big boy. HIT THE FUGGIN' BALL!"

"I don't see how giving a bunch of ne'er-do-wells a season ticket cures anything, man. What's to keep them from beating each other to death with a pitching wedge?"

"Discipline. The game would eventually teach them to use that anger constructively, focus it on a nasty bunker lie or a slippery downhill putt instead. There'd be a certain amount of bloodshed among the high handicappers and violent felons but the game has rules that are self-enforcing. It's all well and good to beat your opponent to death but you've still got to get past that long par four yourself."

"But Billy, what would be the motivation to get out of prison?"

"Well, you brought up that whole getting your brains bashed in thing. Mostly they'd discover that they want to get out to play other courses and have sex with someone besides their cellmate. Then there's the gruel. Awful stuff, gruel. Six months of that and they'll be so busy practicing their short game that they won't have time for shenanigans. You'd make 'em trustees when they hit a single digit handicap and when they get to scratch you cut 'em loose, simple as that. They've got something to shoot for."

"Cut 'em loose? You would release a mass murderer just because he can shoot par?"

"It's impossible to be a scratch golfer and a bad person at the same time."

All three of us paused in the middle of the fairway to absorb the truth of it but long thoughtful silences bug the Hell out of Jaime.

"Was that a slam?"

# Frenchman for the night

Mary picked me so I never really trusted her. She was my cocktail waitress for a couple of years and one night she simply followed me home. Her devotion to me was complete and entirely unjustified.

She was too optimistic and too pretty by half. I've always been attracted to a sort of plain girl with low self-esteem. I have bad posture and post-adolescent acne so I was sure my wife would be looking at her shoes when we were introduced. Mary moved into my apartment and contented herself as my live-in non-girlfriend. After five years my little voice told me that my indifference to her was a kind of cruelty. My little voice said that I should find my wife.

It happened one night at the bar where I work. Jimmy Buffett's song "Frenchman for the night" was playing on the jukebox and a girl appeared at the end of the bar. She had her back to me and was looking out the window of the bar at the creek below. I caught a glimpse of her face reflected in the window and acted on impulse.

I tapped her on the shoulder and said, "I think you're my wife."

Relief washed over me when I came to my senses and noticed her wedding ring. After an awkward silence I asked her if she was a married lady. She looked at the ring on her hand for a weird, long moment and told me that she was. She turned and left without an introduction.

When she showed up at the bar near closing time a week later I knew that we were being moved by destiny. When the "Frenchman for the night" song shuffled into the jukebox again I got a chill.

My boss rounded the corner and I expected him to bust my chops for sitting at the bar but he didn't. He smiled his biggest smile and handed me a videocassette. He told me that Jimmy Buffett had been on Good Morning America so he taped it for me. He excused himself with a bow and left me alone with the nice married lady.

Our conversation was strange and pointed. We interviewed each other like job applicants and when I closed the bar we parted without so much as a handshake. I drove home that night under a full moon that cast enough light to read a newspaper.

When I got home I told Mary I had met my wife. I told her that she didn't have to move out immediately but that she had to go. I told her that ours had been a relationship of convenience and that it must end. I ignored her weeping protests and her prescience in telling me that the girl I aimed at was flighty or confused. I was confident that I was doing the right thing in being forthright with Mary.

I remembered the videotape my boss had given me and popped it in the VCR to distract me from Mary's audible grief. Jimmy Buffett and The Coral Reefer Band were gathered on a black soundstage. Brother Jim was dressed in white from neck to toe. They performed an uncharacteristically haunting song called "Frenchman for the night."

"By the light of the moon, he's a Frenchman for the night..." The song spoke to me directly. Each verse seemed to chronicle my strange odyssey with the married lady. "The girl he knew, with eyes of blue, waiting on the shore..."

This could not be simple coincidence. Mary moved out a month later.

———————

I was alone with my Labrador on the 4th of July when the thunderstorm struck. The dog was usually good company but she was a nervous wreck that night because of the storm. Emmy had doggy epilepsy and I feared the storm might trigger a seizure. She'd emerge from the episodes unharmed but they were a horror to witness.

My little house was rocked by the storm, Emmy was a basket case and Mary's shadow wouldn't leave me alone. I did what seemed the only sensible thing and called my mother. Mom said that Mary was the best thing that ever happened to me and that I was an idiot for letting her leave. She told me that I was probably not a knight in shining armor, that I was more likely an adulterous scoundrel who may soon be answering to a jealous husband. She told me not to shove.

I shoved.

The married lady called me that night from a campground up north. She told me that, while she was camping with her husband, she was thinking about me. I told her she wasn't doing her husband any favors by hanging around a loveless marriage and that Independence Day would be a good time to bag it. She asked him for a divorce that night in the tent.

Lightning struck my little house a couple of hours later as I lay in bed with my epileptic Labrador. Not metaphorical lightning, the real kind, which bathes you in a strange blue light and makes your hundred pound dog stand bolt upright on your chest. It melts the phone jack into the wall and turns the stereo system into so much cooked plastic.

...The kind of lightning that mysteriously cures your dog's epilepsy.

Mary and I used to watch her seizures through wet eyes. We called them her "wiggles" to make them sound less serious and wished them away with all of our might. I wept now wishing that Mary was around to hear the good news.

"Emmy and I were struck by lightning and we've both come to our senses. Please come home!"

The married lady fell off the radar after an ugly year or so. I found my Mary waitressing in a diner on the north side and begged her, on bended knee, to be my wife. To her credit she spurned me but her maternal bond with my dog clinched the deal. We were wed the following month. Emmy hasn't had a seizure since the storm.

My brother Billy told me that the same song that directed me to my soulmate made him go home with the trashiest chick in the bar.

Go figure.

# You don't need a reason to cry

S he was what most people would call a middle-aged woman, although that designation has always confused me. If the average life span hovers around seventy-five, then middle aged would be about thirty-eight. A braver man than me will call a thirty-eight year old woman "middle aged" to her face. This lady was fifty something, bumping up against sixty something and it was unlikely that she'd live to see her 120th birthday.

It seemed to me that by the time someone had bopped around the orb for a half a century or more he or she would have nailed down most of the variables. Life's frustrations would be predictable and manageable by then, I thought, or mechanisms for coping with the roller coaster would be firmly in place.

There were five of us around the blackjack table, including the dealer, an Asian couple and the nice middle aged lady. The other players were experiencing the steady bloodletting that is the casino's stock in trade but I was on a rampage. I couldn't lose.

The Asian pair seemed to be an old married couple with a well-practiced routine for when the luck went south. The casual observer could ascertain nothing from their stony expression but I watched them pass several hundred dollars across the felt in the wrong direction. They were obviously veteran gamblers so they were backing off their bets gradually in the face of a strong dealer and a bad run. They would survive the downturn through careful money management.

The nice middle-aged lady was taking a pounding with every accounting of the cards. When she doubled down her eleven she'd hit a three. If she held pat with her pair of face cards, the dealer would flip over a blackjack. She excused herself three times to hit the magic money machine and pleaded with the dealer each time to hold her decidedly unfortunate spot, in the nearly empty casino.

I was firmly in my happy place, zigging when I should zig, zagging when I should zag and getting paid on twelves and thirteens as often as twenty-ones.

------------

Billy and I were there at the outset of casino gambling in Minnesota. He'd drive down to the Indian Reservation to play bingo and I'd tease him about buddying up with the blue-haired set. One night he came back with nine hundred dollars in cash and I was forced to reevaluate my definition of cool pastimes.

The Indian reservations are predominantly self-governing entities and are left to their own devices on everything from law enforcement to tax collection. When they discovered that the cash bingo game was drawing customers from off the rez, they wisely expanded their trade.

The expansion began in earnest, with something called a "Peg Wheel." It was a large "Wheel of Fortune" kind of thing with a leather strap that clipped across the pegs until it arrived at a number. The device was much simpler than a roulette wheel in that there weren't any colors or null spots for the house, simply odd and even numbers counting up to forty-two. The player layed down money on odd or even, they gave the wheel a spin and the house would be pay even money for a lucky guess.

The peg wheel was a dream bet as far as serious gamblers are concerned and you'll never see anything like it in Vegas. It was absolutely even money, like the toss of a coin.  There isn't a professional casino manager in his right mind that will offer you anything resembling an even money bet.  To someone unaccustomed to the craft it might sound stupid to bet on the flip of a coin but it's a far better wager than any casino game that you will ever see.

We had an absolute gas while it lasted.  Wads of twenty-dollar bills in each hand, betting up to eighty dollars at a whack and beating the ill-conceived game more often than not.  We left with bulging pockets nearly every night until the reservation hired a gaming consultant from Nevada.

Billy and I were on our way through the back of the bingo hall one night, flush with folding money from our new hobby, when we stumbled over the future of casino gambling in Minnesota.  The professional gaming consultant developed a new game, exactly like blackjack in every respect, save a slight difference in the appearance of the cards.  Each deck was numbered normally but instead of pasty white royalty adorning the face cards, they had pictures of eagle feathers or buffalo.

The game was given a different name but the rules were identical to blackjack and a billion-dollar cash cow was born.

———

The gambling casinos sprouted like mushrooms, almost over night, on Indian reservations throughout our state and the rest of the country.  At one point there were as many as seventeen such casinos in Minnesota alone, generating revenues estimated in the billions.  Exact accounting would be a private matter, as the casinos operated on the soil of a sovereign nation and were not subjected to normal taxation.

The good old days of peg wheels and even money bets at the little teepee were gone forever; replaced by massive Las Vegas style casinos, ten thousand car parking lots and humorless pit bosses.  The attraction of the game ebbed for me as the Native American's attention to the profit margin increased.  It was becoming much harder to separate them from their wampum so my trips to the casino became increasingly rare.

I never thought worse of the noble tribes for cashing in on their sovereign status. Our father pummeled us, as children, with the truth of the atrocity the white man perpetrated on these serene people. "Don't criticize a man until you have walked a mile in his moccasins." The success they were enjoying with the acceptance of the casinos was small compensation, I thought, sweet revenge. I became less willing to toss my own hard-earned bartender bucks into the pile but more power to 'em if they could harvest the rubes.

At some point a more aggressive gaming consultant was hired and it was decided that the profit margin for blackjack could be nearly doubled by changing one little rule. In traditional blackjack the dealer must hold on a "soft seventeen," that is an Ace and a six. The game would simply be altered to allow the dealer to take a hit on this particular combination of cards, presumably bettering his hand. The players would barely notice such a subtle change in the game but the accountants in the cash cage were soon up to their necks in filthy lucre.

I started to get a bad feeling about the Indian casinos. Before the dramatic rule change I could leave the teepee with my head held high on a losing night, confident that I had contributed to their survival as a race. When they changed the rules of a centuries old game to nearly double the house advantage with the stroke of a pen, I changed my opinion. It seemed they had been successfully assimilated to the white man's ways of blind avarice and no longer required my sympathy.

Those infrequent trips to the teepee were now a purely adversarial endeavor.

———————

My duties at the bar demanded a sort of super-human perkiness that didn't fade at last call. At the end of a busy shift I'd be wide-awake and looking for action. My wife would be asleep at that hour, as would most decent people, and nothing good could come of disturbing her. I started going back to the casino just for something to do in the middle of the night when there was nobody left to play with.

I had long since come to grips with the fact that the cards were stacked against me so I was stingy with the blood money from the bar. That night at work had been a grueling exercise in thankless beverage delivery and when I gave last call I had only fifty-seven dollars in my tip jar. Within a few minutes at the first blackjack table I had more than ten times that amount.

The sky's the limit when I'm playing with the casino's money so I upgraded to the exclusive use of the hundred-dollar black chips. I tipped the dealer with the twenty-five dollar green chips and the waitress with the red plastic fivers. I was absolutely on fire that night and at one point had twenty-five black chips in one pocket, in addition to my healthy table stakes.

I was so focused on my own thrill ride that I barely noticed my companions at the table. I knew that the Hmong couple was doing a steady bleed but they seemed to have no end of fresh blood. The husband was uniformly morose but the wife chirped a happy song, in a language I didn't know, every time she went back to the well. The cute little woman would set her enormous hand bag on the padded edge of the blackjack table, interrupting play, and fish around in it for reinforcements. She'd pull out a fistful of hundred dollar bills and slap them down on the felt with a broad smile.

The other lady at the table was breaking my heart. She was incapable of taking a hit without busting and the lines on her face and the mist in her eyes indicated that the well was running dry. She had excused herself three times, always in the middle of a hand, to negotiate with the instant cash machine. The game of blackjack often requires additional wagers for splitting Aces, or doubling down, so play would be halted while she retrieved the money. The magic money machine quit speaking to her by the fourth trip and she returned to the table empty handed. She hit the twin Aces because she couldn't pay to split them and watched what would have been her first two blackjacks of the night become a busted twenty-two.

She stayed and watched us play for fifteen minutes or more, openly sobbing, no money left to wager. The lady seemed in no hurry to leave the casino or even the table that had been her Waterloo. One got the impression that she was in much deeper than she could afford and that she might not have a happy home to return to. The dealer seemed sympathetic to her plight and since there was nobody clamoring for her unlucky chair she was allowed to sit and watch and weep.

By the time she left I was up about three grand and the nice Hmong couple were out at least that much. The husband who had been mostly silent throughout the evening spoke to the dealer in halting English.

"That lady was crying. Why that lady cry so much?"

The young dealer was now concerning himself with the emptying casino, his tip jar and the reshuffling of the cards and answered the Hmong man with an inattentive shrug. The man's wife, who held the purse strings during their own plunge into the abyss, answered his question more succinctly.

"Look around dum-dum. You don't need a reason to cry."

# In front of God and everyone

I make an appearance in more wedding albums than Elizabeth Taylor. I'm not a frequent partygoer or a chronic groom but if you tied the knot in Minnesota there's a pretty good chance that I reluctantly attended the reception. Look carefully at that photograph of Uncle Leo groping the best man's girlfriend on the dance floor and you'll see me over in the corner, behind the portable bar. The benign expression on my face masks the fact that I'm planning to use my corkscrew to disembowel the deejay the next time he plays the Macarena.

Some demented genius has cornered the market on wedding reception planning and rendered them all identically horrific. It doesn't matter if your party is at the local VFW or in the ballroom of the finest hotel the result will be the same. I would plead with you to reconsider for the good of your marriage. The exorbitant price you'll pay for loveless food in a big room with sour carpeting could be better spent and about half of the people in attendance would rather be elsewhere anyway. Henry David Thoreau wisely warned us to "distrust any enterprise that requires new clothes" and I would expand the admonition to include rented ones.

With the divorce rate hovering around in coin toss territory the wedding itself is an exercise in ritualized insincerity. Whether you make your vows in a church in front of God and everyone or quietly in the office of a Justice of the Peace, you are as likely as not engaged in a fraud. I say bag the entire ordeal and fly below the radar on the matrimony thing. Quiet promises are easier to keep, like a resolution to diet or to quit smoking. If you want to insure failure in either of those endeavors you need only spout your grand goals from the rooftops. I attribute the low success rate of marriage to the pomp and circumstance that surrounds it.

I advocate a secret ceremony involving only the two principle parties. You'll save a pile of money if you whisper the oath to your prospective mate and you'll save face if it turns out to be a pack of lies. You might just save yourself from a one way ride on the bullet train to Hell by not breaking promises to your God. At the very least you'll emancipate me from my place behind the bar and the living nightmare of watching another drunken aunt shake her misshapen booty to the medley from Grease.

Every marriage represents one more woman I'll never get to lay down with and another guy who is more likely to cancel his tee times. It's a somber damned occasion and should be treated as such. Any God worth worshipping and breaking vows in front of would prefer that we frolic like otters and the constrictions placed on us by formal matrimony are decidedly unotterlike. I believe it's an inherently evil social construction and would beg you to abandon the idea altogether.

If you must take on a spousal unit, for Heaven's sake keep it to yourself.

--------

We stopped at the mall and bought a couple of gold rings and pretty much laid out the ground rules during the car ride on the way to the boat. I promised her that she'd always be my Mary and she promised me that she'd always be kind to dumb animals. We could iron out the little details as we went along. We had been given a rusty old houseboat called "The Sandbucket" as an advanced wedding present and since I was the Captain of the vessel I felt qualified to perform the ceremony myself. We stood together on the deck of the boat in dry dock, I made some kind of vague oath to the golf gods and we were wed.

"Doesn't the boat have to be out to sea for the Captain to marry people?"

"I think you're sucking the beauty out of this blessed event by harping on silly details."

"Well, somebody's got to sign the marriage certificate or it won't be legal. It'll look pretty funny if you sign it yourself."

I was aware of the dubious legality of maritime nuptials but felt that the spark of plausible deniability would add zest to our union. The thing about having to be out to sea seemed a debatable detail. The boat was elevated above the snow on blocks of wood after all, so it wasn't really on dry land either.

"Yeah, I guess you've got a point there. I had planned to make my signature illegible but I suppose that doesn't seem right either."

The clever little vixen was covering all of the angles, savvy as an old sea dog she was.

"And what's up with the spiel to the golf gods? I don't even play golf."

"Oh now there's where you're wrong, Mary. Everybody plays golf eventually, you should start now while you're young and limber."

"In Minnesota in February?"

Christ, if I had known the appeal to the golf gods was going to be a deal breaker I'd have kept my mouth shut. I was just trying to make it sound official. She was squirming a little now, apparently coming to her senses so I knew I had to act quickly.

"My grandpa's a preacher, we can get him to make it legal."

"Your grandpa's ninety years old and he's been retired from the church for over forty years. That doesn't sound kosher either."

"We'll get him reinstated or reenlisted or whatever they call it. I'm pretty sure it's like the Mafia or the Hotel California, you can check out but you can never really leave."

————

Mary and I are probably not the first couple to be married in a nursing home but I'll bet that we're the youngest. We sent away to the Church archives for a photocopy of my grandfather's proof of holiness papers and paid fifty bucks to make him a licensed clergyman in the state of Minnesota. Just to cover my bases with the golf gods I held a closest to the pin competition in the snow to determine my best man.

Mary bought a red dress at the thrift store for two dollars that was worth at least ten times that amount and I was a vision of purity in my white linen suit and pink carnation. I put a daisy in her hair and we drove to the nursing home to wake up my grandfather.

"Hey grandpa wake up, we want you to marry us."

"Wha...what? I can't marry you, I don't know the service, besides I retired from the ministry decades ago."

"No, it's cool grandpa, here's your paperwork. We already made our vows, you've just got to make the 'I do' part official."

Grandpa put his best suit coat on over his pajamas, balanced in his walker and performed his last ministerial act. It was a moment of great symmetry for him because it mirrored his first duty as a cleric. Seventy years before he had nervously performed a marriage ceremony only a day or two after his ordination and he hadn't done one in English since. He was shipped off to a mission in India and married hundreds of Indian couples in the Tamil language but hadn't a clue what to say at an American wedding.

"It's okay grandpa, you're tight with God. We just need you to say that you approve."

"You promise to be nice to one another?"

Grandpa had a powerful affection for my Mary and his eyes welled up with tears at his surprise role in our union. When he tried to dry his eyes he wavered unsteadily over the walker so he just let the saltwater flow. My bride and I answered in unscripted harmony.

"We do."

"Well then, I pronounce you man and wife. Let's have a drink."

# The Bicycle Missionary

Walter wanted to be a farmer in the worst way but it would not be permitted. His father was a preacher, as was his grandfather so his path was preordained. They immigrated to Iowa from Germany by way of New Zealand and Australia to spread the word. They were stern German Lutherans and though he lacked their religious zeal, he could not defy his father's wishes for him to follow in their footsteps.

The night before his graduation from the seminary, Walt and his roommate stayed up all night drinking beer and spinning grand dreams of how they might save the world. Walt vowed to go to India, his roommate to China. The comfort of their dorm room at the midwestern seminary and their ironic Christian optimism compelled them to seek out those less fortunate.

Foreign missions were not highly regarded by most of the seminary students. Some said they would flatly decline such a call. "It's one thing to be drafted, it's quite another to volunteer." Their ridicule would insinuate that a volunteer must have some ulterior motive, perhaps a selfish desire to see the world. Walt was undeterred by the loose talk but it caused him to probe his own motives.

A couple from his father's congregation in Fort Dodge, Iowa offered to drive his folks down to St. Louis for his graduation. Following the ceremony, Walt joined his parents for the ride back to Fort Dodge. As they passed through a suburb of Des Moines, their Packard was struck head-on by a driver who was accelerating around a city bus.

Walt managed to climb out the back door of the demolished car and tried to open the driver's door from the outside but it was jammed. The couple who had offered them the ride suffered the worst of it. The husband was inert with his head resting on the steering wheel. His wife leaned motionless against him with a terrible injury to her scalp. He saw that his father, also in the front seat, had been thrown into the windshield and he rushed around the car to his aid.

As his father flopped back onto the seat, jagged pieces of glass cut gashes in his neck and blood streamed over his clerical collar. Walt completed a Red Cross emergency first aid class only two weeks before, in preparation for his mission to India, but he knew that his training was not equal to the current crisis.

His dad's head wounds seemed minor, thanks to a stiff hat that he wore, but Walt worried about the blood flowing from the wounds in his neck. He struggled to remove his father's collar to no avail. The collar was buttoned tight and his own badly gashed and broken finger hindered Walt's efforts. He pulled at the stiff white collar with both hands but it would not give.

It became apparent that his wounds were superficial when his father regained consciousness and gave Walt an irritated look for tugging at his neck. Walt helped to load the injured into the cars of benevolent witnesses who gathered around the crash. His mother was only winded by the collision. His father's legs were badly injured and he spent several weeks on crutches before graduating to the life-long use of a cane. Walt emerged with a game knee, a badly mangled finger and a new determination to serve the God who had spared his parents.

Any weakness in his missionary zeal was eliminated by his father's stubborn clerical collar. He saw poetry in it that cemented his faith and affirmed his calling. He saw God's hand in the Red Cross training he had completed only weeks before the accident. Although he hadn't the means to do anything tangible for the accident victims, he felt that his training kept him from succumbing to helpless panic.  He was told later that dispatching the victims to the hospital by private car rather than waiting for an ambulance might well have saved their lives.

Walt knew in his heart that his life had been spared in the accident so that he could serve his God in India.

————

The mission in India lasted about twenty-three years.  The hopelessness of the famine-ravaged country was not resolved during his tenure but I know it wasn't for lack of effort on his part.  I once asked him if he was over there whacking those poor people with the Bible and he told me, with moist eyes, that he never had the time.

He built schools to teach them to read and write Tamil, the local language and used the meager mission allowance to keep a handful of the sad millions fed.  A mother and her children would routinely make a days walk for the often empty promise of a coconut shell full of milk.  The hungry masses gathered around his family's compound while his own children enjoyed an idyllic, well nourished Rudyard Kipling childhood.

His mission was futile and thankless and depressing.

————

We were with him in his Minnesota home several years before his death when he showed us a Christmas card he received from a stranger in Texas.  The stranger's name was Benjamin and he was studying civil engineering at the University of Texas.  He sent Walt the card to thank him for his efforts in India fifty years after the fact.

Benjamin wrote that he was the grandchild of an "untouchable" who, without Walt's intervention, would have sired another untouchable and then another.  He said that fifty years before, Walt provided his grandfather with the means to acquire a bicycle. The bicycle gave him the ability to cross great distances to find work and food. The work and food broke the cycle of poverty in his lineage, which in turn allowed Benjamin to take an advanced degree at one of the best Universities on Earth.

My grandfather drew his last breath in a nursing home in the happy land of Minnesota. He was halfway through his 92nd year when he was finally "called home." Mary and I smuggled in brandy to toast him on a life well lived and he reacted as if we'd brought the cure for old age.

In his last days he believed the nursing home was a steam ship heading for exotic locales and we saw no reason to correct him.

# Half of the Empire

You can laugh and mock me now but some day it will happen to you. Just when you least expect it a little voice in your head will command you to action in spite of yourself and you will never be the same. Your friends and family will see it coming but if you're burdened as I am, with a Y chromosome, you'll probably be the last to know.

I was a bachelor golf guy when it happened to me. Happy as a duck, a fridge full of beer and Chinese take-out, I couldn't think of a soul that I'd trade places with. I shared my space with critters; a dog, a cat and a bossy parrot but I was definitely Bwana. As the King of my castle and the sole architect of my little scene, I had stumbled onto my happy place.

One night I was stretched out on the couch with my loyal hound coiled at my feet and the cat purring on my chest, just sipping a brewski and reading the articles in Playboy. The bird was sitting on my shoulder showing off his vocabulary in exchange for bites of my pizza and everything Jimmy Buffett ever recorded was waltzing through the stereo. I didn't have to tee off until noon the next day and my biggest concern in life was whether or not I should try out my new sand wedge. My world was whole and perfect and serene.

I loved being me.

Then it happened. The little voice in my head spoke to me so clearly that night that I feared I was suffering a schizophrenic episode or a very bad batch of Budweiser. At first I thought it was the parrot talking so I stuffed a piece of pizza into his craw. When the voice spoke again it was more insistent and since the bird was still chewing, I knew that it wasn't him. It sounded like my own voice and startled me with its commanding tone and clarity.

"It's time to take a wife."

The outrageous edict rang in my ears and jolted me upright. The cat freaked out and jabbed all twenty claws into my chest before diving directly onto the sleeping dog and repeating the violence. The hundred pound mutt spazzed sideways off of the couch and fell to the floor with a dreadful thump, rattling the coffee table and tipping over my beer.

When I made a futile attempt to save the suds the parrot went into a squawking fury and began pecking madly at the side of my head. I reached around to swat the feathered menace and he batted me with his wings, his efforts at flight inhibited because his claws were deeply embedded into the flesh of my shoulder. My screaming upset the pup and she started barking and howling while the parrot shrieked his own displeasure about an inch from my eardrum.

I tripped over the coffee table in an effort to escape the squall and slammed directly into the stereo system, upsetting the needle on the record player and scratching the useful life out of my favorite album. The infectious optimism of the Jimmy Buffett song "Volcano" gave way to haunting synchronicity when the stylus got caught in a skipping groove.

"…when the volcano blows...SKIP...when the volcano blows...SKIP...when the volcano blows..."

———

I don't write to dissuade you from matrimony but to leave you better prepared for the consequences of your actions. I was woefully ill equipped for the terrible thatch of negotiation and compromise when it happened to me.

Everyone knows that your spousal unit gets half of the Empire just by signing up so I understood that I would sacrifice financial autonomy. I actually prepared in advance for such a trauma by maintaining a sizeable debt and always living slightly beyond my means. If I did fall to marriage I would automatically come out ahead because the lucky filly would be saddled with half of my burden. Love me love my liabilities, baby.

What I never fully considered was that when the Empire is divided, a momentary vacuum is created in the throne room and since nature abhors a vacuum it must be quickly filled. Well meaning idealists might tell you that the marital ship of state can be sailed by two captains, working in harmony for the good of the voyage but these people have never been married. There can be but one captain and if you're the one with the Y chromosome it's probably not going to be you.

Show me two married men who actually call the shots in their relationship and I'll show you a naive guppy and a filthy liar.

———

My wife scares the Hell out of me so she's in charge. Mary seems to know what I'm thinking a few seconds before I think it and moves with the calm assurance of someone who has seen the big picture. I had heard people make reference to women's intuition before but always suspected it was a political ruse to keep men in line. My mother seemed to know when I was doing something wrong before I did it but I always attributed it to our shared genetics. When my wife started going psychic on me, I threw in the towel on behalf of my entire gender.

It started innocently enough with foodstuffs. She had the uncanny ability to predict precisely what I would want to eat, hours before I had given it a thought myself. If I had a hankering for chicken and mashed potatoes, that's what I got for dinner. When I remembered I hadn't had spaghetti in a while it would magically appear on my plate. I began testing the phenomena by picturing more exotic dishes and within a day or two they'd show up as well.

One day I was driving home from the golf course and saw a billboard with a tantalizing image of a large bowl of blueberries. I had eaten them in bagels and in blueberry pie before but it had never occurred to me to try them solo. A naked blueberry had never crossed my threshold. I thought about my Mary for a moment and her strange gift and then returned to musing over those tasty looking berries.

When I got home and plopped down in the Lay-Z-Boy to watch real golfers on TV, Mary plopped the bowl of chilled blueberries down next to me.

———

The skeptic in me rationalized the food episodes as simple coincidence, or foreknowledge based on familiarity. The blueberries were easily explained by the fact that she didn't know me well enough to know that I never ate them. They were in season, after all, so were probably displayed prominently at the market. I had heard of old married people finishing each other's sentences and transforming to bear a physical resemblance to one another. Guessing what your spouse wants to eat, it seemed to me, must simply be the result of sharing close quarters.

The full scope of my wife's treacherous prescience didn't become apparent until after we had been married for a few years and were past the point of no return. I was closing the bar one night and a lovely customer with ample cleavage was the last soldier standing. She flirted a bit and chatted me up as I did my closing chores, her bosom heaving to and fro. I saw little harm in stealing an occasional glance at her chest and she busted me more than once with a coy smile. I explained that it was time to leave and she must have noticed that I was talking to her breasts because she whipped them free of their harness on the spot.

"You've been trying to catch a peek all night, well here ya go!"

I was struck dumb as they wobbled there in front of me, mocking the death of my bachelorhood and taunting me with a lusty jiggle. I was morose when I told the nice lady to put them away and go about her business. I skulked home that night, feeling slightly guilty for having gazed at another woman's flesh and slunk into the darkened bedroom so as not to wake my wife. She stirred when I nestled in next to her and was groggy when she spoke.

"Oh, honey you're home...I was having the weirdest nightmare...All of the girls at your bar were naked."

———————

I can't speak for the entire breed of bartenders but I can guarantee you that this one marries for life. That woman has been inside of my head and there's no telling what she's seen. There are only two ways to insure her silence and since one of them comes with a lengthy prison term our blessed union is secure in perpetuity.

I will never know exactly how many of my innermost thoughts have been compromised but I'm not taking any chances. She's a lovely woman and you'll never hear me say otherwise. It's far too late to make her sign a non-disclosure form or a prenuptial agreement and divorce is simply out of the question.

She knows too much.

# The Sandbucket

There is a venerable maritime superstition that warns against changing a boat's name. Once a boat has been christened she has taken on a life of her own and must be treated with the same respect afforded a person. This admonition is widely known to sailors and is referenced in popular literature at least as far back as 1881:

"He was hanged like a dog, and
sun-dried like the rest, at Corso Castle.
That was Roberts' men, that was,
and comed of changing names to
their ships, Royal Fortune, and
so on. Now what a ship was
christened, so let her stay, I say."

Robert Louis Stevenson
*Treasure Island*

She was a forty-two foot steel-hulled houseboat called "The Sandbucket." At least fifty years old, she'd been tied to the same slip since my childhood. The Sandbucket had a reputation as the marina party barge when I was a kid and I drank my first beer on that very boat at the age of twelve.

The son of the original owners inherited her and subjected her to all manner of debauchery before a financial crash compelled him to sell her to Ben. Ben and his wife were English professors and they needed a boat that was big enough to live on during the summer. The Sandbucket could sleep twelve and the galley was as well equipped as any residential kitchen.

Ben is a Joyce scholar and literary critic who resembles a cross between Mr. Magoo and Groucho Marx. Everyone on the dock referred to him as simply "the professor" and wouldn't think of having a cocktail party without him. He was my mentor and I loved him like a father.

When the time came for him to give up boating he offered us the Sandbucket as a wedding present. The marina was a condominium arrangement by which the docks were bought and sold as real estate and her slip was worth considerably more than she was. If we agreed to buy the slip from him, he'd toss in the Sandbucket for free. I didn't have the means to buy the slip but felt I was destined to take the helm of this boat I had known since childhood.

Try to borrow fifty thousand dollars using eleven boards as collateral and you will learn the limits of a banker's sense of humor. By leveraging a new mortgage on our house we were just able to swing it. I convinced Mary that the slip was an investment and that in lieu of an actual wedding present I would name the boat for her.

The Sandbucket sat in dry dock for the rest of the winter while we sweated out the arrangements for the purchase of the slip. As the meetings with dour bankers grew more intense so did our anxiety. Every day brought to light a new expense or responsibility that we hadn't considered. The property tax alone was over one thousand dollars per year, not to mention insurance and marina fees. The boat was giving us a headache and we didn't even own her yet.

As spring approached we were confident that we could finance the slip so the day before our wedding we gathered with a small group of friends to re-christen the boat in dry dock. Mary shattered a bottle of cheap champagne against her hull and the Sandbucket became the Maria Angelene.

————————

The Maria Angelene fell to the bottom of the St.Croix River like an anchor, minutes after they lowered her into the water. The insurance company said the hull had rusted through due to years of neglect and they would pay nothing for the loss. Ben had to hire a crane to salvage her from the bottom and then had to pay someone else a small fortune to drag her carcass off to the boneyard.

We never told him that through my ignorance of maritime tradition I had changed her name and doomed her to the deep. While we felt bad for Ben and the Sandbucket we were joyously free of our burden. The casual observer might see it as a bad omen for our marriage but if it's possible to wish a boat to the bottom we had done it.

The papers were all but signed in blood at the bank when Ben called to tell Mary that her boat sunk.

She had the presence of mind to tell the semantics professor that she didn't own a boat.

# Grow where you're planted

Emilie kept the dried carcass of a headless salamander hanging from a piece of string on the wall next to her kitchen sink.  If you asked her why she hung it there, she'd give you the hint of a guilty expression then look away quickly like a little kid who feared the secret was written on her face.  I must have asked her a dozen times before I ever got a straight answer.

"Really, Grandma, why do you keep a dead lizard dangling above the sink where you wash the dinner plates?"

"Oh, I don't know.  Do you think I should hang him somewhere else?"

"No, what I mean is, why did you bring it into the house in the first place?"

"Well, I found the salamander next to the fence behind the huckleberry bush."

"... And? "

"And I brought him in the house.  Have you seen that huckleberry bush?  Last year it didn't amount to anything but there will be enough berries for a pie this year.  I told Harold that it's been stunted ever since they put up those power poles next to the fence.  I wrote them a dozen letters about it but they never even answered them.  You know

Harold, my mailman, he says that he's never even seen a regular letter from the electric company, just the bills from the computer. They use a super computer now; a man named Seymour Cray invented it right here in Minnesota. Have you ever heard of him, Jonathan? What a bright man, a genius really. So many things were invented here, Scotch tape and sandpaper and snowmobiles and microwave ovens..."

You didn't have to put a nickel in Emilie; you didn't even have to give her a nudge. Her mind moved at a frantic pace and demanded constant narration. As children we marveled at her ability to go for ten or fifteen minutes straight without breathing but came to discover that she was secretly inhaling between syllables. We'd put the dining room chairs in a circle when Grandma Emilie telephoned and then pass the handset around, taking turns at pretending to pay attention.

"Yes, grandma, uh huh, yes grandma..."

If you visited her house you had to allow at least forty-five minutes for the extraction period in her driveway. The conversation continued while you climbed into your car and didn't skip a beat when you put the transmission in gear. It was a science really, backing out of the driveway with grandma hanging on to the open car window, rolling the window up gradually so as not to pinch her fingers. It could be forty below with the wind chill and Emilie might be wearing only a bathrobe and slippers but the ritual never varied.

You had to keep the car moving steadily enough so that you could eventually achieve escape velocity but not so fast that you might run over her feet or spin her to the ground with a broken hip.

———

We couldn't blame Emilie for being chatty. She spent twenty-three years as a mission wife in South India with nobody to talk to but monkeys and toddlers. Her children were packed off to boarding school as soon as they were waist high and the monkeys had a very short attention span. Her husband was busy with his mission and had little patience for a verbose wife at the end of a fourteen-hour workday.

She found solace and company in the pages of books that she ordered from America, which only gave her more things to talk about. Two decades of being shushed by the busy missionary and all but ignored by the monkeys made the woman a ticking time bomb of pent-up conversation. After his tour of duty my grandpa pined for peace and quiet and they were divorced.

Emilie was a deeply religious woman but confided in me once that she wished her husband had never taken up the Indian mission. With their divorce it seemed that all of her hardship was for naught, that things might have been different for their marriage had they only stayed put in America. She told me that she had always felt a little guilty for trying to talk him out of going but he wouldn't hear of it anyway.

"My husband was called to India and I was called to follow my husband."

————

The idea of missionary work seemed so noble to me as a child that I never questioned the mechanics of it. The willingness of mission families to sacrifice the comforts of home and the company of like-minded people is evidence of their sincerity. It's not as if they choose to go to the darkest corners of China or Borneo to spread the word to the godless commies, it's their calling.

I was proud of my grandparents for their decades of service in India but bothered by a recurring theme in cartoons. The cartoon missionaries often wound up in a boiling cauldron and were ultimately eaten by headhunters. Since even the wackiest farce contains a grain of truth I worried that our own missionary relatives might risk a similar fate. I wondered why the natives would be so angry with helpful visitors.

After being stalked at my inner-city apartment by a pack of rabid Jehovah's Witnesses I began to alter my opinion on the subject of proselytizing. What on Earth did these people think that they were doing trying to sell me their flavor of Christianity? I come from a long line of Lutheran missionaries, pal. Get the Hell off of my porch! I don't care if the God of Abraham is sitting in your car at the curb, it takes a pile of nerve to knock on strangers' doors and tell them whom to worship.

My missionary grandfather was pushing ninety before I screwed up the courage to ask him if such a thing wasn't presumptuous. He answered me without a second's hesitation or a hint of holier than thou.

"I wanted to stay in Iowa and become a farmer but my father wouldn't let me."

———————

Emilie had a poster on her kitchen wall with a mod flower power feel and a quasi-religious message. It read, "Grow where you're planted" and had a picture of a Day-Glo daisy growing alone in a thatch of thorns.

"I saw that poster at church the day after I moved the huckleberry bush and I knew that God put it there for my benefit. I should have left well enough alone but no, I had to have huckleberries for pie, had to have my way. Now look at what I've done. Just look at it!"

"Look at what, grandma? You said the huckleberry bush has never been bigger."

"Not the bush, that poor salamander. I chopped his head clean off with the spade when I dug out the bush. I should have let that huckleberry grow where it was planted like the poster says."

"So grandma, you hung up the poster to remind you not to dig up any more bushes but why did you hang up the salamander?"

"He reminds me to look at the poster."

# Play it where it lies

Easter is the perfect holiday to signal the beginning of spring because its arrival is as fickle as the season itself. Nailing down the exact date is a mind-bending exercise for even the most disciplined ecclesiastical scholar. I've read the conditions three times and I still have to consult a calendar to confirm the correct date.

The rules for determining Easter are based on something called the "Paschal Moon," which is when the fourteenth day of the new moon falls on or next follows the day of the vernal equinox. In short, Easter is the first Sunday after the first full moon on or beyond March 21st but never later than April 25th. What any of this has to do with the crucifixion and presumed resurrection of Jesus is a complete mystery to me.

Springtime in Minnesota is a promise that is not always kept. The reward for a grueling winter, more often than not, is a sleety, cold trudge to June and spring exists as little more than words on a calendar. We can only cross our fingers in March that adequate penance was served during the winter and that we will be delivered before Mother's Day.

Cabin fever and Seasonal Affective disorder conspire to elicit a giddy mania in most Minnesotans by the time March 21st rolls around and if it isn't warm by Easter we simply pretend. The first time the thermometer breaks forty degrees Fahrenheit you will see people in shorts and shirtsleeves, shivering in denial, crazy as loons.

The golf clubs come out of storage even if we have to swing them with mittens.

––––––––––

We always manage to play golf on Easter, one way or another but it isn't always on a golf course. They won't let us out if there's frost on the greens so we sometimes have to resort to "park golf" with pitching wedges and frozen balls. We invented the game on a snowy, thirty-five degree Easter morning as a means to escape a dark family gathering and place a demand for an end to winter.

We had just buried our Grandmother and the rest of the clan was planning a morbid assembly around the coffee urn in the church basement but Billy had a better idea. He made an optimistic tee time for just after the funeral but the weatherman lied and the golf course was frozen shut. Determined to escape the gloomy roomful of relatives, Billy proclaimed that we golf on Easter no matter what.

All of the rules for park golf were developed that morning and we've played by the same ones ever since. The wager never varies, a quarter a hole with carryovers and double for aces. Park golf can take you in any direction at all, in a setting not designed specifically for the game, so most of the rules are based on avoiding injury to spectators or arrest of the participants. Anything immobile can constitute a valid hole but you must always hit the target below head height as a safety precaution and must be willing to pay for damage caused by an errant shot. Pissed off pedestrians and lawmen are the responsibility of the golfer who does the offending.

Billy teed up his ball on a pile of snow in the church parking lot and pointed at the stop sign on the corner as our first goal. The winner of the hole gets to pick the tee box and the next target and that morning Billy was inspired. He was winning every hole and kept picking shots that led us further away from the heavy scene at church. We were at least a mile from familial obligation before we paused for our own memorial. Church or no church I thought we should speak to the occasion so I gave Billy a gentle nudge in that direction.

"Grandma would have been happy to go so close to Easter. She was big on the Jesus thing."

"Yep."

"Do you think the relatives are gonna get pissed at us for ducking out?"

"Yep."

He was killing me in the game, already four bucks ahead and he seemed a little miffed when I reminded him of the holiday and our loss. He shanked his next shot badly and it rattled against the undercarriage of a minivan at the four way stop. We hid the golf clubs behind our legs as the angry driver scanned the area for the source of the projectile and finally drove off unsatisfied.

"Do you think that they have golf in Heaven, Billy?"

"Yep."

––––––––––

We originally set out to make our way toward Mound's Park, a strip of land atop the hill overlooking St. Paul that actually looks a lot like a golf course. When we ran out of park we set our sights on the tall buildings. Park golf became neighborhood golf, then railroad yard golf and downtown sidewalk golf. When we started losing our daylight and freezing our asses off we found an open door and invented "skyway golf."

The skyway system was once unique to the Twin Cities but I'd be surprised if it hasn't been imitated elsewhere. A network of heated, windowed tunnels at the second floor connect nearly every major structure in downtown St. Paul. This human "Habitrail" makes it possible to crisscross the entire urban center without ever buttoning your coat or braving a crosswalk. It's obvious that the designers of the skyway system didn't have golfers in mind because you can't hit anything resembling a full pitching wedge but the cozy warmth of the carpeted hallways more than compensated for limited shot selection.

Walking around with a golf club in public buildings is something like carrying a clipboard in the deference you are shown by passersby. It might have something to do with the fact that the thing could be used as a formidable weapon but when they see that you're actually golfing, fear is replaced by curiosity.

The skyway system was mostly vacant due to the major religious holiday so we had very few human hazards to avoid. Occasionally somebody would attempt to pick up one of our golf balls and we'd startle them with our alarm.

"No, don't touch that! It's a ball in play."

They'd ask us why we were golfing in the skyway on Easter and we'd tell them it was too cold outside; irrefutable logic to any long suffering Minnesotan. We started to develop a gallery of curious onlookers and fellow golfers who followed us from shot to shot down the carpeted fairways.

When a hapless security guard bent down to pick up the Titleist that smacked into his shin, no less than twenty spectators voiced their own outrage. When he meekly suggested that we take the game outside, the gallery grew ugly in our defense and for a moment I feared a lynching.

———

If people are allowed to follow the events on Earth after their death, I'm sure that our grandmother was walking around with us rather than hovering over the sad scene at church.

Billy has an odd gift for making anything he does seem like the right thing to do at the time. Hanging around with him feels like being in a movie where the protagonist gets away with outrageous behavior because the audience is rooting for him and has suspended disbelief. He has the courage of his convictions so nobody's opinion has any bearing whatsoever on his own.

We played the skyways with little interference that day and I'm certain that if I attempted such a thing with anybody else we'd be rousted immediately. A little boy approached Billy at one point during our game and offered his services as a caddy, to help clear the fairways and carry Billy's beverage.

"Are you famous, mister?"

I answered before Billy could.

"No, kid, he ain't famous, he just acts like he is."

Before his mother finally called him away, the little boy inexplicably asked Billy for his autograph. As far as I know it was an unprecedented event for my brother the factory worker but he signed the kid's baseball cap like an old hand.

"To Adam from your friend Billy. Play it where it lies little buddy."

# Not rain, nor sleet, nor Mandy

Truth is stranger than fiction so there is never a shortage of sensational news stories but it used to be that those were left to True Detective Magazine and the dime novelists. The fact that Andrea Yates and Chandra Levy are household names speaks to how far we've fallen from an accurate representation of our world. The term "Congressional Intern" conjures images of sex and violence even though the reality is far more mundane. If you follow the television news you have reason to believe that your sister with postpartum depression is a baby killer in waiting.

The best illustration of the destructive effect of sensationalizing isolated tragedy is the stigma suffered by employees of the United States Postal Service. The first image generated in our collective mind when someone is introduced as a postal worker is a disgruntled civil servant teetering on the edge of homicidal mania. The statistical reality is that there have been only eight such recorded incidents since the Continental Congress appointed Benjamin Franklin Postmaster General more than 225 years ago. Add to that the knowledge that the Postal Service is among the largest employers on the planet with some 800,000 presumably non-homicidal people on the payroll and you begin to appreciate the breadth of the baseless slander.

The Post Office has always been a fair and decent employer and to combat the negative image of overblown tabloid attention they have redoubled their efforts to create a serene work environment. A job at the Post Office is a great gig if you can get it, comprehensive health and life insurance, a retirement plan and an additional savings program augmented by a generous employer contribution. The service even offers something called "flextime," that allows employees to divide their shifts around personal necessity.

The disgruntled postal worker is by and large a fictional creature and it might surprise you to learn that applicants often spend years on a waiting list to join their ranks. The Letter Carriers Union is among the most powerful and well-financed trade unions on Earth so it is unlikely that employees would suffer for long under the thumb of a capricious Postmaster.

Once you have secured a job with the Postal Service it is all but impossible to get fired.

———————

Mandy wanted to be a letter carrier in the worst way and she finally got her wish. She had worked on the assembly line of an electronic component factory since her graduation from high school and pined for the freedom of movement and relative independence of a mail delivery route. When she told her friends at the factory that she had taken the test for a position at the Post Office they teased her mercilessly about "going postal" and warned her that she was making a terrible mistake.

She received a score of ninety-five out of a hundred on her examination and was tentatively accepted for employment but had to wait nearly two years for the first job opening. When she finally got the letter in the mail that invited her to interview for a carrier route she felt as if she had won the lottery and put in her two week notice at the factory before the new job was even secured.

Mandy despised the spirit crushing monotony of the assembly line at the factory job and came to refer to it as "Henry Ford's Curse."

She wanted to take pride in her work but every effort that she made to that end was greeted with hostility from the floor supervisor who desired that she remain a featureless cog. She had, at one point, been written up and suspended for two weeks for adding the words "with love" to the little adhesive stickers that said "inspected by #10274."

Her greatest frustration at the factory was that the management made it all but impossible for her to feed her gnawing nicotine habit. They closed the employee smoking lounge several years before and told the employees that they must endure the elements and smoke outside near the loading dock. The foreman on the dock was a virulent anti-smoker and soon became irritated with the huddled fumigants and their debris and they were further exiled to the parking lot. Mandy's breaks were only fifteen minutes long and it took nearly seven minutes to make the trek to the Siberian smoking area, which left only sixty seconds to hot-box the heater before the long walk back to the loveless assembly line.

When the Postmaster asked if Mandy had any questions about her new route the only thing that occurred to her was the care and feeding of the monkey on her back. Negative publicity about the working conditions at the postal service made her new employer eager to please and they assured her that the mail delivery vehicle came equipped with an ashtray and that she was free to smoke between deliveries.

Mandy finally found her happy place.

———————

A veteran letter carrier accompanied Mandy for the first week on her new route and his supervisory report indicated that she was the most conscientious employee that he had ever encountered. Mandy arrived early every single morning and on her own time separated the mail for her route into neat little piles tied with a shoestring bow. She carried a small notebook and jotted down all of the names on her route and by the end of her first week of training had memorized all one hundred and twelve of them. She wanted to be able to greet her patrons personally should they ever meet her at the mailbox.

After two weeks of supervision Mandy was scheduled to run her route solo for the first time and she could barely sleep the night before for her giddiness. She stayed up later than she should have, scrutinizing the map of her route and testing her memory to make sure that she knew the name associated with each address. The bit of restless slumber that she did get that night was seasoned with surreal dada-esque dreams of jumbled names and numbers.

General nervousness and lack of sleep that first morning on the job took their toll and Mandy very nearly ran over the dispatcher when she backed her delivery vehicle out of the carpool. The near miss and the scowl that followed made her more nervous still and her hands were trembling on the steering wheel as she pulled away from the postal depot. Her own heartbeat was thumping in her ears as she merged into traffic and realized she had forgotten to bring along the bundle of mail for her route.

After a dangerous U-turn in rush hour traffic and an awkward exchange with the man she had nearly run over in the postal garage, Mandy was on her way to her appointed rounds. When she reached in her pocket for a cigarette to soothe her nerves she realized that she had left them on her kitchen table, right next to the map of her route.

————

Mandy steeled herself against the urge to break down and cry and pulled into a convenience store to buy more cigarettes. A line of people formed behind her at the busy counter before she realized that her purse was on the table at home, right next to her cigarettes and map. The Post Office uniform must have inspired confidence or the tears welling up in her eyes engendered pity because the young man at the counter let her have a pack of generic cigarettes in exchange for an IOU.

When the nice old man at her first stop on Maple Street greeted her cheerfully by name she felt that the worst was behind her.

"Howdy, Mandy, you're out on your own today, huh?"

"Yep, Mr. Chamberlain, flying solo today for the first time. Sorry I'm running a little late with your mail."

"Gee, I don't mind. It's all bills anyway. You can keep them for all I care. Say, I didn't know that you smoked. That's a terrible habit for anybody, much less a pretty young girl like yourself."

Mandy forgot that she had the lit cigarette in her hand and was mortified when he reminded her of it. Her supervisor made it clear that she was to confine her smoking to the vehicle and was never allowed to smoke during her actual deliveries. Her first impulse was to drop the cigarette right then and there but she didn't want to mess up Mr. Chamberlain's sidewalk so she ran back to the truck without a word and butted it out in the ashtray.

"I'm sorry Mr. Chamberlain, I'm not supposed to be smoking on my route. I've had such a mess of a morning and my nerves are shot. I didn't even realize I had it in my hand. I hope you won't say anything about it."

"Don't be silly, I wouldn't rat you out but you really ought to kick the habit."

"I know I should, my mother rides me about it all the time but today isn't gonna be the best day for me to quit smoking."

The kind old man could see that Mandy had already had her fair share of stress for the day and offered to walk along with her on the first block of her deliveries to keep her company. He stayed by her side through three more blocks, until her mailbag was nearly empty. He was such a joy that she wished she could drag him along to the next neighborhood to help her finish her route.

As they rounded the corner of Mr. Chamberlain's block and saw the fireball engulfing her mail truck, Mandy realized that her route was probably already finished.

———

Government contracts go to the lowest bidder and mail trucks are not immune. The decision to include any ashtray at all was likely a reluctant one so when pennies could be saved by rendering them from plastic, the die was cast. Mandy wasn't really to blame for the loss that day but she put the lie to the urban legend that it's impossible to get fired from a solid union gig. Apparently the postal service is a little touchy about setting the mail on fire so there wasn't any collective bargaining over her immediate termination.

Mandy wanted to make her mark on the new job but she couldn't have dreamt that her short term of service would have such a far-reaching impact. The United States Postal Service operates tens of thousands of similar vehicles and every last one of them had the ashtray removed on Mandy's behalf. Contracts for new vehicles must conform to the new Mandy standard.

The next time you meet a mail carrier on the street, you might want to keep the "going postal" remark to yourself. There's a pretty good chance he's having a nicotine fit and is not to be trifled with.

# The penthouse or the gutter

Craps is a beautiful thing. An aggressive player on a happy run could potentially turn one white chip into a thousand purple ones in the space of ten minutes and a dozen rolls of the dice. It is the most complicated game in the casino but reaps the greatest potential rewards for the player who can master it. The game is unique in that it allows the player to play as the house or against it, positive or negative as the mood strikes. Odds of up to ten times the amount of your original wager can be placed in large casinos, allowing for the geometric acceleration of wealth or poverty.

A methodical craps player can build his empire slowly over several hours of careful mathematical jousting and approach the unthinkable, a level playing field. The house advantage in craps can be theoretically reduced to something approaching zero but the casinos aren't worried. After half an hour of gratuitous adrenaline and free drinks, most of us can't even pronounce "theoretically" much less do the math.

The party atmosphere around the craps table and the promise of quick riches appeals to our lusty passion, not our analytical mind. You may walk into the casino planning a faithful strategy of pass line and come bets, tweaking the odds on the strong numbers and betting against the weak ones but the bones are a fickle mistress. Before long you'll find yourself tossing desperation bets on "Any Craps" or "Big Red 7" with the rest of the tourists.

With craps you are either sleeping in the penthouse suite or crashing in the gutter.

––––––––––

The police killed both of the last two occupants of the apartment across from Billy in separate incidents. I'd bug him about living in a dangerous part of town and he'd shrug it off as the calculated risk of being a city dweller. The first guy was gunned down during a hold-up at the Taco Bell on the corner but the latest one had his ticket punched right there in the hallway in front of Billy's door.

The circumstances surrounding the second incident were fuzzier but the guy definitely had it coming. His name was Tommy Green and there was a good deal of evidence to indicate that his death resulted from a case of mistaken identity. Most urban guerillas assume a nom de guerre or several and "Green" is a common one because it's the color of money and it's easy to remember when you're high. The cops were looking for *a* Tommy Green the day that they came to serve the fugitive warrant but later conceded that it was most likely a different one.

The bad luck apartment across from Billy's was comically tiny, euphemistically called an "efficiency." It looked like it had been converted from a walk-in closet; toilet, bed and kitchenette all crammed into an eight by twelve-foot space. Tommy was a mammoth man and had to turn sideways just to get past the kitchen counter to the little bed in back. His toilet was an open throne right next to the kitchen sink. The little room appealed to the kind of person who had spent time in a cell, so it suited Tommy Green just fine.

Tommy was a career criminal, he was going on forty years old and had been outside of prison for less than two weeks since his fifteenth birthday. He was sent to the reformatory in Red Wing for raping his high school English teacher and then to grown-up prison for killing the rogue who tried to rape him. Tommy did his seven years on the second-degree manslaughter rap and was released to the world at age twenty-five, for the first time since puberty. On day two of his parole he killed a liquor store clerk for the contents of a cash register and went back inside for murder.

Tommy served thirteen years of a twenty to life sentence at Oak Park Heights and then moved into the apartment across the hall from my brother.

———————

I thought Billy lost his mind the night he invited his dangerous neighbor over to play craps with us but it was just another in a long line of calculated risks. Tommy was flashing a big wad of dough from some nefarious activity or another and Billy saw the profit potential in being neighborly. Our new friend had the same luck with gambling as he had with life in general so Billy eventually separated Tommy from his green but not without a terrifying roller coaster ride of wacky field bets and hard ways.

Billy bought the full sized craps layout and chips in Las Vegas in the hopes of mastering the arithmetic of the game in the relative safety of his home. Most of his sessions were among friends and rarely went beyond a five hundred-dollar bank but things took a serious turn the night that we played with his dangerous neighbor. Within the first few rolls of the dice, Tommy tossed boxcars, hitting a fifty-dollar proposition bet and just about breaking the bank. Billy's expression was uncharacteristically grave and his hand shook a little as he paid out seventeen hundred and fifty bucks just ten minutes into the game.

Tommy freaked out when Billy paid the wager with plastic chips instead of folding money and demanded that the game be switched to cash. Billy's face went pale and he appeared to shrink in the shadow of the aggressive gambler. I worried that my brother didn't have enough cabbage laying around to make good on the boxcars and when Tommy stood up to demand payment I saw the pistol sticking out of his back pocket. Billy had already raked me over the pass line for everything but cab fare so I was in no position to help him cover the bet.

I couldn't tell if Billy was pissed off or scared when he sat back on the couch and started taking off his cowboy boots. I was afraid he was going to go into some kind of Kung Fu karate man deal against a guy with a gun and come up short again. Tommy was hitting on a crack pipe between every roll of the dice and his eyes were wild and murderous from the smoke as he loomed over my brother. To my great relief, Billy shook a pile of greenbacks from his boot onto the craps table and counted out enough to cover Tommy's twelve.

The reckless gambler's eyes are drawn to the little boxes with the big odds but even at 35 to 1 the boxcars and snake eyes are a sucker bet. You might just as well throw your money at the roulette wheel. Any croupier will tell you that the hard ways and proposition bets are for dreamers and that the field is for fools so Billy eventually got all of his money back and then some. Tommy left with empty pockets at about four o'clock that morning looking sullen and desperate. He told us, with twitchy bravado, that there was plenty more where that came from and made my brother promise to host another game the following evening.

Five hours later they drew his chalk outline just outside Billy's door.

———————

Rationalization is the gambler's best friend and the only way to beat the house. If you can't explain away a losing streak then you don't belong in the casino. The way Billy sees it none of us gets to take anything away from the table so we aren't really playing for keeps anyway. We were standing over a winning game one night and I asked him how much he was ahead. He did the confused puppy head slant and told me that he didn't understand the question.

"I'm gonna count it when I'm dead."

Tommy Green most likely had violence in his heart when he left his efficiency apartment that day so there wasn't much weeping when the cops cashed in his chips. The gun was in his hand not his back pocket when he met them in the hallway and they dispatched him without controversy.   When the fates directed the police to the wrong address that day they did everyone a favor, especially Tommy.

Billy is a penthouse or gutter kind of guy and he majored in rationalization at gambler's college.  He had lived in the tough Midway area of St. Paul for decades and was accustomed to the gritty underbelly but I thought that the flying lead outside his door might finally nudge him out of the hood.  When our mom heard about the shooting she telephoned him every night with a frantic plea to consider the suburbs but he wouldn't hear of it.

"Mom, the cops hardly ever kill bad guys in the suburbs.  It's much safer here."

# Kermit's luck guides our puck

Every one of us, American or otherwise, can claim a kinship with the scattered, struggling Native Americans. The sorrowful condition of the noble tribes is the human condition condensed and accelerated, their fate is ours foretold. We are systematically civilizing everything soulful and laudable from our collective being and the Cherokee or Navajo can tell you exactly where we are going. We sent them on ahead as scouts.

The prairie University I attended took the name of the Dakota Sioux as its mascot and despite uniform displeasure from the tribe itself, a core group of stubborn white alumni are loathe to give it back. Our sports teams are known as "The Fighting Sioux" to this day and the stylized profile of a Sioux Brave still adorns the uniforms and letterhead.

One wealthy alumnus in particular, Ralph Engelstad, has made it his business to perpetuate the identity theft and the hurtful irony of the moniker, "Fighting Sioux." His threat to rescind a large cash contribution to build a new hockey arena was enough to stall the overdue mascot change and the singing cash registers drowned out the righteous complaint of the original Americans.

Ralph Engelstad was a backup goalie for the University of North Dakota's hockey team in the bad old days, the late 1940s, when

Indians knew their place. He made his original fortune in the 1960s selling a parcel of land in Nevada to Howard Hughes, who used it to build the North Las Vegas Airport. He was the primary developer of the NASCAR racetrack near Las Vegas and also owns the Imperial Palace Hotels and Casinos in Las Vegas and Biloxi, Mississippi. Suffice it to say that Mr. Engelstad has very deep pockets.

When a commission was formed at the University to address complaints about racism in the use of the Sioux tribe as a school mascot, UND's biggest benefactor made the conditions of his philanthropy clear. He was in the process of gifting the University with an 85 million-dollar hockey arena when the mascot change was being considered. In a letter to the President of the University who was heading up the commission, Mr. Engelstad wrote:

> "...If the logo and slogan are not approved by the above-mentioned date, I will then write a letter on December 30, 2000 to all contractors and to everybody associated with the arena canceling their construction contracts for the completion of the arena..."

I've met the University President to whom the unseemly threats were delivered. His name is Charles Kupchella and he seems to be a bright and virtuous man. He presides over a University that can humbly claim preeminence in sensitivity to the plight of Native Americans but would likely be the first to admit that there is plenty of room for improvement. Approximately three percent of the student body is composed of Native Americans, the largest minority on campus, and there are numerous academic avenues for their specific betterment.

The University of North Dakota provides 25 different American Indian programs and even offers a degree with a major in Indian Studies. UND can boast that it has graduated one in five practicing Indian doctors through an innovative project called "Indians Into Medicine."

———

A natural rule emerged from Internet discussion groups called Godwin's Law, which states that in any argument it is inevitable that one party will eventually compare the opposing party to the Nazis or to Hitler. This will be the climax of any debate and whoever calls the other one a Nazi first loses. We must add a new exception called "The Engelstad corollary."

Godwin's Law presumes that your opponent might not like being compared to a Nazi.

Any discussion of the biggest benefactor to my old school cannot escape his famous fondness for Hitler memorabilia. His Imperial Palace Casino in Las Vegas once housed a macabre display of his Third Reich collection in what he called the "war room." Ralph ran into a little bit of trouble with the state gaming authorities after the second time he threw a birthday party for Adolph Hitler.

A life-sized portrait of Adolph himself loomed over the proceedings, inscribed, "To Ralphie from Adolph, 1939." A German oompa band played marching tunes for the guests, who noshed on a swastika shaped birthday cake as they perused his multi-million dollar collection of morbid artifacts. According to the investigation by the Nevada Gaming Commission, his shrine had matching paintings of Mr. Engelstad and Hitler in uniform, flanked by authentic Nazi flags. Ralph was the proud owner of a six-wheeled Nazi staff car and a Mercedes-Benz once owned by Gestapo chief Heinrich Himmler.

Gaming Control Board agents also found a plate used to print hundreds of bumper stickers with the message "Hitler was right."

Ralph Engelstad has the peculiar distinction of being accused of moral turpitude in Sin City itself and was assessed a fine of 1.5 million dollars for disgracing the state of Nevada.

———————

The current protest over the mascot at the University of North Dakota is not the first. The indignation of the affected group has always rumbled just beneath the surface on that campus. The last big blow up happened in 1972, when some spunky frat boys created an ice sculpture that resembled a naked Indian woman with her legs spread apart. A Native American man wound up in the Grand Forks jail after he discovered the artwork and beat the living crap out of all three of the artists.

Go Fighting Sioux!

The ripples from that incident and the protests that followed had all but calmed by the time I arrived at the school eight years later. I ran into the occasional racist slogan on a tee shirt, or an old drawing of "Kermit," a jolly, pot-bellied Indian caricature similar to the Chief Wahoo mascot of the Cleveland Indians. Kermit looked more like a drunken white guy with feathers stuck in his hair than a fearsome warrior. He always held a beverage and his cheeks appeared red from whiskey not race.

The crusty old grad students and the professors could even recall the bygone chant, "Kermit's luck guides our puck" and the little whooping war dance that was performed every time the home team scored a goal. The racist connotations of the school mascot were gradually downplayed and the image of the proud Sioux Brave in stoic profile was accentuated. Kermit faded into history but for some reason the natives on campus never seemed to buy into the idea that the name "Fighting Sioux" was meant to honor them.

If Kermit was supposed to represent the actual Sioux Indian, the hockey coach had better hope they don't have his luck.

————

The new hockey arena was nearly halfway complete when Ralph wrote his menacing letter so he had to remind them of the fact that he still had some control over his gift. He sounded less like a major philanthropist than like the petulant child who threatens to end the game by taking his ball and going home.

> "If I walk away and abandon the project, please be advised that we will shut off all temporary heat going to this building and I am sure that nature, through its cold

weather, will completely destroy any portion of the building through frost that you might be able to salvage."

The North Dakota Board of Education pulled rank on the commission charged with studying the mascot and logo change. The day after they received copies of the threatening letter from Ralph Engelstad they voted unanimously to keep the name that was never theirs to begin with. One line of that notorious letter stands out to me as the distillation of the entire issue. The philanthropist with a fascination for Nazis betrayed his scorn for academia with an ad hominem attack on the President of the University.

"...It is a good thing that you are an educator because you are a man of indecision and if you were a businessman, you would not succeed, you would be broke immediately."

The fact that the comings and goings of sports bucks holds so much sway over the direction of a University speaks to our cultural decay. The year I enrolled at UND they were struggling to come up with a million or two for expansion of the library but the alumni immediately coughed up several times that amount for construction of the old hockey arena.

The new Engelstad Arena is by any description one of the finest hockey stadiums in the country, if not the entire world. The facilities can accommodate more than 11,000 hockey fans with an additional 48 luxury "skyboxes" and a second rink for Olympic-style play. The eighty-five million dollar contribution for its construction was at the time, according to Mr. Engelstad's own letter, "one of the 10 largest ever made to a school of higher education."

What any of this enormous waste of resources has to do with higher education completely eludes me.

The objectification of a race of human beings would be bad enough if it rang true but I'm afraid that calling a team "The Fighting

Sioux" places a warped veneer on American history. The smart money in Las Vegas would have been all over the US Cavalry in that game.

The administration at my alma mater is in the awkward position of rooting for the real Sioux to stop fighting.

# Part Three

# Behind Bars

Ididn't choose to be a bartender. I got the idea from my father, who tended bar on purpose after several professional careers. A thousand late cocktail meetings and a thousand more three martini lunches and he developed a natural envy for the simple man behind the bar. He was the child of missionaries, schooled in the seminary and the bar was the bully pulpit that was his birthright.

I, on the other hand, greatly overestimated the demand for eager young political scientists. My life behind bars was destined through the necessity to pay off loans on a college degree of dubious value. I rationalized my situation by viewing the bar as the ideal locale for a modern Socratic discussion of the world of ideas; in vino veritas and all that.

Most of the time, however, I serve as a pharmacist or a drug dealer with an inadequate stock. The liquor always acts as a social lubricant for awhile but by its very nature invites excess. This excess makes my only medication a sedative and the enemy of useful discussion. There is truth in wine but there is also a chaotic, self-destructive buzz.

I have to make a living so I fill their glasses, empty my tip jar and pay the light bill. The downside to my profession is obvious and inevitable. The product I sell gradually diminishes the consumer. Good customers diminish more quickly. The positive side of my trade is that my product is highly addictive, rendering my niche recession proof.

Mine isn't the kind of bar where the bartender leans on his elbow and listens to your problems. I tell people what's bothering me. This model has several benefits over the traditional bartender/patron paradigm. The customer in hearing my problems is distracted from his own sad life but more importantly the concept of the 'pity tip' is introduced. My bartending method has the collateral benefit of better engaging my interest in the conversation.

I read a fortune cookie once that said it is better to talk about ideas, than people or things. I have adopted this truism for my interactions across the bar. I don't often burden the customer with the details of my problems but rather with the greater concerns, which they'd certainly share. Things like entropy and gravity, life and death. My methods meet with mixed reactions from the masses. The poor sap who spent the day wrestling with carnivores in business suits is searching for sedation and small talk.

I will always furnish the sedative but they don't pay me enough for small talk.

# Alex and the ICBM

The piano player at the bar brought in a board one night and we played during his breaks. I knew how the pieces moved but that was the extent of my knowledge of the game. He beat me twice within the first four minutes or so, using two variations of "the fool's mate" and I was hooked. I've kept a chessboard on every bar I've tended since that day.

We play a version in the bar that I call "Gentlemen's chess." You are not allowed to lose a piece accidentally. If, due to the ravages of bourbon, your queen should unknowingly stumble into the path of my bishop, I will warn you of the faux pas. The player is allowed to return the queen to safety and subtly encouraged to buy another cocktail. Everyone's a winner and I come out looking like the benevolent guru.

If you beat the bar you win a drink but beating the bar is a rare occurrence. Give me a strong chess player and a bottle of rum and my money's on the rum every time. Every so often a rocket scientist or a rated Master will strut in, order black coffee and unceremoniously kick my ass. These matches are my favorites and are the only games that are etched in my memory.

————

It's not as if I had just fallen off of the turnip truck. When I heard the Russian accent I knew I was in for a humbling exchange on the chessboard. There are some generalizations that can be safely adopted. You should never tug on Superman's cape, spit into the wind or play cocky chess against a cat from Russia.

Alex thumped me soundly, five games straight, before we were even introduced. In my defense, I was playing black but that was hardly a relevant factor. I castled early and often but his ruthless aggression laid waste to my battlements every time. The worst of it was his arrogant sneer. There were far too many witnesses for my taste and all of them would attest to his irksome air of superiority. At one point he called one of my moves "foolhardy" and shoved the piece back into position with a huff. I was beginning to feel like a bitch-slapped wolfhound and I didn't like the feeling.

"Ah, that's sound advice Alex. In America we have a name for your type of player...obnoxious shithead."

You could have heard a ruble drop.

He politely pretended not to understand the vernacular but his demeanor softened considerably from that point forward. I acknowledged his superiority on the chessboard and asked him if he was a rated player. He told me that his rating was below that of Master but that he trained his ten-year old son to be the Australian chess champion for his age group. He explained that he had taken a job with British Aerospace and they relocated him from Moscow to Sydney.

"British Aerospace? What are you man, some kind of rocket scientist?"

He sheepishly admitted that he was exactly that. Alex's job in Moscow had been to solve trajectory equations, which would guide Inter-Continental Ballistic Missiles to specific locations in the United States. He was expressionless when he told me that he performed the calculations for the missiles that were now targeted at Minneapolis and the bar we were in at that moment.

He explained that Minneapolis was a central food distribution point and that it was near enough to the Strategic Air Command in Grand Forks, North Dakota that the entire region was designated for "overkill." Several dozen ICBMs were poised to eradicate everybody but the cockroaches in my home state within the first twelve minutes of the last war.

We both stood mute under the weight of his words for a long moment.

Alex broke the silence and brought us back to the smaller battle. "You are not a terrible player. Your concentration on defense is your undoing." His harsh logic and faint praise stung a little. "You are a man without arms in a fist fight."

————

I followed Alex's suggestion to come out of my castle and kick a little ass and it worked. Our final game dragged out over two shifts at the bar and ended in a draw. At various times during the sixteen hour grudge match I assumed the advantage and actually got to see him sweat. I look for small victories in this life and playing black to a draw against the rocket scientist is one of my favorites.

I wanted to bust his chops a little so I told him that he played pretty well for a guy with all of those missiles aimed at him.

Alex replied, without lifting his gaze from the board, that since he had accepted a position in Minneapolis he must learn to ignore them.

# The importance of being Ernie

*"Golf is of games the most*
*mystical, the least earthbound,*
*the one wherein the walls*
*between us and the supernatural*
*are rubbed thinnest."*
- John Updike

Two friends and I played the first nine holes at a public course in Minneapolis and were grouped with a fourth at the turn. Ernie was about 80 years old and he told us that he could golf his age with regularity. He never hit the ball more than 175 yards but it went straight toward the target with most every shot. Us young bucks would smash the ball as hard as we could off of the tee, often doubling Ernie's distance but by hook or by crook the wise old guy would end up penciling in a lower number.

Ernie was a great influence and we commented throughout the round on what a positive effect his serenity and steadiness were having on our own games. By the end of the round we had all learned to mimic his humble address and slow, thoughtful swing.

In talking to Ernie we learned that he was a retired songwriter and that he had earned his living writing jingles for advertisers. We prodded him further to see if he had written anything we may have heard and he owned up to one very famous beer commercial. My buddies and I were all raised in the happy land of Minnesota and were pummeled in our youth with the Hamm's Beer jingle.

> *"From the land of sky blue waters,*
> *from the land of pines...*
> *comes the beer refreshing....*
> *Hamm's the beer refreshing."*

The word "Minnesota" derives from a Dakota Sioux phrase meaning "Land of sky-tinted waters" so the jingle became our unofficial state anthem. If you grew up in the 50's or 60's in the upper Midwestern United States you cannot read the above lyric without generating a mental image of the Hamm's bear. The commercials were delightfully infectious cartoons starring a black bear that played the tune on a tomtom with his tail. Ernie wrote it! We were impressed.

We thanked Ernie exuberantly for being a charming part of our childhood but more importantly for fixing our suspect golf swings. My friends and I all bettered our handicap that day at Meadowbrook, a feat that we never accomplished before and haven't repeated since.

--------

There is a wonderful book that speaks to the spirituality of golf called *Golf in the Kingdom*. It's a novel that explores the metaphysical side of the grand game. Great truths are revealed in the story through the teachings of a mystical golf professional named Shivas Irons. I recommended the book to my wife to provide her with insight into my passion for the game.

When I returned home from golf I told Mary all about my brush with greatness. The Hamm's Beer bear was as much a fixture of her youth as mine and she was duly impressed. She grinned hard and rushed into the other room to retrieve the book she was reading that day. She shoved it into my hands and told me to read the four or five pages that preceded her bookmark.

Just behind the dog-eared page I found the passage in which the sage Shivas explains the great wisdom of advertisers. Shivas points out to his golf pupil the simple truth that wisdom is merely remembering. The job of the advertisers is to make us remember so they are among the great masters of the Universe. The author makes particular reference to the Hamm's Beer jingle as an example of their power to plant imagery in the mind.

If I could bottle a substance that produced the tingling in my spine I felt at that moment, I would be a popular bartender indeed.

# The Rodent Roundup

"A guy died in the bar one night. He fell stiff as a board, right behind where you're sitting...heart attack, I guess."

"Did anyone try to help...you know, CPR or anything?"

"No, it was spooky how everyone just stood there and watched him go. The Gophers were playing the Badgers in a night game at the dome and the place was lousy with football fans. The guy was waiting to be seated in the restaurant, standing over there by the host stand. His arm went rigid and knocked the clipboard out of the host's hand and into the wall with a thwack. Everyone stopped what he or she was doing when the clipboard hit the wall and turned in time to see him expire. We knew he was dead before he hit the floor."

"What do you mean you knew he was dead?"

"Everybody knew. There had to be a hundred souls in that room, and not one stepped in to break his fall. The ones who were closest to him jumped back as though they were avoiding a falling tree." I cleaned the dirty glasses and ashtrays as I spoke.

"His death was tangible."

———

The bar and restaurant staff learned to dread the nights that there was a game at the dome because the stadium was so close and the football fans were the wrong kind of busy. The Minnesota Gophers play the Wisconsin Badgers frequently enough that we came to call it "The Rodent Roundup," almost reverent in our level of loathing. It was a hurricane of bad karma.

The sports fans were known to bring dead critters to the games to throw on the field at half time to intimidate their opponents. It started with dead badgers and gophers, of course but soon grew to include a variety of mammals with no real relationship to the combatants or their mascots.

Disturbing as it was to realize that one of our patrons might be packing a rotting badger carcass, there was a more dreadful foreboding that night. It was close to Halloween and a shadowy kind of amateur pagan chaos was in the air.

Before the sports fans arrived en masse, I had only one customer at the bar. I didn't bother bonding with him because I knew that we were going to be in the reeds at any moment. I'd hand him his Gibson, he'd look at his watch and ask me if anybody had called for him on the phone. We repeated this exchange three or four times before the guy broke step and asked a new question.

"Have you ever heard of the Eastern Onion?" Slightly slurred by the Gibsons.

"Yeah, I think it's a Thai restaurant over on Hennepin...four and a quarter for the drink." No time to chat, pal.

He shoved a twenty at me to cover the drink and his tone became more insistent, "No, no, it's a messenger service, like Western Union, get it? You know, singing telegrams, people in costumes, that kind of thing." He looked at his watch again then back at me in time to catch me making my escape to the cash register. He increased his volume to accommodate our distance but overshot the mark in his drunken state and nearly screamed, "HE WAS SUPPOSED TO BE HERE AT 6:00!"

The sports fans descended on us and the Gibson guy was lost in the crowd.

They arrive at about the same time and when one of them dies they leave in a hurry. That's not to say they didn't stay for the freakshow; the doors thrown open to the street, the paramedics' heroic but futile efforts, the removal of the body. They weren't about to let it dampen Game Day, though, so at the end of the show they were gone as they arrived, as one. I was surprised that none of them felt the tug of the bar to drink and brood and talk about the death of their fellow, rather than going to the game.

It was a devastating blow to the evening's receipts but a mercy to the oppressed staff.

––––––––

One sports fan remained after the storm. The Gibson guy, who preceded the tumult, was left, much worse for the effects of the freakshow and the gin. I was actively ignoring him when the waitress at the end of the bar held up her hand and pointed at her palm in the universal "look behind you" gesture.

Bartenders learn young to watch for weapons and the guy who just walked in the back door of the bar was packing a doozey. I saw the blade first, at least two feet long, curved like a scimitar, attached to a knotted wooden shaft about five feet long. The man wore a hooded black robe that obscured both his face and his feet. The robe, draped to the floor, made it appear as though he was floating across the room directly toward the man at the bar.

I stood petrified, incapable of reaching for the telephone to call 911. When I opened my mouth to yell a warning to the guy at the bar about his imminent beheading, my vocal chords were paralyzed as well.

In my trance, I'm certain I was the last to realize that the assailant was dressed as the grim reaper as a Halloween prank, hired by the Gibson guy to go to the game and loom over the proceedings.

The waitress, who was a veteran of much stranger scenes than this, shrugged and told the reaper that he was about twenty minutes late.

# As a matter of fact I did invent the Internet

There is a marvelous scene in the Woody Allen film "Annie Hall" in which Allen's character, Alvy Singer, is waiting on line in a movie theater. An obnoxious man behind him is pontificating on the real meaning behind the writing of Marshall McLuhan so Allen turns to confront him.

"...Marshall McLuhan? You don't know anything about Marshall McLuhan."

"Oh really? Really? I happen to teach a class at Columbia called "TV media and culture" so I think my insights into Mr. McLuhan, well, have a great deal of validity."

Since the film director is all-powerful at blurring the line between reality and fiction, the real Marshall McLuhan happens to be standing behind a pillar in front of Woody Allen in line at the theater.

"Well that's funny because I happen to have Mr. McLuhan right here ... Come over here a second (To McLuhan). Tell him.

"I heard what you were saying. You know nothing of my work...How you ever got to teach a course in anything is totally amazing."

Woody Allen turns to the camera and delivers one of the all-time classic movie lines directly to the filmgoer.

"Boy, if life were only like this."

---

I call them "pufferfish," the boastful or self-aggrandizing types who visit the tavern for no reason other than to impress the occupant of the next stool or the poor bastard stuck behind the bar. I've endured them in their thousands and am largely unimpressed. In my experience it's the quiet ones that you've got to watch out for.

The most interesting person at the bar, or in real life for that matter, spends more time listening than talking and rarely makes a spectacle of themselves. The prim, quiet woman across from you on the train this morning might well have been a Nobel Prize winning chemist but you will never know because she didn't advertise. Genuine Earth shakers don't pine for attention, you've got to draw them out.

When the dot com craze began, the bar was lousy with geniuses all of a sudden who were eager to expound on the real significance of the scene and their role in it. You couldn't swing a cat without hitting an Internet millionaire or a Silicon Valley entrepreneur with a limitless expense account and a falsely inflated sense of self worth.

The Internet phenomenon to them was little more than a vehicle of commerce, so their wealth was adequate evidence of their genius. I had to stand mute and prepare cocktails, enduring aggressively wrong-minded people blustering about the real importance of the Internet. I started to feel very alone in my poverty and my idealism.

It seemed to me that World Wide Web was the ultimate realization of the Open University, the death of elitism and proprietary knowledge. Focusing on the network as an agent of commerce is like saying that the automobile is a great invention because you can sit in the driveway and listen to the radio. I felt that they were missing the point.

---

I stopped making judgements about people based on their livelihood the third or fourth time that I ran into a savant washing dishes. It never occurred to me to ask John what he did for a living or for a rundown of the highlights of his resume. I gathered that he was a computer person of some description and most likely a good one because he was quiet about it. If you sit at my bar I'll ask your name and what you're good at but how you make your money seems irrelevant.

John was the best kind of regular, the kind who shows up often enough that I can remember his name but with sufficient rarity that I'm genuinely happy to see him when he does. Business called him to Minneapolis a couple of times a year in the mid-1990s, during the heyday of Internet awareness and since he shared my enthusiasm for computers in general and the Internet specifically we formed a conversational bond.

I was afire with enthusiasm for the Internet and never tired of discussing its potential. When the National Science Foundation lifted the commercial restrictions on the Net they couldn't have anticipated the wacky growth of the thing but I did. A moment of epiphany showed me a world with a billion hosts communicating freely and I knew in my heart that it was the most important development in human affairs since language itself.

The most interesting thing about John was that in spite of his expansive technical expertise he did nothing to quell my childlike exuberance for the magic of the machines or the potential of the Internet. I felt my worldview vindicated when John was around because he knew more about computers than anyone I knew but had not yet given in to cynicism over their potential. I could spout the most outrageous opinions without fear of ridicule.

"I think the Internet is the end of war."

"You may be right."

----

It was a quiet night at the bar, one pufferfish, his bootlicker and a young woman in a business suit who was alternating between admiration and disdain for the pufferfish. When the man paid her tab with a loud flourish she pretty much locked onto admiration. The woman was in town to interview for a job with General Mills, traditional industry and breakfast cereal, solid but lacking glamour. The vocal success of the dot com millionaire was throwing her off a little and she seemed to be contemplating a career change right there at the bar.

"You own the company? That must be very exciting."

"We went public in July," then a knowing wink to his bootlicker, "little beans compared to the merger we're working on."

The pufferfish was buying her drinks for all of the wrong reasons and the poor woman thought that she was interviewing for a job. I've been a reluctant voyeur to this kind of icky scene too many times and was wishing them all away when one of my favorite regulars showed up.

John took a seat at the opposite end of the bar from the other three and ordered his typical glass of red wine. I was eager to escape the spectacle at the other end of the bar so I bent John's ear about a story in that morning's newspaper. It was a funny piece about the fragility of the nascent Web. A group of winos and transients had gathered beneath a bridge at the University of Minnesota, built a fire to stay warm and melted the fiber optic bundles that connected the Gopher State to the rest of the world.

He had seen the story on the Web and was opening his mouth to comment when the pufferfish loudly intervened.

"Give us all a Zima, set up the whole damn bar!"

Quite a gesture, I thought, on a Sunday night with four people in the lounge. I looked at John and rolled my eyes and he waved off the free Zima. I fetched three bottles of the nasty stuff from the cooler and delivered them to the loud man and his cohorts.

"What about the guy at the other end, give him a Zima too! Put it on my tab, son."

"No, thanks just the same, I'll stick to the wine."

"You should try Zima, it's awesome. Everybody's gonna be drinking it before long. I own a company that has the exclusive rights to advertise it on the Internet."

The bootlicker made a loud slurping sound as he extracted the last of his Tom Collins through a straw and eagerly grabbed his bottle of Zima.

"This stuff is awesome."

The businesswoman sipped the transparent beverage from Hell and grimaced.

"It's, uh, different."

"You bet it's different, sweetie, that's what people want. I'm gonna have the whole world drinking that stuff before long. Banner ads are the wave of the future."

I returned to the other end of the bar and John resumed the conversation interrupted by the rush on Zima.

"Maybe those winos knew what they were doing when they knocked out the Net."

————————

My idealism about the Internet surfaces whenever John visits the bar. I've always believed that avarice and ignorance were the tag team enemy of mankind and that the best of all possible worldwide webs could defeat them both. If information is freely exchanged people will become too smart to be taken advantage of. I could talk to John about possible futures and he'd play right along.

"I can see a world where a complete University education is free on the Internet."

"It will probably happen sooner than you think. I saw an article on the wire today that the Library of Congress has devoted billions to scanning documents for free display."

The pufferfish overheard John and his sensibilities were offended.

"That's not free, friend, that's my tax money they're being generous with. This whole 'open source, let's all share' mentality is as dead as the dinosaurs. The Web will be all about counting eyeballs and making money."

"I wouldn't bet on that if I were you." John was confident but polite, "that bubble might burst."

"Well, I appreciate your advice, friend but I already bet on it and won big. I've been on the Net since they opened it up back in '91 so I think I know what I'm talking about. Get me another one of those Zimas, son."

The man had been playing the game of Internet longevity one-upsmanship so long and so successfully that he considered 1991 a conversation ender. John couldn't resist claiming seniority.

"Well, with all due respect, I've been on the Net since it was developed, closer to 1971 and I can tell you with certainty that it wasn't designed for commerce. The whole intention was the uninhibited exchange of data packets. Open source isn't a mentality, it's the nature of the beast."

"Yeah right, everybody's an expert. I suppose you invented the Internet like Al Gore."

"Well, I wouldn't say I invented it. I was node number 12 at Urbana so the guys at node numbers one and two should get the real credit."

"Nodes? What are those, some kind of geek BBS you used in college?"

"No, the ARPANET project that created the Internet. The initial hosts were referred to by node number and mine was number 12. I was on the team that wrote the TCP/IP protocol though, so I suppose you could say I was there at the beginning."

"The T.C.I.C.P what? What the hell is that?"

"It's the language of the Internet. It's kind of complicated, you probably wouldn't understand."

# I hate Minnesota Nazis

Tending bar has always reminded me of the guy who hits himself in the head with a hammer because it feels so good when he stops. It isn't masochism in the purest sense because the satisfaction is only loosely attached to the beating. It's sort of an enhanced masochism with the additional pain of delayed gratification.

Bartending comes with a fair amount of actual physical risk, usually right up there with cops and cabbies on the list of the ten most dangerous professions. I have had a good run so I won't relay too many violent episodes but I could provide the names of two dozen bartenders who would. I could account for a few more who didn't live to tell about it.

I did some independent study in college on the effects of various recreational substances and I can report without equivocation that alcohol is by far the most potent. It's a startling paradox that the crazy juice is legal and socially encouraged while a mellowing herbal agent that grows like a weed is verboten, but such is war.

The barman dwells in the gray area between getting you liquored up enough to piss away your children's inheritance and hoping that you don't kill an innocent on the way home. Most states provide for his prosecution as an accessory to murder should the latter occur but the moral dilemma is much scarier than the law.

There is no feeling in the world like surviving a twelve hour stint in a busy bar, to the satisfaction and physical well being of all concerned. A thousand variables conspire each night to menace the barman's serenity so, in the parlance of aviators, any landing that you can walk away from is a good landing.

————————

I've always had a soft spot for night auditors. We're usually the only two people stirring in the entire hotel by the time I close the bar so we are kindred spirits. It takes a certain kind of person to work the graveyard shift for any length of time and I almost always hit it off with that type of person. We share a quiet pathos.

It's rare for me to exchange more than a sentence or two with my counterpart at the front desk but these ships passing in the night have always been among my favorite relationships. I'm usually in a hurry to finish my chores and the night auditor is in a hurry to have my paperwork, so he can begin his. Ours is a perfectly benign symbiosis, we simply exchange pleasantries and say goodnight.

On a lark, I once asked a cute new auditor if she had ever fantasized about sneaking off to a vacant room with the bartender. To my shock and eventual regret she confessed that she had. As it turned out, her particular pathos was seasoned with violent psychotic outbursts so I learned to keep a cool professional distance in all future exchanges.

————————

I'd heard the rumors about Carrie but I've been around the block enough times to know that gossip is usually only half-true and is almost always mean-spirited. I'm sort of like the FBI when it comes to loose talk; if you make a report on your neighbor, I want to know what's in your garbage can. I dismissed most of the speculation about Carrie as idle innuendo. A wiser man would have recognized that the other half of the truth was worse than the gossip.

Carrie was a recovering heroin addict and former prostitute from the mean streets of Los Angeles. She didn't jive well with the wholesome midwestern work ethic at the front desk and by the time I met her she had alienated all of her coworkers, one by one.

She was hired, with the assistance of her parole officer, to work as a desk clerk in the hotel but her shrill voice and disturbing manner necessitated a lower level of customer contact. By the time I collided with Carrie, she was being trained in for the graveyard shift.

As I handed her my paperwork she glanced at the signature on the bottom and emitted a screech that would make Fran Drescher flinch.

"I know this name, this name on your report...It's Shute isn't it?"

The timbre of her voice was almost comically grating, like a cross between the Wicked Witch of the West and Joe Cocker. Carrie was fifty-something and the topography of her vocal chords bore the ravages of almost a half a century of Marlboro Reds, loveless blow jobs and cheap wine.

"Umm, yes, that's my name...It's, uh...nice to meet you?"

"It's you alright! Your father was a Catholic Priest and he killed my brother driving drunk!"

Her eyeballs were cranked open so wide there was no evidence that she even had lids for them. Her pupils were tiny little dots that darted constantly from left to right, alternating their pinpoint focus on each of my own. I've faced angry men with loaded weapons and pissed off girlfriends with golf clubs but I've never been as disquieted as I was at that moment.

"Umm, I think you have me mistaken for someone else...I come from a long line of Lutherans and we'd have certainly noticed a drunken Papist in the mix."

"No, I'm sure of it, your father killed my brother!"

———————

Carrie wasn't your run of the mill delusional psychotic; there was some method to her madness. I had plenty to fear from her fixation on the imagined murder of her brother but it wasn't the only cause for alarm. She was hate filled in general but she had fine-tuned her rage to fit within the ideological dogma of the white supremacist movement. Her arms were decorated with Aryan Nation tattoos to demonstrate her devotion to the cause.

Sometimes she seemed to forget that my father had killed her brother and she'd take me into her confidence about someone else's transgression.

"You know that little bitch Julie who works the three to eleven has a black baby don't you?"

"Umm, yeah...he's a cute little bug, his name's Anthony but they call him 'The Ant'"

"Cute my ass, he's an abomination, so is the race traitor bitch that spawned him!"

"Umm, goodnight Carrie."

Crazy is as crazy does so we must forgive people with an extreme ideology. If Fred Phelps tells you that "God hates fags," you may wish to forego debate and simply nod and smile. When you encounter a worldview that is shockingly dissimilar to yours and in total contrast with good sense, don't be quick to assume that it's as well reasoned as your own. They might just be a nut case.

Carrie swore herself to my undoing and made daily subversive attacks on me and mine. She called the police on me one night because I smelled like beer and the nice policeman explained to her that bartenders often smell like beer after swimming in the stuff for ten hours at a time. He further explained that they were currently investigating a rape and that she was wasting their time needlessly.

The poor cop winced when Carrie shrieked, "I was raped once!" then he quietly excused himself.

Her reign of terror eventually culminated in her firing but not before she'd done real emotional and monetary damage to a dozen different coworkers over a period of six months. In the final analysis I got off pretty cheap. I dropped a couple hundred bucks to paint over the racial epithet she scratched into the side of my car and I had to replace a set of brand new radials.

Geno at the garage was a real mensch about it and he cut me an amazing deal on replacement tires. He said I broke the record with fifteen roofing nails in four wheels and he was giving me his "victim discount." You can find comfort and wisdom in the strangest places and I found mine in my automobile mechanic. Geno told me with sage certainty that I must have angered an idiot and I should be proud, not upset. His mother told him that he could always judge a man by his enemies.

When I explained that I'd been targeted by a rampaging white supremacist, he gave me the first good belly laugh I'd enjoyed in months.

"Yeah, I hate Minnesota Nazis."

# The regular

It was an upscale hotel in a decidedly downtrodden corner of the city.  A single night's stay in one of the rooms would cover a month's lease at the nearby welfare squats but the barstools could be rented for the price of a bottle of beer.  Our proximity to squalor guaranteed a blurring of the line between the haves and the have nots and the bar I tended had a door that opened to the street.

My tour of duty at that particular lemonade stand was happily brief but in the space of ten months I lived through enough chaos to last me a lifetime.  I didn't stick around long enough to endure armed robbery or serious bodily injury but that clock was definitely ticking in the background.

Hotel bars rarely employ bouncers so I served as the court of last resort when things took an ugly turn and man, things took an ugly turn almost every single night at that watering hole.  I only suffered actual physical violence a handful of times but a couple of those were enough to teach me not to underestimate any foe.

Under the best circumstances regulars are a mixed blessing and this particular gin joint was not among the best circumstances.  The only people who made multiple appearances at this bar were icky or dangerous or both.

―――――

The guy had to be eighty years old, a crusty wino known only as "Stinky." When his monthly stipend ran as dry as his gullet, he'd shoplift cologne or perfume from the drugstore on the corner. It had to be a devastating blow to his taste buds and stomach lining but the stuff had a high enough alcohol content to soothe his Jones and calm his tremors. The perfume exited his pores, merged with ordinary bodily secretions and created a noxious cloud around his person, like Pigpen in the Charlie Brown comics.

Stinky always showed up at the beginning of the month, when he was still flush with the government's largess. The dole rarely lasted beyond the sixth or seventh day on the calendar so his nuisance to me was marginal. He pretty much kept to himself at the bar and all things considered he was probably among my best-behaved victims. Stinky would have made my A list if he'd lay off the Aqua Velva for awhile and take a bath from time to time.

On the street he was a derelict but on the days that he had folding money in his pocket he moved with exaggerated dignity. Stinky occupied his barstool with perfect military posture and sipped my crappiest whiskey as though it was a rare French cognac. I even taught him to tip sort of, sometimes only a dime and a few pennies or a crumpled up bus transfer but it was a start. On a bad day, when the well was dry, he'd leave me pocket lint or a tube of hemorrhoid cream he'd stolen from the drug store that morning.

Stinky wasn't bad people necessarily but his hygiene was a quiet threat to my trade. My secret fear was that he'd show up one day with all of his friends.

―――――

I had never seen the woman before that day but my little voice told me that she was gonna be bad news. The first indication that something was terribly wrong was when she parked herself on the stool right next to Stinky and tried to strike up a conversation. Stinky could make my eyes water from six feet away so at the very least the woman had a badly flawed olfactory.

She was sixty-something and every bit as ragged as the odoriferous octogenarian next to her. Small tufts of greasy gray hair bulged out from underneath her soiled pink stocking cap and it looked as though Helen Keller had applied her make-up with a brick. She wore a tattered green parka, patched with duct tape and missing one sleeve at the elbow. Leopard pattern K-mart stretch pants and unmatched Keds tennis shoes made her assault on fashion complete.

"Uh, howdy ma'am, what'll ya have?"

Her breath was a fair match for her smelly counterpart at the bar and her gooey slur made it clear that she was already medicated. The dozen or so teeth in her mouth were puce colored and broken. Only one of her two front teeth remained and it was chipped so as to resemble a fang that jutted out of her gum at a forty-five degree angle, giving her a whistling lisp.

"Thith fuchhin' plathe is nuthin' thinthe they took out the piano bar...yer prolly waterin' down yer likker too. Thtupid fuchhin' bathtardth..."

Big wads of opaque saliva jettisoned from her pie hole with every utterance so I grabbed a bar towel and kept my distance.

"Uh, they took out the piano bar when Eisenhower was President, ma'am, maybe it's time to get over it. What'll ya have?"

"Well that all dependth now, don't it buthter?"

She swooned clumsily against Stinky, who had been doing his best to ignore the spectacle on the neighboring stool. She jarred his drinking arm in the process and spilled his precious bourbon.

"Get this crazy broad away from me, sheesh! I'm mindin' my own business here and payin' good money for a drink. Ain't you got rules to keep out the riff raff? I want compensation dammit! Crazy hooker spilt my whiskey!"

"Who you callin' a hooker? I'm a rethpeckable lady and a real gennleman would buy me a champagne cocktail."

"Calm down, calm down." I splashed a little more rot gut into Stinky's glass to cover his spillage and was about to give the woman the bum's rush when I was distracted by a hotel guest at the other end of the bar. He was a generically well attired business traveler and the single malt scotch he ordered cost more than the combined net worth of the odd couple at the opposite end. To my horror, the fanged menace noticed him too.

"Now thath a gennleman over there...You wooden let a lady go thirthty now wudya, hanthom?"

"Certainly not."

Oh dear God, I thought, don't buy her a drink or we'll never be rid of her.

"Bartender, put the nice lady's drink on my tab."

––––––––

She began wobbling toward the soft touch in the suit and I reacted quickly by placing her champagne cocktail down next to Stinky. As a dog's glance will follow a Milk Bone, her rheumy eyes adhered to the beverage and to my great relief, the rest of her followed dutifully. Class conflict was the last thing I needed in that deteriorating scene and if my boss walked in to see street people commingling with his precious hotel guests he'd blow a gasket for sure.

I had planned to leave the indigent lovebirds to their own devices at the far end of the bar, in favor of chatting up the hotel guest, when Stinky started shrieking.

"She's grabbin' at my wiener! Make this old hag let go of my wiener!"

By this time there were about a dozen hotel guests seated at the various tables in the lounge, all within earshot, each visibly shaken by the geriatric genital grab. I moved quickly to defuse the situation but it was too late. By the time I made it back to ground zero, Stinky was on his unsteady feet and the fanged crone had fallen backward off of her barstool in a drunken heap on the floor. She was motionless for a minute or two and as much as I hate people dying in my bar, the prospect provided me a moment of guilty comfort.

As luck would have it, she survived the fall and returned to her barstool. The side of her face that hit the filthy barroom floor had bits of debris lodged in the liberally applied pancake makeup but beyond that she seemed no worse for wear and tear.

"That thmelly bathtard thpilled my cocktail...Gimmeanotherone dammit!"

"I think you've had enough, you're going to have to leave now."

"Yer gonna kick me out, you thkinny little fuchhher, you an whoothe army?"

She picked a stack of three glass ashtrays off of the bar before I could react and had her arm cocked like a catapult by the time I fully evaluated the threat. With all of the fury of a Nolan Ryan fastball she unloaded directly at my head from less than five feet away. Either the patron saint of bartenders intervened on my behalf or due to substance ravaged motor coordination her aim really sucked. In slow motion, like a gun battle in a Peckinpah western, I watched the glass missiles pass centimeters from my head. The ashtrays divided in flight with one whizzing past each of my ears and the third just grazing the cowlick on top of my head.

My relief was temporary, perhaps a nanosecond or two, interrupted by the ashtrays shattering the twenty-five foot mirrored wall behind the bar. Shelves full of festively colored, ridiculously expensive joy juice cascaded to the floor or ruptured as they struck the back bar. I stared dumbstruck at the devastation; thousands of dollars worth of broken glass and spilt spirits with me smack dab in the middle of it.

Some wrongs are so egregious that you have to just stand there for awhile and shake your head. My boss lost sleep at night worrying that cigarette smoke was gradually yellowing the ceiling tiles in the bar. I knew that he had to have heard the squall of shattering glass from his office and was en route to the bar at that moment with the veins bulging in his neck and forehead. He was a high strung cat to begin with but this tableau was gonna be aneurysm material.

My only hope would be to lay my hands on the culprit, as a sacrificial offering to deflect his anger but when I turned, she was gone.

Stinky returned to his stool as though nothing had happened and was trying to get my attention when my manager rushed into the bar. The boss stopped in his tracks just inside the doorway and trembled as he surveyed the aftermath, crimson growing in his cheeks, apoplexy testing the limits of his cardiovascular system. I stood frozen in place on the sticky pile of expensive debris, waiting for the second explosion of the night.

Stinky started banging his empty glass on the bar, momentarily distracting my boss from his homicidal rage.

"Whaddya gotta do to get a drink around here?"

# The right path

If you've ever worked in the service industry, specifically in a hotel or restaurant, you will empathize with my hatred of national holidays. The hotel never closes so duty demands that I hold down the floor whether anybody is feeding the tip jar or not. Normal people with real jobs look forward to holidays as paid vacations but for my kind they are a lonely, penniless purgatory.

Quasi-religious holidays are the worst because they hang around longer and come with their own baggage. Easter sucks because business travelers add a Thursday to Good Friday and usually bug out by Wednesday. Easter Monday sits too close to Sunday so it's shot to Hell as well.

The only lingering grudge I hold against Abraham Lincoln is for his Thanksgiving Proclamation, setting aside the last Thursday of November as a national holiday. That sucker's worse than Easter because Thursday's so close to the middle of the week that it throws a pall in both directions. As far as the hotel bartender is concerned you might just as well tear the whole week off of the calendar. I love the Great Emancipator more than most but I'll never forgive the inconsiderate ape for not commanding us to be thankful on a Saturday.

None of these minor horrors can compare with the Christmas/New Year's drought. Normal people quit showing up at the bar about halfway through December and I generally don't see them again until the second week of January. To worsen my woe, some genius attached increased financial obligation to this holiday so I bleed at thrice the normal rate while my income all but vanishes.

New Year's Eve is amateur night and it's probably just as well that I avoid the fray. I'm sure plenty of bartenders make hay but nobody in his right mind rings in the new year in a boring hotel lounge. The slow bleed that starts around mid-November runs right through the Stupid Bowl near the end of January and I'm never flush again until Valentine's day.

"Happy Fuckin' New Year to you too."

————

By the time Christmas Eve rolled around, boredom and poverty had pummeled me into whimpering submission. I brought only the heaviest tunes to work that night and resigned myself to dwelling on dark matters with Leonard Cohen in the empty tavern. I planned to watch for the taillights of my boss's car in the parking lot. I'd close the lemonade stand the minute the coast was clear.

"Why the Hell are we open on Christmas Eve anyway? It's a major religious holiday, for chrissake!"

The boss was perky and salaried and smug.

"Well, the hotel's at twelve percent occupancy and we can't very well slam the door in their faces, now can we?"

He always asked rhetorical questions that only fueled my feelings of uselessness. The manager gets paid the same amount whether there are victims in the bar or not so it's easy enough for him to be full of the holiday spirit.

"Now put on a happy face, you don't want the customers to think you're a Scrooge do you?"

I looked around the vacant scene to emphasize the fact that there weren't any live ones around to see me scowl and I was about to say "Bah Humbug," when a lone hotel guest approached the bar.

The boss puffed out his chest and gave me an "I told you so" wink, as he made a beeline for his car. On his way out the door he thumped the somber customer with his cheeriest non-sectarian assault.

"Happy Holidays!"

Aw Christ, I thought, it was nearly ten o'clock and I had hoped to be closed by eleven. This cat was gonna get the cold-shoulder no matter what. There wasn't gonna be any food service and the God damned blender was broken if he was looking for a strawberry Margarita. If he starts chatting me up, even a little bit, I'm turning the lights up to 7-Eleven intensity and killing the tunes completely.

I growled my own greeting as Leonard Cohen groaned in the background.

"What'll ya have, bub?"

———————

There's only one thing worse for a bartender than an empty room and that's one that's nearly empty. If the joint is completely dead I can plop down on the couch in front of the idiot box, or crank the tunes and pretend I'm not at work. If there's even a single live one I have to stay on my toes.

This guy sounded like double trouble because he told me that he was meeting a colleague who would be arriving on a later flight. In addition he explained that he didn't go to bars very often, which made him an amateur, the very bane of my existence. Novices always order stupid drinks and lean on the barman for direction and small talk and I wasn't in any mood for a high maintenance relationship.

"I'm not much of a drinker and I rarely go to bars but I've had a rare day."

"Yeah, you and me both. What'll ya have?"

"I heard that Absolut Vodka is kosher so I better stick with that...no ice please. Is that Leonard Cohen singing on the jukebox? I believe that's the first time I've heard him played in public."

This guy might not be as bad as I thought. Only one in ten thousand digs Leonard Cohen and he ordered spendy liquor in an empty glass like an old pro. His use of the word kosher hinted that he probably wouldn't burden me with a lot of Christmas cheer.

"Kosher? Is that a figure of speech?"

"No, no, I'm an Orthodox Jew...A guy on the plane told me that Scandinavian vodka is kosher and I'm taking him at his word...My name's Moshe, what's yours?"

"Jon's my name." No time to chat, pal. "Six bucks for the firewater, kemosabe."

"You may as well run a tab for me, my colleague won't be in for an hour or more and he'll want something when he gets here."

Lovely.

———

I started closing the bar around him and blunted Moshe's every effort at conversation with stern silence or a curt "yep" or "nope."

"Have you been a bartender long?"

"Yep."

"Will you take time off for the holidays?"

"Nope."

For a guy who didn't frequent bars Moshe was making quick work of the booze. I replenished his glass three times in the first fifteen minutes and he ordered the fourth without slurring. I began to worry less about falling into the morass of useless conversation and more about the other curse of the novice drinker, public puking.

"Hey, you might wanna go easy on that stuff, Moshe. It might be kosher but it hits your stomach like turpentine just the same."

"I'll be ok, Jon. I've drank enough to know that I'm a sleepy drunk, not a sloppy one."

"Suit yourself amigo, they're your intestines."

He knocked back the fourth Absolut in one swallow and handed me the empty glass before I had set down the bottle from pouring the third. He sounded as sober as Moses when he spoke and removed any lingering fear of small talk.

"Do you ever think about death?"

————————

Asking a bartender in an empty bar if he ever thinks about death is like inquiring whether or not fish can screw underwater. It's sort of their job. Contemplation of the abyss, while in the abyss is a tautology and when Leonard Cohen is moaning out "Tower of Song" in the background, it's just a stupid question.

Moshe began staring off into space in such a way that I presumed it was rhetorical. It was just as well that I didn't start ranting on the subject because he was willing to carry the conversational burden solo.

"I study Buddhism and find it interesting that death is so closely attached to rebirth that the two are inseparable."

"Umm, I don't want to split hairs here, but I thought you said you were an Orthodox Jew."

"Oh, I'm observant. I have to travel with a suitcase full of kosher food because I'm not allowed to eat in most restaurants but Buddhist thought isn't prohibited. My copy of the Gita was a gift from my Rabbi and we discuss it often. Buddhism is a discipline, not a theology."

"Well, all I know is what I read in the papers but it seems to me that old Yahweh might have a problem with the whole reincarnation theme."

"You might be right but the Rabbi seems to think it's harmless enough if we steer clear of idolatry. The discipline parallels Judaism in remarkable ways."

"I'll have to take your word for it, Moshe. I don't worship anybody."

"You would make a good Buddhist. The master says that if you meet the Buddha on the road you should kill him as a false prophet. Each man must be his own Buddha so any who claim to be yours are lying."

Moshe seemed to have a superhuman immunity to the joy juice and he went on and on about Nirvana and Holy Epiphany, about Heaven and Hell. His perspective was foreign to me, and compelling. Here I was spending Christmas Eve with my first Orthodox Jewish Buddhist Leonard Cohen fan and I had forgotten all about giving him the bum's rush. He seemed to share my pathos in spite of the comfort he found in his faith and I was just growing fond of him when the liquor started to hit.

He began to falter after his seventh drink and his oratory deteriorated to short, definitive bursts.

"God must love Buddhists."

He sounded more like the novice drinker and less like a serious theologian when the hiccups kicked in.

"The Buddha ... hic ... must love God ... hic ..."

Then the light left his eyes as if someone had thrown a switch. The last of his "Johnny Walker wisdom" escaped in a drunken slur just before he passed out.

"There can be ... hic ... more than one right ... hic ...path ..."

————————

It was nearly closing time when Moshe's colleague arrived at the hotel. I had cleaned up around my sleeping patron and was turning up the lights when the man walked into the bar. He motioned toward the snoring heap next to him and spoke in a hushed tone.

"How long has he been that way?"

"Oh, not long, I'm in his debt really, for keeping me company on a dead night. You must be Moshe's colleague."

"His boss. I'll have what he's having."

"He didn't tell me he was meeting his boss or I'd have kept him sober. I hope you don't think worse of Moshe for getting shit-faced, it's mostly my fault for chatting him up. Moshe's a thoughtful cat and you're lucky to have him. He told me that he seldom goes to bars."

"Seldom? Moshe's never been in a bar in his life. He's an Orthodox Jew and a teetotaler as far as I know."

"He said that he had a rare day."

Moshe's boss threw back his glass of vodka in one gulp and signed the tab, doubling the amount with my gratuity. He moved to help his blissfully hammered employee to bed and answered me over his shoulder as they wobbled toward the door.

"You only lose your father once so it was a rare day for him."

He paused at the door, balancing his drunken employee on rubbery legs, and almost whispered his politically incorrect farewell.

"Merry Christmas."

# A life after death

W e've all got our tragedies but Tommy's was complete. He used to have a lovely wife and beautiful twin daughters. All three were safely strapped into the Saab when an eighteen-wheeler ended their existence about a thousand yards from his driveway.

They diagnosed him with post-traumatic stress disorder and saw to it that the government would subsidize the little rat hole he ended up in downtown. He gets a check every month for seven hundred and eleven dollars, which just about covers the basics.

His plan on the night that I met him in the blizzard was spontaneous and beautiful in its simplicity. He was listening to news on the radio in his apartment when the weather advisory about dangerous wind chills was broadcast. Tommy would simply take a long walk after midnight when the streets were clear of meddlesome good Samaritans.

As I waited at a stoplight that night I saw a man wandering around in circles in the middle of the intersection and guessed that he was dazed by hypothermia. It was fifty below with the wind chill and ten or fifteen minutes out in the open could have put him to sleep forever. I pulled up next to him, threw open the passenger door of my car and beckoned him inside. When he thawed out he told me he had an apartment nearby so I drove him to his door. He asked me what I did for a living and I told him I tended bar in the hotel across the street from his place.

The following Tuesday he showed up at the bar and explained that he wasn't much of a drinker but he'd try a glass of red wine. He said it was a mystery to him how people developed a taste for the awful stuff. I told my new regular that people don't really use the liquor because they like the taste.

"It puts some space between you and the world."

Tommy listened intently as though he had never considered the chemical effects of alcohol. "Does it really work?" He asked innocently.

"You bet it does, a little too well I'm afraid. Too much, too often will put such a distance between you and the world that you'll never make it back. I can wreck your life with one bottle of rum."

"No you can't."

There wasn't a hint of irony in his sad expression.

The wine provides only temporary relief from his tragic reality but it's enough to help him regain his perspective. To quell my fears that I had created an alcoholic he promised he would only drink on Tuesdays and then, only in moderation.

A decade of Tuesdays has passed since then and Tommy is fine. I wouldn't say that wine saved his life but it seems to have given him a tolerable point of view. The wine works its magic, the world falls away and he casually starts a conversation with something like,

"Do you believe in a life after death?"

# Get back to where you once belonged

**M**innesota is as progressive as any of the fifty American states in the arena of social equality so if you insist on being an oppressed minority you might just as well do it here. My friends in Texas call us "drugstore liberals" because we haven't earned our bullshit when it comes to the cohabitation of the races but their criticism is weakened with each new census.

I look forward to the seamless social blending of Earthlings but will be pleasantly astonished if it occurs during my watch. I'm ashamed to say that I'm still burdened by some lingering racial stereotypes myself so I was taken aback the first time I encountered a black man in Minnesota with a British habit.

"Hullo, may I have a cuppa tea?"

---

The hotel bar was a non-scene so I did what I could to liven things up. Among my most powerful weapons in this pursuit was a gorgeous black lacquered medium grand piano. We didn't have a house musician so the thing was little more than an expensive piece of furniture but it was available to make a scene at a moment's notice.

The occasional hotel guest or bold employee would tap out a tune but even when it rested quietly the piano exuded an elegant ambience. I would ply talented visitors with free drinks to play for the assembled patrons, sometimes creating a glow equal to the finest salons in Paris. The gorgeous musical instrument may have been under utilized but it was not unappreciated.

The hotel was a large property and it contained three such pianos scattered throughout the building. All three were treated as decorative accessories and moved from room to room as necessary, to class things up and ruin their tuning. I would often arrive at the bar on Monday to discover that our piano had been "borrowed" over the weekend and moved to some remote corner of the facility. It required eight housemen and a good deal of effort to move one of the pianos up and down the stairs to the lounge so, once borrowed, it was never eagerly returned.

I'm sort of like the Rain Man when it comes to keeping things in their place so I would throw a well-scripted conniption fit every time the piano disappeared. Fortunately the night manager was a right thinking cat and would round up his minions to see to the piano's rightful return. The obvious logic that one of the instruments should live in the lounge at all times never sunk in with the cretins who ran the hotel so as often as not it was absent without leave.

I eventually paid the ultimate price for their impertinence. They will never be forgiven.

———

I could tell there were rock stars in the hotel that day because the caravan of luxury busses was being corralled in the employee parking lot. When I checked out the bar keys the desk clerk told me that Ringo Starr & His All-Starr Band were performing at the Minnesota State Fair and would be staying with us for three days. Two-thirty in the afternoon is pretty early in the morning for bartenders so my thrill over the arrival of the celebrities must have been subdued.

"Didn't you hear what I said?" The desk clerk was aghast at my apparent lack of enthusiasm. "You might have a Beatle in your bar!"

"Hey, don't get me wrong, it would be kickin' to pal around with Ringo but I seriously doubt that he'll make the scene."

"Don't be surprised if he does, they're eating in the restaurant right now."

This struck me as odd because the restaurant didn't usually open until five o'clock but I suppose being a Beatle has its privileges. When I got to the bar I could hear voices around the corner and sure enough one of them was Ringo's.

I'm certain that every level of fame has accompanying weirdness and that the depth of this weirdness is proportional to the individual's notoriety. Famous people have every reason to be a little spooky. I read a story once about two women coming to blows over possession of one of Bob Dylan's discarded cigarette butts. Ringo and his party were keeping a very low profile in the back corner of the empty restaurant.

I had three people at the bar by the time they had finished dinner and we were all punchy over our impending brush with greatness. The only egress from the restaurant was through the bar so we knew that we would at least catch a close up glimpse of the former mop-top. As I predicted, Ringo didn't linger and if any of the people at the bar blinked they would have missed his Greta Garbo impersonation entirely.

For years afterward I would do my impression of the former Beatle, which consisted of pulling a hat down over half of my face, covering the remainder with my hand and practically running through the bar.

———————

If you want to get a rise out of an American bartender ask him for hot tea. Despite the growing popularity of herbal tea among the neo-hippie, Earth Mother set the beverage is largely unappreciated in the former colonies. Hot tea is a huge pain in the ass to the average American bartender because the facilities for its preparation aren't kept handy and the revenue for your effort is scant.

If you ask me for hot tea in a busy bar I will generally turn my head like a confused puppy and move on to the low maintenance, bourbon swilling fellow next to you. When the black gent with the British twang put in his polite order I was standing in an empty bar so I was obliged to fetch it.

As I made my way back to the kitchen, cursing his impertinence just under my breath, I pondered the oddity of a black man in Minneapolis doing teatime with the Brits. His face seemed familiar so I wrestled to make the association while I prepared his tea. He thanked me graciously and when he gave me a broad smile I recognized him instantly.

"I'll be damned, you're Billy Preston. You're the fifth Beatle!"

"I've been called a half Beatle before and I think I'd rather be called the fifth."

I admit I was star struck for a moment but I'm proud to say that I regained my wits immediately. Instead of fawning over him I wanted to know what was in it for me.

"Hey, Billy, could you give me a little Jo-Jo?"

The song, "Get Back" was an enormous hit for the Beatles and Billy Preston held down a piano stool right smack in the middle of it. The man must have been exhausted to the brink of insanity over requests to play that tune and a free cup of tea was little incentive to a cat who plays in stadiums. I was shocked speechless, when he blithely agreed.

"Sure, man, I'd love to..."

I've replayed the scene in my mind a hundred times since then and the soundtrack is always the same. I make the turn to gesture toward the now absent piano stool in slow motion and the theme from the shower scene in psycho screeches in my ears.

"...Where's your piano?"

# Bartender's ear

It may or may not surprise you to learn that people bleed on the bartender. I have unwillingly absorbed confessions on everything from marital infidelity and incest to embezzlement and income tax evasion, from gimlet-eyed penitents across the upper Midwest. Sometimes they are bragging about misdeeds but more often than not they are only bending my ear to purge their conscience. I am physiologically incapable of keeping a secret for any length of time so if you have something shameful to confess I recommend finding a priest.

There is no holy sacrament or attorney client privilege in effect when you cleanse yourself across my bar so you always run the risk of becoming a character in the dramatic retelling. I would never betray a humiliating secret told to me in confidence by a gentle soul, without masking the identity of the confessor but assholes are always fair game. Since the doors of the tavern are thrown open to the general public there is rarely an asshole shortage.

One of the bars that I hid behind for a while was a watering hole for corporate lawyers and stockbrokers, to the exclusion of nearly every other profession save the occasional hooker. Happy Hour at that scene was like an out and out competition to see who had the most flexible ethical framework and the usual winners appeared to have none whatsoever. These soulless freaks had even despoiled the congenial custom of buying a round of drinks, so that it eventually resembled an arrogant taunt. I am hesitant to generalize about specific livelihoods but if Hell fire rained down on that room to eradicate the lowest ninety-percent on a scale of moral rectitude, the prostitutes would have been the only ones left standing.

They weren't all icky people but I grew fond of only about two dozen from two thousand over the course of three years. The rest of them might just as well have had targets painted on their backs and my greatest source of amusement was shooting arrows at their bloated, self-important intrigue. I would overhear the stockbrokers murmuring about a secret deal and I'd walk straight across the room and blurt it out to one of the lawyers. While the lawyer was slipping me twenty bucks for the scoop I'd overhear one of his colleagues mumbling about pending litigation and simply repeat the process in reverse.

Another bartender might have given the hookers the bum's rush but I developed an affection for many of the working girls and turned a blind eye to their trade. Unlike the rest of my clientele, they were at least sincere and guileless in their desire to screw people out of their money. The prostitutes at that bar were usually a notch or two above the girls who walked the street so, as far as I was concerned, they were good for business.

It was common for the happily married stockbrokers and attorneys to skulk off to a hotel room with one of the ladies but the deed was usually done in shamed silence toward the end of a bout of serious drinking.

———

Jasmine wasn't like the other girls and when she showed up for the happy hour rush she caused a bidding war among the suited wolves. It was obvious that she was a hooker because she smoked Newports and rubbed her tits on everything that moved but she looked more like a Vogue model than a slattern for hire. Jasmine was clean enough to eat off of and I'm certain that the going price was above five hundred dollars by the time she finally picked a victim.

The winner was the slimiest stockbroker in the bar and instead of sneaking off to the hotel room as was usually the case, he proudly escorted his conquest to the elevator, basking in the congratulatory hoots and wolf calls of his less fortunate colleagues. He crept back to the bar about fifteen minutes later as pale as a sheet, trembling as he ordered a double scotch without ice.

"Hey, Jimmy, you look like you've seen a ghost, pal. When you left with Jasmine I figured I'd lost you for the duration, what the hell happened?"

"I don't want to talk about it. Make the scotch a triple."

"What do you mean you don't want to talk about it? She's the most gorgeous working girl who's ever set foot in this joint. Half of the damned bar wanted to dip into her bloomers and you don't want to brag a little?"

"Listen, man, Jasmine is a dude. She had a lip-lock on the lobster before I reached down and found out that she had one her own."

"You've got to be kidding me! That's one of the most beautiful women I've ever seen in my life. Are you sure?"

"Am I sure? Am I sure? I know a dick when I see one."

Jimmy noticed his volume was increasing to elicit nervous looks from the lady on the next stool so he toggled it back to a shamed whisper.

"She took it out and showed it to me. It's twice as big as mine."

I think after that he said something like, "If you tell anybody about this you're a dead man," but I was far too busy telling everybody to hear him. Whispering secrets and keeping the confidence of slippery people is a scoundrel's game and I'll have no part of it.

"Hey everybody, Jimmy says Jasmine's got a package and it's bigger than his."

————

I must have bartender written across my forehead or something because people tend to pour out their souls to me even when I'm off duty. The most startling confession I've ever been burdened with visited me when I wasn't even standing behind a bar. I had never met the man before so I don't know what made him think that I wouldn't go straight to the police but I'm pretty sure that he was admitting to murder.

I was shooting pool in a working man's tavern and the guy was hanging out around my usual table in the dark corner of the bar. Every time that there was a lull in the action on the pool table he engaged me in conversation and I did nothing to discourage him. He was a rough looking character but so were half of my buddies in the bar so I didn't hold that against him.

The man spoke with an urgency that led me to believe that he had something he wanted to get off of his chest. Every time I missed a shot on the pool table or waited for my opponent to rack the balls he would pick up right where he had left off, as though he was steering our sporadic conversation toward a definite conclusion. I'd seen it a thousand times as a bartender, the confessor speaks in a circuitous spiral around the real issue without ever losing sight of it, hoping to be drawn out by a sympathetic ear.

The guy began tipping his hand overtly when I mentioned my long-standing grudge against one of the bouncers. Every time the aggressive doorman passed by the pool tables to collect debris he would grab active beverages to pump up liquor sales.

"If that asshole grabs another one of my half empty beers I'm gonna call him out. Somebody's gonna get tired of his badass routine one of these days and take that prick down."

The bouncer was twice my size and I was obviously talking out of my ass but my companion in the dark corner took my words at face value.

"Have you ever been mad enough to kill somebody?"

"Well, I was thinking more along the lines of making him buy me another beer but I suppose that killing him would provide some satisfaction, yeah."

There was a weight in his tone that raised the small hairs on the back of my neck and I was greatly relieved to be called back for duty on the pool table. I managed to stay active for a couple of games straight and so avoided the foreboding conversation in the corner but when I returned to protect my beverage from the over-zealous bouncer, the penitent grabbed my ear and became heavier still.

"Sometimes people deserve to die, don't you think?"

I noticed for the first time that the brooding tough guy at my table was a little bit teary eyed and it made me uneasier still. I tried to lighten up the conversation to no avail.

"Aw, there are plenty of nasty people in the world but killing's too good their kind."

"What if somebody's messing with your wife and kids? What if there was no way to stop him without ending his miserable life?"

I was now certain that this was a conversation that I didn't want to be involved in any longer. Ordinarily closing time came too early for me but that night the clock seemed to be moving backwards.

"Well, killing your enemies always seemed kind of counter-productive if you ask me, sort of gives them the easy way out. I think prison is worse than dying so if they're really nasty you should make them rot in jail."

The man pounded his fist on the table hard enough to scare the cigarette butts out of the ashtray and wobble the beer bottles so I knew that we were no longer talking about a hypothetical situation.

"That bastard would have hired a lawyer and nothing would have come of it. I'm glad that I..."

"Whoa, whoa, whoa, wait a minute, pal! I ain't a priest and for all you know I might be a cop so we'd better just stop right there."

"I really need to tell somebody about this. It's eating a hole in my gut. I just wanted to teach the guy a lesson, I never meant to actually..."

"Hey, hey, hey, there you go again! I've really gotta get going now, you know, to beat the bar rush. You ought to go talk to the bartender; he's just standing over there not doing much of anything. I hear that bartenders are, like, sworn to secrecy or something."

"Really?"

# Walk like a duck

W e always watch for the big monsters, the malignant melanoma or the airplane crash. The small puddle of water on the kitchen floor was a threat I had never considered.

I was in the living room sweating a seventy-five dollar electric bill when I heard the terrible thump. Mary was finishing some chores in the kitchen before bed, turned too quickly on the wet ceramic floor and lost her balance. When I found her she was face down in a growing puddle of blood.

As I knelt over her I experienced a kind of tunnel vision. The emergency operator was giving me instructions but they may as well have been in Swahili for the attention I devoted to them. Mary's stillness made me fear the worst, that in one second's carelessness she was gone forever. When I rolled her over a small jet of blood spurted from near her right temple. I put a pillow under her head and pressed a towel over the wound. It had been about three minutes since I heard the thump and she didn't appear to be breathing.

We've all heard the stories about a devoted spouse following his mate into the abyss. A long time couple is separated by death or disease and the remaining mate simply withers away in their absence. In a recent newspaper article I read of an otherwise healthy man falling dead from heart failure hours after hearing of his wife's death in a car accident. At that moment I felt hollow and that my own heart might sputter and stop. I held little doubt that if my Mary was gone I was going in after her.

She was unconscious for the duration of the 911 call and was scaring the hell out of all concerned when the paramedics arrived. They took her to the hospital by ambulance and I followed by car not knowing if she was alive or dead.

———

Hospitals are different than they were when I was a child. The Hippocratic Oath now hides behind managed health care and the fear of litigation. The doctors reacted with alarm when they removed the first aid gauze and Mary's head spurted like a squirt gun. The blood soiled their clothes and the wall behind them when they jumped out of the way. Rather than moving to stop her bleeding, both went for the intercom to call a surgical team. After a small eternity one returned to cautiously replace the gauze. The doctors were visibly miffed, presumably fearing exposure to AIDS. For a moment I thought that they were going to berate her for the impertinence of her blood vessel.

We spent the rest of the night at the hospital having her coconut scanned for internal bleeding or loose marbles but neither was apparent. My heart sang when Mary joked that they would see cartoons if they gave her a CAT scan. When she was able to name our five pets, in order by size, I felt as though I had won the lottery. She wound up with a lump about the size of a golf ball near her temple but was otherwise no worse for wear and tear.

There's not much room for love at the hospital these days. Doctors and nurses are loathe to assume responsibility for anything and the comforts they offer are mechanical and minimalist. When the doctor told me that Mary should have some Tylenol I asked if they could give her a couple to get her started. Her head was throbbing and we hadn't so much as an aspirin tablet at home. The doctor looked at me as though I was a homeless person asking for the keys to his Porsche.

I explained to them that she was brought to the emergency room almost totally naked and they had to think about it long and hard before they let her go with their scrub pants and bloody gown. I had to remind them that it was February in Minnesota before they would part with a couple of disposable booties for her bare feet. Hospitals have come a long way from the days when they insisted on taking you to your car in a wheel chair. They simply said she could leave, without so much as pointing the way to the exit.

It is far better to avoid the nastiness altogether. We are now more attuned to the tinier catastrophes that wait for the careless. I have little doubt that the asteroid will strike while I'm wiping up a potentially deadly puddle on the bathroom floor but I am ever vigilant. Every day I remind Mary to walk like a duck because ducks rarely tip over. She is very precious to me and for the few moments I thought she was gone, I am forever affected.

For all of our guile and vitamins we are fragile critters and I am left to wonder how people can be so casually cruel to one another. As your bartender, I would advise you to hug your spousal unit like there's no tomorrow.

I further recommend that you always walk like a duck.

# The Country House

When Mary cracked her skull open on the kitchen floor I developed a slight nervous condition. She had the great good fortune of being unconscious throughout most of the freakshow so she came away with little in the way of lingering trauma. I was a basket case for awhile. The frail human condition hit me right between the eyes and I noticed, for the first time, the full range of dangers that awaited us around every corner.

Mary's doctor suggested I get a hobby to distract me from my paranoid obsession so I started drinking. I had been a bartender for nearly twenty years and it had never occurred to me to use the stuff myself. When I discovered that sufficient quantities provided total distraction, I was hooked.

The bottle of Budweiser I took at the end of the night as a shift drink became two, then three. The suds distracted me from my worry for awhile but I discovered, to my chagrin, that I was a melancholy drunk. If I ventured into that fourth bottle of Budweiser and John Prine happened to be playing on the jukebox, it was all over but the crying. I had increasing difficulty finishing the paperwork and closing the bar through my weeping fits so I decided to take a leave of absence and start drinking full-time.

I whacked the 401k and started spending my retirement at a working man's tavern down the street from the hotel. By way of odd symmetry the joint was a fixture of my youth and was, in fact, the first place I had ever bought a bottle of beer. My brother Billy had an apartment near The Country House when I was fourteen years old and he sneaked me through the back door when nobody was looking. The place hadn't changed a bit in twenty years and the minute I walked through the door I was surrounded by the ghosts of my misspent youth.

---

I was born with a gift. I'm a scary good pool player. I can beat just about anybody using only one hand and with two I can clear the balls so quickly most people are still chalking their stick when I bury the money ball. My best time on clearing a fifteen ball rack, with called shots, is twenty-two seconds. I'm not bragging because it's not because of anything I did, I've never practiced or made an effort to improve my game; I was born with the geometry. I was fourteen, going on forty-five when I first discovered my special purpose.

I started haunting the Country House every week when I found I could sneak in through the screen door in the basement. By the time I was sixteen they had become so accustomed to my presence that I was never bothered to prove my age. I scared the hell out of grown-ups who spent decades trying to master the game and always left richer for the effort. Skinny and unarmed, save my pool stick, I specialized in the gentle separation of men from their money. Having seen the film "The Hustler" a dozen times, I would always forestall collection of a wager in the face of hostility.

"That sucks man, you'd have kicked my ass if you hadn't scratched, let me buy you a drink."

The bar held an eight ball tournament every Thursday night and I was always the favorite. The prize money was something like a hundred bucks and I made it a point to spend the whole damn thing buying people drinks before I even won, as a show of good faith and to keep from getting banned or beat up. The real action was on the side games anyway; the tournament itself was purely public relations.

I soon discovered that buying people drinks was a win/win deal. Adult beverages were spendy so they saw it as no small favor and showed kindness in return but the stuff dulled their senses and rendered them ripe for the slaughter. I sipped my Coca-Cola and marveled at the potential.

The downside became obvious the night I lost the tournament. I don't know if there was a full moon or what but it was one of those nights that the universe is slightly askew and I felt a strange uneasiness from the minute that I walked into the bar. There were many new faces that night and among them was a young Native American woman named Annie, who had come to the Country House with the sole aim of kicking my ass on the pool table. Annie was the best pool player on the Rez since the age of twelve and when I ran into her at twenty-one she was nothing short of world class.

Annie routed her first six opponents without stopping to chalk her stick and stole glances at me between every match. She was quiet and respectful of her opponents and was the only other sober soul in the room. When she met me in the last bracket of the tournament she introduced herself in a polite tone and told me she had hoped to play against me in the final. Annie was the picture of sportsmanship when she looked me in the eye and wished me good luck on the game.

One of the victims for whom I had been buying drinks had crossed the line from boisterous to obnoxious and began making distracting noises and comments every time Annie took aim. I had unwittingly created a monster by getting the stranger liquored up and Annie was paying the price. She wasn't fazed by his bad behavior and to her credit she made quick work of me and won the first two games of the best of five series.

His taunting increased in volume and venom until he was appending every comment with "Squaw Bitch." I'm not a specialist in Native languages but I'm pretty sure those are fighting words on the Rez and I felt Annie had every right to smash the idiot's melon with the end of her pool stick. Annie ignored him with a stern serenity and continued to out class me on the pool table, seemingly unperturbed.

I felt responsible for the spectacle since I helped lubricate the stupid monkey so when he started in with the "Squaw Bitch" thing, I intervened on Annie's behalf. When I confronted him he focused his rage on me instead. When I asked his buddy if he could do anything to control the guy they both stood and wielding pool cues like clubs they menaced me into the back corner of the bar. There was no reason behind their drunken glare and without my guardian Angel I would certainly have taken a brutal beating that night.

A crusty old bartender once told me that there is a special place in Heaven for people who pick up the tab. He felt that buying a drink for a stranger, expecting nothing in return, was the height of human nobility and that it bestowed a sort of pedestrian sainthood. The crowd of people who watched the growing spectacle weren't moved to action by the racial slurs and bad sportsmanship but the prospect of me being subdued before I could pay the bar tab was unacceptable. The entire population of the bar rose as one to my defense and made it clear to the scoundrels that they should reconsider beating me to death.

I steered clear of the Country House for about twenty years after that.

———————

The cops waited at the end of a street that led away from a tavern at closing time so they didn't have to wait long. They said that they stopped me for rolling through the stop sign at the end of the street. The legal limit for alcohol in your bloodstream while driving in Minnesota is .10 and I blew .10 exactly. The debater in me longed to point out the fact that I had apparently gotten to the legal limit and stopped, as the law demanded. I wanted to discuss their reason for pulling me over because I was sure that I made a full and complete stop at the intersection in question.

I had, by this time, graduated to the use of Long Island iced tea for its general efficiency and tastiness. It's a drink that keeps on giving long after closing time and is a certain cure for sobriety. I can be damned articulate at .07 but at .10 with a belly full of tea, forget about it.

At around .084 I begin to lose the ability to control my lips and tongue and at .097 I sound exactly like Mush Mouth from the Fat Albert Show. The Long Island iced tea inspires grand oratory that crosses my mind with stunning celerity but the words gurgle out of my pie hole like an infant dribbling oatmeal.

I called my Mary from jail.

At the police station they told me that I was their most cooperative DWI suspect ever and that in the future, silence might be a useful ally. The cops were charmed by the fact that a lifelong bartender would be so unaccustomed to strong drink and were hugely impressed with my Mush Mouth impersonation. They gave me the Breathalyzer test three times in the hopes it would drop to .099 but it seemed to be going the other direction. They generously submitted only the lower test results.

The arresting officer whispered to me that I shouldn't go to the expense of hiring a lawyer. He said that if you were right on the line they would plead it down to a careless driving instead of the dreaded DWI. The kindly cop went on to tell me that I was a hilarious drunk but that I wasn't very good at the mechanics of drinking.

He suggested I consider a new hobby.

# My African Friend

Daniel was so fresh off the boat he didn't realize that his every utterance was a cliché. "America is the land of opportunity, my friend. Every man is free to work and to feed his family, to live in peace." I was merely making small talk with a cabby when I asked him what he thought of America so far. "In my country it is difficult and dangerous. Every man must struggle every day to survive. We are all blessed to live in this place." His enthusiasm and sincerity told me that the hackneyed rhetoric was new to him.

"You look like a kid, Daniel, don't tell me that you have a family to support." His eyes were smiling behind his sunglasses when he turned to me in the backseat and said, "I am twenty-two years old. I have four children and each is an American!" Daniel held my gaze until he was certain I gathered the weight of his words and in that moment I realized I had met my first perfectly happy human being.

Daniel made the crossing from Ethiopia when he was eighteen, accompanied by his wife and younger brother. He and his brother Samuel had both taken jobs driving cab for the same company within a month of their arrival and had been productively crisscrossing Minneapolis ever since.

I met Daniel as the result of a ruthless conspiracy between the State of Minnesota and The Mothers Against Drunk Driving.

————

The Breathalyzer read .10 exactly so I dodged the full-blown drunk driving charge but received the consolation prize of a "wet careless." It's slightly more serious than a simple careless driving ticket but less stigmatizing than the dreaded DWI. This "DWI Lite" was the result of a compromise between a powerful lobby and a state government that couldn't build prisons quickly enough. I had to pay five hundred dollars and take a cab to the tavern for sixty days.

Getting liquored up in a bar is a spendy proposition to begin with and sliding there and back in a cab is worse. The hidden costs of my new hobby were spiraling out of control so I needed to mitigate the expense somehow. I had already rationalized the tavern going itself as research for my novel but the forty bucks each way in a cab was breaking my back.

I noticed that most of my taxi cab drivers were East African, and many of them were from the same part of Ethiopia. I had been marked in their circle as a long fare and a soft touch so they were the first at the curb when the phone rang. They were a ridiculously friendly bunch and I came to realize that they were tight with one another and that two of them were brothers. It occurred to me that I could get a "value added" cab ride if I pumped them for first hand information about their homeland and language. The ride was twenty-five minutes each way so I'd be getting a safe driver and an Ethiopian tutor for less than a hundred bucks an hour.

Daniel gave me two cell phone numbers and told me that I could call them directly at any time and he or his brother would answer. When I explained that I wanted him to tutor me on Ethiopian to mitigate the expensive ride, he was surprised and delighted. We fell into a pattern of him teaching me vocabulary on the ride to the bar and testing me on what I had retained, through the storm of alcohol, on the ride home. He instructed his brother, Samuel, to speak to me in Ethiopian exclusively whenever he answered my call.

Both brothers were articulate, erudite and eager to share what they knew with one of the natives. Daniel told me that in four years I was the first person to ask about his homeland. Everyone else wanted to remind him how lucky he was to be in America, something he understood far better than they did. What started a couple of months before as a frivolous cab ride, became the center of my summer and among my fondest experiences in this life.

Daniel and Samuel taught me everything I know about Ethiopia and I'm in their debt.

―――――

As you get older your circle of acquaintances broadens and the odds against seeing people you know on television and in the newspaper narrow to even money. When I moved from a small town to a large city I read the accident reports and obituaries from the small town with some trepidation, almost certain I would know the people involved. It seems paradoxical but there is a greater distance between people in a crowd and the big city will desensitize you with nameless tragedy.

I remember the first time I saw someone I knew in the big city newspaper. I would normally flip right past the obituaries but for some reason I glanced at the exact spot in the page with a name that I knew. "Hey Mary, look, that guy I tended bar with at the hotel downtown is dead at 32. Yep, It's the same guy. It says survived by a sister named Tina." It seemed strange that someone I knew should emerge from a swirl of more than two million souls but there it was in black and white.

With the passage of time and the broadening of my circle such an event became tragically commonplace. It was a rare newspaper that didn't contain a friend or a friend of a friend bumping into a bad scene. I didn't have to sift through the little obituaries to get the story on my African friend.

Homicidal mania sells newspapers so they spilled ink all over the front page for the murdered cabby. The story of the killing was all over the previous night's news so I didn't feel I needed to read the gory details. I'm ashamed to say that I was going to ignore the story and look for happier news until the word "Ethiopian" caught my eye. The account of the tragedy triggered recognition slowly, each word harder to read than the last through glazed eyes, "named Daniel, survived by his brother, Samuel, aged twenty-two, four children."

Daniel's wife explained to the reporter that they emigrated from Ethiopia to escape violence.

# Name dropper

Sometimes I'm self-conscious about my status as an under-achiever so I try to suck as much as possible out of my experience behind bars. It is humbling to have to wear a little plastic name tag after seventeen years of schooling and my situation in the tavern occasionally requires me to utter the dreaded mantra of liberal arts graduates everywhere.

"Would you like fries with that?"

It seems that just when I'm ready to throw in the bar rag and search for greener pastures I'm visited with an experience that reminds me of the positive side of my trade and am given a small jolt of enthusiasm to remain behind the bar. I worked a private party in St. Paul not long ago that I would have paid to attend.

The party was given to honor a man who is arguably the greatest Minnesotan ever, Harold Stassen, in recognition of his 90th birthday. If Mr. Stassen's name is less than a household word, it wasn't for lack of trying on his part. His reputation lately revolves around his ten unsuccessful bids for the White House and his extraordinarily bad toupee but he is a truly great historical figure. He has since expired but was at the time the last living signatory of the United Nations Charter, one of its primary architects and most ardent supporters.

Harold, at the age of thirty-one, had been the youngest person ever elected Governor in United States history and he hadn't rested on his laurels for a minute since then. During World War II he joined the Navy and was given the position of Chief of Staff under Bull Halsey in the Pacific and stood on the deck of a warship in Tokyo Bay to help preside over the surrender of the Japanese. He was a great advocate of world peace through world government and the crowd who showed up to toast his ninetieth birthday was impressive indeed. The Chairman and two former Chairmen of the Joint Chiefs of Staff were in attendance, as was The Admiral of the Navy and most of the Congressional Delegation from Minnesota. Nearly every name on the guest list appeared somewhere in the history books or on the front page of the New York Times.

The party was like a trip to Disney World for a student of politics or history. Although I may be a minimum wage slug, I've lived long enough to shoot the breeze with the General Secretary of the United Nations and to sell a scotch and water to a four-star general. Harold was a life-long Republican but I had to go to his birthday party to meet my favorite Democrat, Eugene McCarthy. It turns out that Eugene and I have a favorite human in common and it was surreal chatting with Senator McCarthy about Abraham Lincoln and getting paid for the privilege.

That little scene alone was worth the tuition at bartender college.

———

Billy has worked at the chow mein noodle factory since high school so he hasn't had occasion to meet many famous people. George Hamilton spilt a drink on him once, next to a craps table at Caesar's Palace but that's about the extent of it. Billy was down a couple of grand at the time and was having a little bit of a mood so he just about kicked the pretty boy's ass right then and there. He is decidedly unimpressed by celebrity.

We were standing in line at the clubhouse to pay our greens fees one time and I gave him an elbow to the rib cage when I noticed a luminary standing right there in front of us.

"Hey, Wilbur, that's Sam Shepard!"

I had the good sense to whisper but Billy was half-asleep and responded loud enough to be heard on the practice green.

"That's very exciting. Who the hell is Sam Shepard?"

The famous playwright and actor turned around and gave us half a smile but he was understandably reluctant to pal around with us much after that. Ironically enough it was Billy who started Jaime and me off on a pissing contest over brushes with greatness that day. Our fourth didn't show up, so we had plenty of time to chat between shots while the Shepard foursome played in front of us.

Lord knows I hate to gossip and I'd thank you not to tell anybody I said this but as a golfer Sam makes a pretty good playwright.

---

I was responsible for one of Billy's rare celebrity encounters and it happened to be with one of the few people on Earth who would move him to awe. I had a bartending gig at the 91st U.S. Open at Hazeltine and managed to hook him up with Jack Nicklaus to get his hat signed as a souvenir. Jaime is a fanatical golfer as well and was duly impressed when Billy began boasting for me.

"Jonny's met Jack Nicklaus."

"No shit?"

"You got it, man. Me and Jack are tight."

"What was the first thing you said to him?"

"I think I said something like, 'Hey, you're Jack Nicklaus!'"

"He probably gets a lot of that."

Jaime and I both worked in the hotel and restaurant business forever so it never occurred to me to bring up my encounters with famous people. I presumed correctly that he would have one to match each one of mine and that he would be equally jaded over the thrill of the events. We both agreed that being a widely recognized human would be a real drag after the novelty wore off, everybody wants something from them or expects them to perform on command. Each room that they enter becomes a feeding frenzy and they are the bloody piece of meat in the shark tank. If somebody ever gives you the choice between fame and fortune, I'd recommend going for the fortune.

"So I'm in the clubhouse with Jack and I say to him, 'Hey Jack, you're a living legend and all so when you stand over a three foot putt do you say to yourself: I'm Jack Nicklaus, I'm the best golfer who has ever taken breath?'"

"Yeah, so what did he say?"

"You know I'm not sure, I wasn't really listening. I was trying to think of something else to ask him while I had him there in front of me."

—————

Billy acted as a scoring judge when Jaime and I started trading names, rating our responses with a derisive sneer or nodding with a half-smile when he found the celebrity encounter mildly impressive. He was apparently immune to popular culture and proved as difficult to thrill as the East German judge at the Olympics. The great majority of our experiences received little more than a rolling of his eyes.

"I sold Jean Luc Ponte a cognac."

"Oh yeah, Patti Smith kissed my forehead at a club."

"Anita Baker hollered at me for stepping on her fur coat."

"That's nothing, Joe Strummer dripped sweat on me in Cleveland."

None of the names seemed to ring a bell with Billy so Jaime raised the stakes a little.

"I stood on stage fifteen feet away from Billy Joel's piano stool at a concert."

Billy nodded his limited approval for the first time and started walking closer to Jaime down the fairway.

"Oh yeah, I gave my cab to Ian Hunter and his bass player gave me a backstage pass."

To my horror Billy had never heard of Ian Hunter so I think I lost a point or two. Jaime picked up on my weakness and went in for the kill.

"I danced with Tony Bennett."

"You're a damned liar. He's lying, Billy, he never danced with Tony Bennett."

"Did so."

"Did not."

"Did so, he was pretty buzzed and we didn't dance the whole song but he took me for a little spin, baby."

Damn! We were only on the third hole and it looked like Jaime was going to bury me. Billy was patting him on the back and asking about Tony Bennett's cologne so I knew I had to pull out the big guns.

"I rode in a limousine with Papa John."

Bill and Jaime harmonized in a sarcastic snort.

"The pizza guy?"

"No, man, Papa John from the Mamas and the Papas. I rode with him in the limo to a sound check and shot the shit with him for most of the day."

I remembered too late that Jaime worked at the same hotel and met him as well.

"That's nothing, everybody knows John Phillips. I brought room service up to his ex-wife, Michelle and all she had on was a bathrobe and a smile. Yeah, baby!"

———————

Jaime was crushing me with the likes of Robert DeNiro and Michael Jordan and I was hitting the bottom of the barrel with Tippi Hedren and The Little Rascals. He even managed to top my Jack Nicklaus story with the hilarious recounting of a drunken spectacle involving Chi Chi Rodriguez and Fuzzy Zoeller. I dredged up Tony Curtis and he hit me between the eyes with the double header of a romantic dinner he served to Prince and Kim Bassinger. The little bastard called my Sam Donaldson and raised me a Buster Poindexter.

When I told him I had given Charlie Sheen an aspirin he bragged about giving Joan Jett a back rub and when I got hard up and boasted about Hugh Downs he nailed me to the wall with Barbara Walters. Politicians are the last refuge to which a braggart will cling but I was getting desperate. I gave them the run down of the guest list at Harold Stassen's birthday party and neither one of them recognized a single name.

"Well, how about Wendell Anderson? I tripped Wendell Anderson once."

Bill and Jaime both gave me a withering look, then shrugged in unison.

"You know, Wendell Anderson, the former Governor of Minnesota. He was a rising star 'til he got drummed out of politics for arranging to have himself appointed to Walter Mondale's Senate seat. He was on the cover of Time Magazine for chrissake. You must have heard of him."

Billy already picked a winner in our little contest but decided to humor me a little.

"So how did you trip Wendell Anderson?"

"I recognized him walking through the hotel lobby but I wasn't sure where I knew him from. I asked him if he wasn't the Professor from Gilligan's Island and he got a little pissed off. He gave me a real dirty look and started walking at twice the clip. He told me over his shoulder that he was a former United States Senator and that's when he hit the raised flagstone in front of the fireplace and fell flat on his ass."

Jaime won the gold but Billy gave me points for style.

"Heh, heh, you're a name dropper all right."

# Chess, anyone?

The dream was the same last night. It was closing time and Crazy Joe walked in and sat on a stool at the middle of the bar. He ordinarily took one of the seats in the dark corner at the end, in front of the chessboard and he never came in this close to closing time.

In the dream I give him the bum's rush. "Hey Joe, you're late. I'm closing up the lemonade stand right now."

Joe spent most of his life in a state institution of one kind or another and he understood the discipline of rules and regulations like "last call" and "closing time." During his childhood and adolescence they called them reformatories or hospitals but for most of the last twenty years they were prisons and jails.

His last hitch inside was a sentence at Stillwater for doing something unspeakable to another inmate at some local lockup in Brainerd. Joe was released after serving every last day of his five-year sentence, given a room at the Francis Drake Hotel and 125 dollars in walking around money. He walked around the corner and into my bar about an hour after his release, saw the chessboard on the bar and settled in for the duration.

Chess is a popular game in prison for obvious reasons. It has fallen out of fashion on the outside because people are too busy but these cats have nothing but time. They call it "cheese" and regard a proficiency at it with some reverence. When Joe saw the board on the bar he knew that he had found a home.

Joe was a creepy guy but if I 86'd everybody who was creepy there'd be nobody left to diminish. He had ragged dirty blonde hair to his shoulders and he never removed the dark sunglasses. His ever-present headphones were tethered to a radio he kept in a duffel bag that always rested on his lap. He didn't bother anybody overtly and he always had money to pay for a drink.

I was a little bit relieved when he finally got himself thrown out of the bar for good. I liked Joe, in a way, but his manner was quietly menacing and he had a deadening effect on the two stools on either side of him.

Joe arranged to meet another ex-con in the bar for a chess match, which Joe lost. They were playing for twenty dollars and when it came time to pay, Joe picked up his chair and threw it at his opponent instead. It took five Minneapolis cops to tear them apart and send them off in different directions but not before they tipped over every table and spilled every drink in the place. When the cop asked if we wanted to press charges we declined. They provided the only excitement the bar had ever known, and they hadn't caused any real damage. Crazy Joe was told he was no longer welcome in the bar.

I began having the dreams, nightmares I suppose, shortly thereafter. Joe walks in the bar near closing time and takes a stool near the middle of the bar. I tell him that he's late and that I'm closing the bar. Joe doesn't speak a word in my sleep. He stands and places his duffel bag on the bar in front of me. The bag is unzipped and there is a pistol inside. I think, for a moment, that I could grab it before he does but I stand frozen, staring at the gun. Joe picks up the pistol, levels it at my head and pulls the trigger.

In the loud crack of the gunshot I hear the word "Checkmate." The nightmare always wakes me with a start. I've never been able to fall back to sleep afterward

# Blank space

I had a regular at the bar who builds molecules for a living. He holds twin Ph.Ds in atomic physics and molecular chemistry and pulls in something like a quarter million a year playing mad scientist.

The fact of the matter is that Dr. Brent doesn't really know much about molecules at all. He's certain that they are made up of atoms and that these atoms are in turn composed of protons, neutrons and electrons and that these are really just tightly bundled quarks doing a manic dance in the ether.

Dr. Brent will tell you that an atom has a definable wall and that within this wall the quarks do their dance. He will tell you that all of the known mass in an atom could be equated to a basket of melons in a football stadium, a basket of Buicks in some cases but a tiny percentage of the whole in any event.

"So what's the rest of the atom made of?"

"Blank space."

"The undefined bulk of the building blocks of everything is blank space?"

"Yep. Cool, huh?"

Every time Dr. Brent opens his eyes he sees a world that he knows is not really there. His Volvo, his mother in law and the great pyramid of Cheops are all just so many quarks in a vast sea of nothingness, conspiring to create the elaborate illusion of substance.

The end result of his four decades of study of ultimate physics is that he's not sure why he doesn't fall through the floor when he gets out of bed in the morning.

# Why the willow weeps

I'm sure that the phenomenon goes by many names but I know it as "The crossword puzzle effect." You hit a wall in solving a crossword puzzle and set it aside. Pick up the puzzle a moment later, the answer appears obvious and you wonder how you could have been stymied in the first place. It must be a cross-cultural phenomenon because I've seen it in the fortune cookie sound bites from Lao Tzu as well. The Chinese philosopher didn't address crossword puzzles specifically but I'm pretty sure that he was talking about the same thing when he said, "If one ceases to strive for understanding, one can know without understanding."

I always suspected that the first person to come up with a unified field theory or the cure for cancer wouldn't be wearing a lab coat and a pocket protector. I pictured a man or woman sitting on a park bench listening to the birdsong and watching tree branches bend in the breeze. The layman philosopher would appreciate the essence of the forest from his humble perch while the physicists and mathematicians groped the bark and examined pinecones, slaves to the details they sought. Enlightenment would visit the philosopher on the park bench macroscopically, the seamless amalgam of an intricate universe laid bare to the most casual observation, when viewed from a proper distance with an open mind.

Mathematics and the self-defining laws of physics seem a clunky way to address the delicate latticework of small miracles that conspire to create such a mammoth one. A kangaroo could be defined mathematically but it is much easier and more edifying to simply view the kangaroo as a whole. The creature's peculiar magic is lost in quantum analysis and little of value is gained in the effort. The grandest mysteries, like the parameters of gravity and the cure for cancer, seem far too large to approach with a clinically focused mind.

If you catch me lingering on a park bench or gazing out the window for hours on end, apparently detached, I'm working on a unified field theory.

---

Fred wasn't my uncle but I like to call him Uncle Fred just the same. I know for a fact that he was somebody's uncle, I just don't remember exactly whose and that's not important anyway. What is important is that Uncle Fred was not a biochemist or an Indian Shaman or even a particularly gifted guy. He was a working stiff and a family man who led a normal life in an ordinary town. He had children, his children had children and they were all dosed with an average amount of tragedy and bliss. His life would have been completely unremarkable were it not for the fact that he discovered the cure for cancer.

Uncle Fred's wife took ill in her fifties and expired before her sixtieth birthday. She was still in the thick of it when Fred started solving big problems in his sleep. There was little in the way of cancer treatment in those days so she was left to wrassle with the disease largely unaided. Toward the end she had a terrible fever and thrashed about in a fitful delirium that required the use of the entire bed. Fred took to sleeping on the sofa in the front room and that's when he started having the dreams.

The fact that Uncle Fred was able to connect the dots in his slumber is no more surprising to me than the idea that the best way to solve a crossword puzzle is to look away from it. His days were spent in useless worry over his wife's illness, his plea to the Gods that be apparently left unanswered. A parade of doctors with second and third opinions presided over her deterioration and ultimately her death. The malignant chaos of her decline gave way to the most serene dreamscape imaginable when he allowed his worried mind to rest at night. The questions he screamed into the wind of his waking life were answered softly, unexpectedly in his dreams.

Each night as he fell to sleep on the sofa, the dream would take him to a beautiful park where he'd be seated on a bench near the edge of a placid lake. His wife was not dying of cancer in this place; it was always springtime and the sun felt warm on his cheek. The branches of an ancient willow tree swayed over his head and the fingers of shade moved across his body and comforted him. He'd wake from the dreams inexplicably hopeful about his wife's recovery, only to find her languishing ever closer to the abyss.

The dreams stopped the day that she died.

Fred lived to be a very old man, more than thirty years would pass before he joined his wife, summoned by a similar affliction. He had all but forgotten the dreams of the willow tree and the park bench from three decades before but they mysteriously returned with the onset of his own disease. Fred knew that his night visions were somehow related to his wife's decay but he could never quite make sense of them. They might have remained disjointed forever were it not for an attentive nurse and a series of strange visions during Fred's own deterioration.

Uncle Fred has been gone for quite awhile now and the scientists at the University are still trying to untangle the puzzle he left for them.

————

Janice was a misery junkie. From an early age she saw this world as little more than a theatre of sad circumstances and loss. She had a fraternal twin named Jason who died a senseless death when they were eight years old and she had not been able to summon a happy thought since. They were playing together in the front yard when Jason climbed their favorite tree to untangle the rope of the tire swing. He fell from the branch barely ten feet off of the ground, simultaneously breaking his neck and his twin sister's heart. Jason died in her arms that morning and took the better part of Janice with him. She resigned herself to wait out this life without her brother or her smile.

Her parents did everything in their power to heal the family and mollify their only remaining child after the accident but Janice would not be soothed.

Her mother worked as a nurse in a field hospital during the war and had witnessed the most horrible suffering imaginable; broken men with amputated limbs spurting blood by the bucketful. None of her haunting memories of war torn men compared to the depth of sorrow she saw in her daughter's eyes following Jason's death.

The carnage of war inured her to tragedy, steeling her against despair over the loss of her son but little Janice was as delicate as a flower. She feared that her daughter would never recover without similar toughening. With the best of intentions she visited the little girl with memories of the battlefield hospital, hoping to somehow mitigate the smaller tragedy and thicken her skin. The gruesome pep talks only bolstered Janice's moribund worldview and further distanced her from anything resembling a happy childhood.

The cancer took her father when Janice was eleven and she made the decision to follow her mother's path in caring for the afflicted. She lost her mother to a different type of cancer a month before she received her own nurse's certification.

After graduation, Janice was assigned to an internship in the terminal wing of the hospital's cancer ward, a temporary situation that she never relinquished. Nurses were ordinarily rotated out of hospice duty after six months or so because the hopeless scene bred attrition in the ranks. The death ward was a staffing nightmare, a notorious breeding ground for everything from alcoholism and drug abuse to burnout and suicide. After the fourth time Janice declined rotation from the ward, she was promoted to a supervisory position and never again offered a change of scenery.

Janice found herself singularly well suited to the life of a caregiver for the terminally ill and the dying patients were as much a comfort to her as she was to them.

————————

Fred's excursions were always shorter than he'd like, interrupted by one of the nurses or by a stabbing pain in his legs or arms. He had been burdened with crippling arthritis for the last twenty years and learned to deal with it through immobile meditation. He simply stopped using the afflicted limbs and the pain was kept under control. This world's last gift to Fred was a painful batch of bone cancer that immobility did nothing to quiet.

Doctors rarely visited him after the cancer was deemed untreatable and ultimately fatal. The strapping young oncologist didn't use any soft soap when he delivered his diagnosis to the ninety-two year old man, he simply told Fred that he was going to die and that he should get his affairs in order. Fred received most of his nourishment through a network of tubes and eliminated it through another, so there was little left for the caregivers to do but look after his tubes. The nurses mechanically replaced his morphine patch four times each day and emptied his colostomy bag twice.

The fresh morphine patches were the highlight of his existence because they marked an hour or so of quiescence from the bellowing pain in his bones. Within a few minutes after the application of the patch, he could close his eyes and drift about in the pain-free landscape of his mind and memory. The forays into chemical serenity always began in the same manner. His eyelids drew shut and his hospital bed became a park bench beneath a regal old willow tree. The graceful cascade of willow branches was reflected in the lake and an early summer sun warmed his skin. The scene was oddly familiar to him but the opiates obscured the connection to the dreams that accompanied his wife's sickness thirty years before.

The park was always alive with activity, ducks and geese and swooping gulls, happy children playing tag in the distance as joggers circumnavigated the lake in a sweaty trot. Fred could hear the birds chirping in the branches of the willow above his head and the splash and playful bark of a Labrador fetching a stick that one of the children had tossed into the lake. It seemed odd to Fred that he could contemplate the hospital from that bench, that he could see it clearly through youthful eyes. The old man in the cancer ward would die soon and he wondered what would become of the vital man in the park when it happened.

After an hour or so on that peaceful bench, the dull ache would begin to grow in his arms and legs and build to a throbbing crescendo. His eyes would flash open to find himself in the dark corner of a little room, in a big building where people go to die. He cursed the old man and his cancer and he cursed the limits of the morphine patches that he knew had purchased his fleeting serenity.

The nurses were kind for the most part but were probably relieved as Fred's condition deteriorated. They knew his pain was severe but were only allowed to give him a new morphine patch every six hours, so they did their best to ignore his constant grimace. When his discomfort became intolerable and vocal, the doctors agreed that Fred was near the end. The patches were replaced with an intravenous morphine feed that Fred was allowed to control himself.

When discomfort yanked him back from the serenity of the park bench, he simply pressed the little red button four or five times and drifted right back again.

———————

Janice came to see herself less as a nurse than as a gentle steward for the departing. Any medical expertise she might possess was of little value in the terminal ward and she often felt as though her time at nursing school might have been better spent on theological studies.

If she fancied herself ineffective, it wasn't apparent in her enthusiasm for the job. Her life was devoted solely to the comfortable passage of those in her charge and she was as kind to them as professional decorum permitted. As often as not her days off would be spent on the ward and many evenings she'd sleep off a difficult shift on a cot in the break room in lieu of going home. Janice was the subject of gossip among the nursing staff for not having a life away from work but she was usually too busy to suffer hurt feelings.

Although she tried not to play favorites she had, for the past several months been especially doting on the guy who wouldn't die in 208. Old Fred was down to one of every organ that God had given him two of and was the unhappy host to at least five different flavors of cancer. All manner of disease and attrition were competing over that poor old man's carcass and it seemed to Janice that the diseases themselves must be keeping him alive so they'd have a place to stay.

Fred was the hands down record holder for taking up space on the death wing. It had been over a year since the doctors told him he had a matter of weeks to live and Janice took them at their word. She spent at least one day of each weekend and an hour or two at the end of every shift reading to him from her favorite books. Whether Janice grew attached to Fred in spite of his looming departure or because of it seemed of little importance to her. She hadn't any family left to cling to so she embraced the misery that had taken those she held dear.

Janice knew that her affection for him was selfish.

————————

Time seemed to move in lazy loops from Fred's perspective on the park bench in his mind. If he enjoyed the splashing Labrador chasing a stick he could see it over and over again as though he was rewinding the favorite scene in a movie. Thoughts and people would come at his bidding, some that he recognized as familiar but most of them were strangers, people he had never met in his other life. When he had a pleasant conversation with a denizen of the park it would last as long as he pleased, never interrupted by business or obligation.

The linear locomotive of the real world, the one that was hurtling toward a chasm, felt foreign and unnatural. The lilting arc of the willow's limbs embraced him and provided a sense of well being that he had never known in the waking world. The warmth of the sun and the serenity in the park gave him solace just as the opiates soothed his hopeless counterpart. Nighttime never seemed to fall on the park in Fred's mind.

He struck up a particular friendship with one of the children in the park and their open-ended conversations were his favorite diversion. The boy sat in the crux between two of the larger branches in the willow tree over his left shoulder and spoke with the assurance of a sage across the vocal chords of an eight-year-old.

The boy seemed content to sit on the branch of that tree and talk to Fred for hours, in no rush to abandon their conversation and join the other children playing by the lake. There was something odd about the child, in that Fred could engage him in conversation as though he was an adult, yet he was entirely naive about certain things that every little boy would know. Fred once asked him if he wasn't bored, just sitting in the tree shooting the breeze and the boy didn't understand what the word "bored" meant.

"You know, when things get dull and you'd rather be playing tag or kickball with the other children."

"Why would I be talking to you if I'd rather be playing kickball? That doesn't make any sense."

Fred realized for the first time that he had never once moved from his own spot on the bench; it had simply never occurred to him. He remembered his other self, confined to the bed and wondered if he mightn't be immobilized in this world as well. To test the hypothesis he stood and walked to the lake's edge on strong legs, apparently unencumbered by fragile bones and feeding tubes. He bent down, picked up a stick and threw it into the lake with vigor that his arm hadn't possessed for some seventy-five years. The eager Labrador dove in after the stick, as he had a hundred times before but instead of splashing into the water, the stick made a sound like shattering glass.

Fred was stricken with a terrible dizziness and collapsed at the lake's edge.

———————

The alarm was sounded so often on the terminal wing that that the full code blue teams rarely responded. Usually a nurse or an orderly would check the alert solo and summon help only if necessary. Most of the patients were on a "do not resuscitate" basis, so most of the code blues were something less than urgent. It simply meant that there would probably be a vacancy tomorrow. When the guy in 208 triggered the alarm with his escape attempt, half of the oncology department showed up to see the exhibition.

The poor old guy had climbed out of his bed, ripping out all of his tubes in the process and triggering the code blue. He somehow stood erect on bones as fragile as porcelain, removed the armrest from the wheelchair next to his bed and threw it through the window of his room. The funereal quiet of the cancer ward was shattered with the breaking glass and the subsequent shouting of the orderly and within a few minutes the room was full of curious staff. The attending nurse knew the patient well, he had seniority on the ward and on the planet as a whole, for that matter. Old Fred was just a couple of weeks shy of his ninety-third birthday and he had scarcely left that bed in over a year. He had never done so under his own power.

The presiding nurse thought it curious enough that he should summon the strength and inclination to get out of bed and break the window but more curious still was that, according to his chart, he hadn't walked in nearly a decade. The old man passed out cold after breaking the window, most likely as a result of excruciating pain and had fallen in a heap more than ten feet away from his bed.

"You trying to make a break for it Fred? We've never had a successful escape from 2nd floor west and we're not about to let an old duffer like you get the better of us."

Fred was unresponsive, oblivious.

"Can you hear me Fred? We're going to send you down to radiology to see if you've broken anything."

His vital signs were normal for a man in his condition but Fred was dead to the world, still fast asleep on the spot where he had fallen beside the lake.

———

Fred remained happily sedated throughout the painful ordeal of the full body X-ray procedure. He awoke twelve hours later to a torrent of pain that was grand even by his own high standards. As he reached for the magic red morphine button that had been attached to the bed rail near his right hand he discovered it absent. The effort elicited a tidal wave of agony and he managed to summon a weak scream before falling again into merciful unconsciousness.

Janice had just arrived at the nurse's station when she heard the little yelp from 208. She ran down the corridor to Fred's room and found him sleeping like a baby with his dislocated right arm pulled from its sling and a pathetic expression frozen on his face. She gently replaced the elastic support around his shoulder and he stirred awake as she did so.

"The button's gone, Janie! The button's gone!"

"Calm down Fred, we've moved the button near your left arm since you've all but ruined the right one. I hit it twice just now so go easy on it."

She guided his left hand to the device and he clicked it three times in rapid succession.

"You call that goin' easy, old man? You keep clicking that thing like Dorothy clicks her heels and you're gonna wake up on the other side of the rainbow."

"You promise, Janie?"

The warm comfort flowed through his veins like hot chocolate and the magic button calmed his mind immediately. This nurse was kind and he had taken a shine to her right off. He misread her nametag upon their first introduction and called her "Janie." When she corrected him and said that her name was Janice he told her that he liked Janie better, if it was just the same to her. She laughed and told him that she'd been called worse. Fred called her Janie from that day forward.

Fred had trouble holding a book and turning the pages by himself so Janie started reading to him. Most of the time he'd drift off to sleep after a page or two and awake some time later to find her still sitting in that ridiculous wheelchair, reading aloud to nobody. She would alter her inflection and tone for the different voices in the story in such an animated performance that he felt a little guilty for nodding off.

Janie reminded him of the kid in the willow tree who never seemed in a hurry to go anywhere, content to keep his company alone. If Fred didn't know better he'd have sworn that sweet young thing had a crush on him.

"You've gotta find a fella your own age, Janie, I'm no good for you."

"Aw, Fred, you know you're the only man in my life. It breaks my heart that you'd climb out a second story window to be rid of me."

Fred would have been heartbroken had he known just how close to the truth it was. Janie was smart and attractive by any measure. By all rights she should have spent her evenings breaking handsome doctor's hearts, not mollycoddling an old man with one foot in the grave. The morphine was taking him away from her now and he spoke to her across the foggy expanse.

"I wasn't going to climb out the window, Janie..."

And then he spoke from somewhere between his two worlds.

"I was tossing the stick for that hound and the window broke...and...and..."

As he fell away from her, his face took on a pleasant expression that provoked one of Janice's rare smiles and a tear drifted down her cheek.

Janice spent the rest of her shift at Fred's bedside, watching him sleep and thinking about cancer and death. Fred hadn't broken any of his fragile bones in the fall but the doctors in radiology agreed that he wasn't long for this world. The ravaged cells ran rampant throughout his body now, nearly every bone and each internal organ showed evidence of the malignancy. When the orderlies brought him back to his room on the gurney, one of them pulled Janice aside and said that he'd been told Fred would be lucky to last the night.

———————

"You took quite a spill, old man, you'd probably better stay on the bench."

"You're probably right."

Fred felt different now. His aches and pains accompanied him to the dreamscape this time and the illusion of his youthful self in the vibrant park was clouded over. He doubted that he could summon the strength to get up off of that bench even if his pants were on fire.

"Why are you always muttering about Janie when you pass back and forth? Who's Janie?"

"Janie's my nurse, she's a wonderful girl. You've never told me your name, young man. I'd turn to make a proper introduction but..."

Fred tried to crane his neck around and have a look over his shoulder at the boy but was interrupted by a jolt of pain from his waking world. His vision of the park and the willow's branches reflecting in the lake became blurry, then black. He opened his eyes and he was right back in the hospital, his loyal nurse fast asleep in the wheelchair beside his bed, tortured nerves screaming their objection to the fading opiates. He reflexively reached for the little red button and clicked it furiously until that world fell away and the other returned.

"Your neck hurts don't it? Fred could see that the boy was swinging his feet playfully in his periphery. "The cancer's about finished its run. You'll die soon enough old man."

"Thanks for the vote of confidence. If I could turn around I'd stick my tongue out at you. Do you have a name, or should I just call you sunshine?"

"Jason." The boy's feet stopped swinging. "Dying ain't nearly so hard as living. Your nurse's name isn't Janie either it's Janice. She's my sister."

"Your sister? Janie told me that she didn't have any family."

"I died a long time ago, fell out of a tree just like this one and broke my neck. I came to talk to you because you're Janice's only friend. Did you know that?"

"I sort of got that impression. A pretty girl like your sister should be out kicking up her heels, not wasting her time on a lost cause like me."

The boy resumed swinging his legs back and forth at a happy tempo and Fred could turn his head slowly and just about see the kid's face as he spoke.

"She sees me in your eyes, old man. She doesn't understand how but some part of her knows that you've been with me. When you die she'll lose me too so she's scared to see you go."

"Will I come back to this park when I die?"

"If you'd like. You won't be stuck on that bench either. Your wife is here already but you knew that didn't you?"

"Yes I did. I saw this place when she was dying; the willow tree and the lake exactly like this."

"The willow was trying to tell you a secret when the cancer took your wife but you weren't listening. It told me the same thing on the day that I fell and I tried to tell Janice but she was bawling so hard I don't think she ever heard me."

A part of Fred's conscious mind was intact in his dreamscape because he had the good sense to question these visions and the nature of this place. He knew that the pain medication could trigger hallucinations but if asked to decide which was the real deal, the park in his mind was the obvious choice. The colors were so much more vivid in the dream world and his thoughts had a singular clarity and sense of calm certitude.

"The willow weeps because it's busting to break the big news but nobody ever listens."

"I'm listening now."

––––––––––

The flashing trauma lights in the corridor of the hospital always reminded Janice of the blue light specials at Kmart. "Attention Kmart shoppers, there will be a vacant bed on aisle 4 in just a few minutes." She triggered the alert herself, as she had done for a dozen other dying patients, but this case was considerably more difficult. Janice didn't know why she loved the old man but she loved him and though she'd always known that he wasn't long for this world, she was not prepared for his passing.

The alarm on Fred's oxygen tent disrupted Janice's sleep at 4:30 a.m. and he died a few moments later. There wasn't any time for last minute heroics by the code blue team or a long tearful goodbye for his favorite nurse. He came out of the opiate haze just as the squawking respirator was signaling his last irregular breaths and spoke to his devoted attendant in a hoarse, dying man's rasp.

"Jason says hello."

"Who's Jason you old nut? Lie still until we stop all the sirens."

Janice wrestled with the thatch of tubes that connected the respirator to the oxygen tent through an onslaught of tears and hit the code blue button with a wild swing of her elbow. She was angry that she had allowed herself to love a dying man and she was angry with him for not dying a year ago when he was supposed to.

"Your brother Jason, silly girl."

She grew faint at the mention of her brother's name. The bundle of tubes fell from her hand as she grabbed the bed railing to steady herself. Fred's last whispers in this world were so breathy and hoarse that Janice had to lean over him and position her ear an inch or two from his mouth in order to hear them; her tears cascading onto the dying man's cheek.

"He told me why the willow weeps."

Janice never told Fred that she had a brother, much less mention his name. The old man couldn't have known about the willow tree in their front yard that loomed over her brother's broken body more than twenty-five years before. The day Jason fell from that tree, the last day of his life, he whispered to Janice about the willow tree just as Fred was doing now. As her brother lay dying in the yard that day she was too grief stricken to pay attention to what he was trying to tell her. This time she didn't miss a syllable.

"It has to keep a happy secret, so it weeps."

"What's the secret, Fred? What did Jason tell you?"

The life support mechanism next to the bed sprang to life with flashing red lights and warning buzzers. The commotion of the machine would have obscured Fred's final utterance completely had Janice's ear been more than an inch or two from his mouth. He exhaled his last breath in the form of a barely audible sentence, which fell on her ear as a warm breeze before death's cold calm.

"The willow knows the cure for cancer."

---

Janice started writing the letters anonymously at first. She wrote to the Mayo Clinic in Minnesota and Johns Hopkins in Baltimore using names and addresses that she gleaned from the daily newspaper. She scrutinized the papers each day for word of the discovery of a radical new cancer treatment but saw no evidence that her letters had ever been received, much less taken seriously. Several months elapsed with no progress in her secret willow tree campaign, when the fates added a new urgency to her mission. She attributed her frequent headaches and sleepless nights to stress over the odd turn her life had taken but they were in fact the first symptoms of her own cancerous tumor.

Janice assumed the role of cancer patient and abandoned her nursing career in favor of full-time letter writing. She could now speak with some personal authority on the limitations of radiation and chemotherapy. The traditional remedies seemed to be killing her quicker than the cancer and her rapid deterioration redoubled her resolve to betray the willow's secret.

With the clock ticking in the background she had less to fear for being thought a kook so she signed the next batch of letters with her real name and provided a return address. This time she wrote to Universities with prominent medical schools and teaching hospitals and the response was deafening. Her credentials as a nurse in a cancer ward got the letters opened and read. The earnest appeal to investigate the willow tree as a cancer cure piqued the interest of researchers who had only recently stumbled on the potential truth of her claim.

The healing powers of salicin, from the bark of the willow tree had long been recognized. It is the willow that gave us the miracle drug aspirin. There was nothing revolutionary in the idea that a tree might provide the cure for disease and the willow tree in particular was less than a radical offering.

It was, however, only very recently that the bark of the venerated willow was the target of cancer research and it was unlikely that this nurse would have been privy to the guarded data. The first trial of a substance called combretastatin, from the bark of the African Bush Willow, had shown a remarkable efficiency in starving cancerous tumors of oxygen, strangling them out of existence without damage to neighboring tissue.

Janice's correspondence raised a few eyebrows in the competitive research community because her most recent letters were postmarked three weeks before the publication of papers on that very topic. The series in the medical journal offered preliminary research results that warranted expanded study of the willow bark as a cancer remedy.

It's just as well that she passed away before they involved her in the tug of war over bragging rights to the discovery. A half dozen Universities were prepared to pay Janice's expenses to secure an interview but she was, by that time, far too ill to travel. Before they could visit her bedside, she was gone. Controversy hovered briefly when a local paper made the minor scandal public but was quickly quieted with a stroke of posthumous diplomacy.

As an academic compromise, Janice's name was added to the authorship of the research papers.